Generations in Touch

The Anthropology of Contemporary Issues

A SERIES EDITED BY

ROGER SANJEK

A full list of titles in the series appears at the end of this book.

Generations in Touch

LINKING THE OLD AND YOUNG

IN A TOKYO NEIGHBORHOOD

Leng Leng Thang

Cornell University Press

Ithaca and London

Copyright © 2001 by Cornell University

All rights reserved. Except for brief quotations in a review, this book, or parts thereof, must not be reproduced in any form without permission in writing from the publisher. For information, address Cornell University Press, Sage House, 512 East State Street, Ithaca, New York 14850.

First published 2001 by Cornell University Press
First printing, Cornell Paperbacks, 2001

Printed in the United States of America

Library of Congress Cataloging-in-Publication Data

Thang, Leng Leng, 1965–
    Generations in touch : linking the old and young in a Tokyo neighborhood / Leng Leng Thang.
        p.   cm. — (Anthropology of contemporary issues)
    Includes bibliographical references and index.
    ISBN 0-8014-3843-8 (cloth : alk. paper) — ISBN 0-8014-8732-3 (pbk. : alk. paper)
    1. Kotoen (Age-integrated institution : Tokyo, Japan)   2. Aged—Institutional care—Japan—Tokyo.   3. Intergenerational relations—Japan—Tokyo.   4. Aged—Housing—Japan—Tokyo.   5. Aged—Japan—Tokyo—Attitudes.   6. Retirees—Japan—Attitudes.   I. Title.   II. Series.
    HV1454.2.J32 T657 2001
    362.6'1'0952135—dc21

                                                                                    00-011401

Cornell University Press strives to use environmentally responsible suppliers and materials to the fullest extent possible in the publishing of its books. Such materials include vegetable-based, low-VOC inks and acid-free papers that are recycled, totally chlorine-free, or partly composed of nonwood fibers. Books that bear the logo of the FSC (Forest Stewardship Council) use paper taken from forests that have been inspected and certified as meeting the highest standards for environmental and social responsibility. For further information, visit our website at www.cornellpress.cornell.edu.

Cloth printing   10   9   8   7   6   5   4   3   2   1
Paperback printing   10   9   8   7   6   5   4   3   2   1

FSC FSC Trademark © 1996 Forest Stewardship Council A.C.
        SW-COC-098

To my children and their grandparents

Contents

Acknowledgments

This book is the culmination of the efforts of many people with whom I have the honor of being "in touch." They are too numerous to mention, but I must single out a few to whom I am particularly indebted.

This book is based on research done in the Department of Anthropology, University of Illinois at Urbana-Champaign. My utmost gratitude is to Professor David Plath, who introduced me to the exciting world of anthropology and has since been a great source of guidance and inspiration to me. My deepest appreciation also goes to Professors Clark Cunningham, Nancy Abelmann, Jocelyn Armstrong, and Chuan-Kang Shih for their invaluable criticisms and suggestions.

I would also like to thank colleagues at the Department of Japanese Studies, National University of Singapore, for their wonderful support and especially See Heng Teow, the head of the department, for his encouragement and guidance. I am grateful to Eyal Ben-Ari for his insightful suggestions and enthusiastic support of my work, to Takie Sugiyama Lebra for her encouragement and interest in my project, and to Roger Sanjek and the anonymous reader for Cornell University Press for their constructive criticism and advice. I owe much to the staff at Cornell University Press, particularly Frances Benson and Ange Romeo-Hall for their patience and help, which shaped the final version of this study.

My contacts in Japan were initiated by Mr. Kazunori Yamanoi, who introduced me to Kotoen, and Dr. Wataru Koyano, who led to my affiliation with Waseda University. I am thankful to the faculty, staff, and graduate students at the School of Human Sciences, Waseda University, for their hospitality, particularly the members of the Quality of Life project group.

[ix]

Acknowledgments

My heartfelt thanks go to Professor Haruo Sagaza in Japan, for his encouragement and invaluable support during and after my stay there.

Like every ethnographer, I am most indebted to those individuals whom I have studied. My greatest debt is to the members of Kotoen, who have graciously embraced me into their "big family." I owe a special debt to Mr. and Mrs. Sugi, directors of Kotoen, for accommodating me and helping me in significant ways. The kind staff at Kotoen, too, have provided great assistance and support. The beloved "grandparents" and children, who let me share their lives, deserve much appreciation.

My heartfelt thanks also go to the agencies that have coordinated the individuals whom I have interviewed and surveyed for this book. I am grateful to all of those who have given me their time and opinions.

I thank the Japan Foundation for funding my fieldwork in Japan. National University of Singapore financed my studies and gave me time off from teaching to complete the project. In this regard, I am particularly grateful to Associate Professor Seah Chee Meow, former head of Department of Japanese Studies.

Portions of chapter 4 have previously appeared in *Japanese Studies* 19 (1999): 151–162. They are reprinted here with permission. Portions of chapter 8 were drawn from my article (with Matt Kaplan) "Intergenerational Programs in Japan: Symbolic Extensions of Family Unity," *Journal of Aging and Identity* 2, no. 4 (1997): 295–315.

Many wonderful friends have helped in one way or another to facilitate the study. In Japan, I am grateful to Professor Yasuo Mishima, Dr. Toshiko Otake, the Kasamoto family, the Ichikawa family, and the Mukasa family. In the United States and Singapore, I am particularly grateful to Kate Winkler, Ruth Ann Vokac, Chris Thompson, Jennifer Creamer, Matt Kaplan, Hiromi Mitani, Pauline Snowden, Kazuko Furuya, Kazu and Mika Maruyama, Pang-Liang and Suzanna Ong, and the exclusive Party1 members for their encouragement and support.

Finally, to my husband, Pang Kit, who took leave from his work to move across different countries with me during my years of study, this book is also a product of your efforts and sacrifices. I can never thank you enough. To our son, Justin, who joined us in the midst, I benefit from the added perspective you have given me as mother. Last but not least, I am thankful for the support and encouragement of our families, particularly my parents and my husband's parents. As a token of my heartfelt appreciation, this book is dedicated to them, particularly to the memory of my husband's mother, a loving mother-in-law and grandmother, whose sudden departure was a painful loss to us all.

Generations in Touch

[1]

The Problem: Reengagement

Eighty-five-year-old Mrs. Noyama never gave birth to a child, yet she is "Grandma" to eighty children. Every morning (except weekends) Mrs. Noyama exercises with these children. In the afternoon she helps them change from pajamas to play clothes after they wake up from their naps. She receives birthday presents from them and makes birthday gifts for them. They celebrate the year's events and holidays together.

Mrs. Noyama was "adopted" by these children after she entered an old-age home, which is usually characterized in Japan as a gloomy place. This old-age home, however, is a departure from the stereotypical one. It is part of Kotoen, a larger facility that also houses a nursery, a nursing home, and a day service center that provides meals and activities for community elders. While Mrs. Noyama had abandoned her social identity to enter the home, she acquired a new identity—a resident of Kotoen and, at the same time, the Kotoen "Grandma" for the eighty children who attend the nursery.

This book examines the reengagements of elders like Mrs. Noyama with their "grandchildren" at Kotoen. As more and more of Japan's elders are isolated from their children and grandchildren, many grandparents who might see their grandchildren only once or twice a year would envy Mrs. Noyama's frequent contact with the children. Despite the romantic notion that Japan's strong cultural emphasis on family and filial piety will remain generationally intact in the face of change, Japan shares the dilemma of generational disengagement that Western societies have long faced.

I propose generational reengagement as a viable scenario in an aging society. I examine the unusual case of Kotoen, a pioneering facility with its experimentation in multigenerational living, and I present it not as a model—its success story has already received much publicity in the past decade—but as a case study. Through ethnographic sketches of the activities that bring laughter, joy, frustration, and tears to members of the facility, I consider the limits to which alternate-generation relationships can be made meaningful in extrafamilial form. In so doing, I focus on the ironies associated with the practices and ideals of reengaging the generations and, in a related vein, the advantages and limitations of deliberate attempts to link them. My ultimate goal is to place generational reengagement within a larger sociocultural context. I hope that lessons from Kotoen can illuminate the urgency of generational reengagement and provide some directions to improve the quality of life for all in the twenty-first century.

How Japan, the only non-Western postindustrial society, is coping with the side effects of modernization should be of interest to others, particularly in the United States, who have increasingly perceived Japan as the most significant cultural other. To what degree can the culture prevent the alternate generations from disengaging, and what do the ironies inherent in attempts to reengage them reveal about the broader social contradictions of contemporary Japanese society? As an Asian coming from a Confucius-based culture, I am interested in how Japan's experience may serve as a mirror to Singapore and other newly industrialized societies that must also cope with the consequences of rapid demographic and social changes.

This is the first anthropological study of an age-integrated facility. I hope that this book will generate more research in a significant field of study and benefit both anthropologists interested in aging-related issues and scholars of contemporary Japanese culture.

Background

Sociodemographic Changes in Japan

Postwar sociodemographic changes have occurred very rapidly in Japan. The country's population is aging faster than that of any other today: it has taken only twenty-five years for Japan's elderly population (those age 65 and over) to rise from 7 to 14 percent. Both the United States and the United Kingdom, for example, took 60 years, while France and Sweden took 130 and 85 years, respectively, to double in size. Moreover, the Japanese currently have the highest life expectancy rates in the world: 77.16 for males and 84.01 for females in 1998. Long life expectancy, coupled with a falling fertility rate—the total fertility rate hit a record low of 1.34 in 1999—is further augmented by a changing family structure to generate much anxiety about the future of an aged society.

Let's consider the case of a man who is now eighty. When he married at age twenty-five, he knew that as the eldest son in the family, he would one day succeed his father and eventually become the head of the household. To him, this also meant assuming the duty of supporting his parents in their old age. In imperial Japan, three-generational cohabitation was a cultural and social norm. It was legitimized by the stem family system known as *ie* and supported through Confucian moral indoctrination and the civil and criminal codes, as well as by an urgent demand for elderly support under the barely developed social security system (Kinoshita and Kiefer 1992, 49).

Situations changed by the time this man became elderly. Urbanization, industrialization, and modernization have contributed to the nuclearization of the family and the consequent lower proportion of three-generation households. The new Civil Code in 1946 discarded the traditional family system as feudalistic and replaced it with the conjugal family system. Under the latter system, the children are no longer obligated to live together with their parents, although they have an obligation to support them financially if necessary (Okazaki 1996, 1). Coupled with this decline in traditional households is an increase in the number of single elderly households and elderly couple households. In 1975, 54.4 percent of the households were three-generational, 13 percent had only elderly couples, and 8.6 percent had single elderly households, while in 1995 the percentages changed to 33.3, 24.2, and 17.3, respectively (Kono 1996, 43).

Changes in family structure, lower fertility levels, and increased mobility with modernization have contributed to distancing among the generations and have made it harder for grandparents to have little grandchildren climbing into their laps to listen to a story or simply to enjoy the warmth of the other's presence. This is ironic in an aging society—one with more grandparents and great-grandparents than ever before.

The Rubric of Alternate Generations

In focusing on the extreme ends of the life course, this study is partly related to earlier research on kinship and family in sociocultural anthropology. A. R. Radcliffe-Brown (1952) emphasizes the difference between consecutive and alternate generations. In his famous essays on joking relationships, he posits that the relationships between members of alternate generations are friendly and egalitarian: "An important understanding of the subject is the fact that in the flow of social life through time, in which men are born, become mature and die, the grandchildren replace their grandparents" (Radcliffe-Brown 1952, 96). In contrast, the relationship between the consecutive generations is unequal, for reasons that involve the necessity to discipline and control the younger members to fulfill the social function of transmitting culture and socializing new members in the society. This proposition is challenged by S. F. Nadel (1951), who suggests that informal and intimate relations between grandparents and grandchildren exist only when grandparents do not possess authority over their grandchildren; when they do, their relationships tend to be reserved and formal. Nadel's theory is further supported by Dorrian Apple (1956), through evidence from societies in the Human Relations Area Files. In general, though, the informal, indulgent, and intimate relationships between the alternate generations are more widespread cross-culturally. For instance, while mother-in-law and daughter-in-law tensions and conflicts in Japan are well documented in both academic and popular literature, relations between grandparents and grandchildren are often perceived as naturally harmonious.

Structurally speaking, elders and children occupy a similar social position. As Haim Hazan (1992, 16) has noted, both are in "social categories for which the common denominator is dependency." They have other similarities: both are considered "incapable of engaging in relationships beyond their peers, and are socially marginal" (Hazan 1992, 43). Many scholars have referred to Victor Turner's concept of "liminality" to characterize the structural ambiguity of elders' position "betwixt and between" life and death (Myerhoff 1980; Hazan 1992). This resulted in Hazan's comment that neither human category belongs to the "real world" (Hazan 1992, 43). In traditional Japanese society, too, elders and children were perceived as belonging to the "unreal world" with the gods. A Japanese proverb states that "Until seven, the child is of the gods," which "draws them away from the social order and frees them from the strictures of the society" (Yamazaki 1994, 454). The perceived connection between elders and children has resulted in the "old-young theory" proposed by Toji Kamata (1993), a Japanese folklorist who states that the souls of the young and old are merged: the spirits of youth exist in the old, and vice versa.

Relating elders to children also moves the elders into the arena of *amae*. The concept of *amae* is commonly referred to as "a feeling of total dependence represented by a child's relationship with the mother during nursing and primary care giving" (Doi 1973), which "enables one to presume upon others' benevolence and encourages mutual dependency among people instead of independence" (Tsuji 1997, 200). In a much-quoted phrase, Ruth Benedict describes the Japanese arc of life as "a great shallow U-curve with maximum freedom and indulgence allowed to babies and to the old" (Benedict 1947, 254). Because both have the greatest amount of free time in the life course, it seems indisputable that elders and young children are the best company for one another.

Grandparenthood emerges as one of the few kinship roles individuals acquire in old age. One of the functions of grandparenthood, as Radcliffe-Brown has suggested, is to provide support and refuge to the grandchildren against their parental discipline and punishment.

Pamela Amoss and Steven Harrell (1981) liken the difference between elders and children to that between culture and nature, wherein the former are fully socialized and encultured after many years of engagement with the symbols and meanings of their culture. Grandparents are the "wardens of culture"—guiding, preserving, and transmitting the knowledge, experiences, and skills to the next generation to "help craft the new myths on which acculturation should be based," thereby ensuring the maintenance of social equilibrium (Guttman 1985). Grandparents are also the authority in family and community religious and ritual affairs. Vern Bengston (1985) identifies an interpretive and identity-molding function of grandparenthood, wherein family elders help to position the younger generation by "the building of reasonable autobiographical connections," enabling the young to connect their present with the past to help place their futures. Grandparenting is important for the development of grandchildren as well as for the personal development of grandparents (Bengston and Robertson 1985, 276).

Grandparents in Japan are valued as socializing agents. The traditional family system encourages multigenerational cohabitation, which helps promote interaction among generations. Robert Smith (1974) sees grandparents as the best suited to this role because, as the eldest members in the household, they have the closest link with the ancestors. Cohabitation may also fulfill the practical function of providing childcare. Ella Lury Wiswell observed that children in Suye Mura in the later 1930s grew more attached to their grandmothers at about three years old, when their mothers became occupied with a new baby (Smith and Wiswell 1982, 236).

More than half a century away from the world of Suye Mura, the situation is more complicated. More and more grandparents and great-grandparents are likely to be alive and well—and residing at a distance from their children and grandchildren. Propagandists for electronic mail services (at least in the United States) argue that today's "Good Grandpa" is the man who can hop onto the Internet and join in virtual play with his grandchildren. This is no doubt useful in its own way, but it is still second best. The vastly more serious issue is this: How can members of alternate generations be brought together in face-to-face encounters that allow them to build on their much-posited urge to merge?

Conceptual Framework

Sociocultural anthropology contains scant literature on connecting the generations. As I have noted, the discipline has paid attention to alternate generations, but mostly to the formal, organizational aspects of kin ties between grandparents and grandchildren (Firth 1936; Radcliffe-Brown 1952; Fortes 1960). Moreover, earlier research tended to take a structural and ahistorical stance. But already in the twentieth century we have seen drastic shifts in the age patterning of industrial populations, and all indications are that more change will come in the twenty-first century. One of the first to call attention to this issue was Margaret Mead, in a series of lectures published in 1970 as *Culture and Commitment*.

Mead posited a sequence of three types of generational relations, as humankind moves from pre- to postindustrial eras. In what she called a *postfigurative* culture, elders have high status, children learn primarily from them, and the future is expected to be largely a repetition of the past. In a *cofigurative* culture (after the industrial revolution), both adults and children learn primarily from their peers but still look to elders for final approval.

In today's *prefigurative* culture, however, elders must learn from children, for children are growing up and discovering a world that elders never knew. Such cultural style will only develop with "the existence of a continuing dialogue in which the young, free to act on their own initiative, can lead their elders in the direction of the unknown. It is only with the participation of the young, who have the knowledge, that we can build a viable future" (Mead 1970, 88).

Mead has contributed greatly in raising the issue of generational re-engagement. Her perspective also suggests new ways to restore generational linkages beyond kin ties. However, it is easy to dismiss her cultural scheme as simplistic. Elements of all three types of relations can be found in Japan and other industrial societies. Moreover, declaring the young to be leaders of the future seems unviable as well. Although children may serve as teachers to the elderly in aspects of new technology, such as using the computer and "surfing" the Internet, the knowledge possessed by the elderly is still valuable to the society. Instead of a future in which elders follow the young, it is perhaps more viable to visualize a future in which both the old and young reconnect and learn from each other, possibly through the efforts of the middle generation.

Generational Reengagement

Social programs designed to bring the generations together are increasingly being implemented in Japan, as they are in America. These programs have grown in variety and scope in recent decades. American programs range from the Retired Senior Volunteer Program (RSVP), the Foster Grandparent Program, and the Senior Community Service Program to the more problem-focused Intergenerational Programs for At-Risk Youths and Intergenerational Arts for At-Risk School-age Children (see Robertson et al. 1985; Newman and Brummel 1989). Japan's intergenerational programs have also gained momentum in recent years—Kotoen being an example of an age-integrated facility.

This study refers to the merging of elders and children in such an extrafamilial context as *reengagement*. I use *reengagement* to emphasize the dilemma of alienation between generations in contemporary societies—a dilemma that calls for conscious attempts to link these generations. This concept forms the focus of my ethnographic portrait of Kotoen.

In the chapters that follow I ask in what ways the old and the young are in touch. Is generational engagement a phenomenon that will naturally happen when the generations stay in close proximity? How does the administration of an institution define and "measure" engagement? Does the role of "grandparent" help elevate the resident elders from the "betwixt and between" position that many studies say characterizes residents in old-age institutions? Does it help ease the social stigma associated with institutionalization? Do these institutions help enhance elders' sense of purpose in life? Are there differences between older men and women? Are there differences among different age groups of children and elders? Is there a balance in reciprocity in the exchanges between the old and the young? Do the centerwide ceremonies promote familial connection

[7]

among the elders, the children, and the staff? What kind of social world is created through interaction with the young? What similarities and differences are there from natural grandparent-grandchildren interaction? Do these children grow up to have more positive perceptions of elders?

Two idioms through which generational reengagement is articulated emerged as highly relevant in late-twentieth-century Japan: *daikazoku* and *fureai*.

Daikazoku ("big family") literally means a family with a large number of members. But the term also implies a multigenerational family, deriving from the image of the traditional Japanese family. Kotoen's leaders hold a vision of the facility as "A *Daikazoku* with Eighty Grandchildren," the title of a NHK (Japan Broadcasting Corporation) documentary made at Kotoen in 1988. In this case, the "Kotoen *daikazoku*" is defined as both a big and multigenerational entity. Resident elders thus are considered to be grandparents to the children who come to Kotoen's day care facility.

The adoption of the *daikazoku* ideology in an age-integrated facility raises interesting issues. *Daikazoku* evokes a romanticized image of multigenerational cohabitation in which elders, surrounded by lively grandchildren, are honored and well respected by their offspring. This image departs from the contemporary social structure, however. Earlier discussion on sociodemographic changes has not only shown that Japanese families are shifting toward nuclearization, but it has also revealed that more elders are expected to live separately from their children and grandchildren in the future. Thus, despite its deviation from reality, the *daikazoku* ideal continues to hold some kind of sway in contemporary Japanese discourse.

Fureai implies another form of ideal—the ideal of encounters between people. Compared with *kōryū* ("interaction"), which is emotionally neutral and suggests some degree of formality, *fureai*, defined as "coming in contact" or "touching each other" (Kenkyusha 1983), implies spontaneous interaction involving feelings and emotions. It depicts the qualities most desired in openhearted encounters.

One hears the term *fureai* in public discourse more commonly now than thirty years ago. The rest areas or lobbies of some government offices or train stations, for example, are called *fureai no ba* ("contact place"). The Japan National Railway's "Discover Japan" tourism campaign of the 1970s used the term widely in its advertising. This campaign was in some ways responsible for the widespread use of the term now. These advertisements emphasized the rediscovery of the self in travel through *fureai* with nature and tradition. In this rhetoric, *fureai* is defined aesthetically and sensually as a fleeting, treasured chance encounter that captures "the moment when different worlds touched," such as the *fureai* of the present and the past, the artificial and the natural, the modern and the traditional (Ivy 1995, 43).

The rhetoric of "Discover Japan" seems appropriate for *fureai* between elders and children, who, after all, belong to two different worlds. However, I believe the intergenerational programs and activities in Japan connected by the theme and objective of *fureai* refer more to warm and openhearted encounters. One meal program for elders, served by a group of students, is called the *fureai bento* ("*fureai* box lunch") program. The newsletter of Kotoen, published five times a year, is called *Fureai*, which shows the center's emphasis on engagement.

Kotoen's ideal in generational reengagement becomes clear when relating *daikazoku* to *fureai*. In adopting the *daikazoku* ideology, Kotoen draws on the ideal image of the traditional Japanese family as one in which the ultimate goodness in interpersonal relationships exists, and there is harmony, mutual help, and empathy across the generations. In other words, instead of mere interaction between the old and the young, Kotoen emphasizes *fureai*, where keeping in touch becomes a positive and emotional experience similar to grandparent-grandchildren relations in a family.

When related to generational reengagement, both concepts raise some ironies. These ironies reveal a gap between the ideal and actual practice. On the one hand, there is the irony of "programming" *fureai:* How can the "spontaneous" be encouraged to happened? How is spontaneity measured? On the other hand, *daikazoku* is structurally ironic: How can an ideology almost obsolete in society be created and structured inside an institution? I return to these themes several times in the following chapters.

Theoretical Approach

This study focuses on alternate-generation relations in an age-integrated facility. I describe situations I have observed and participated in, sometimes quoting directly on what I have heard, sometimes asserting my own commentary; sometimes I highlight survey and interview responses to emphasize an issue and sometimes refer to the work of others. Along the way, I introduce some social gerontological notions and theories, such as activity, disengagement, social exchange, and person-environment fit theories, to help me frame the concept of generational reengagement. In some cases, I challenge these predominantly Western theoretical perspectives with a non-Western cultural point of view. I hope an inclusion of such discussions will contribute to the understanding of aging and generational reengagements cross-culturally.

Specifically, I situate the work within the sociocultural anthropology of aging. Much has been written in this field since Margaret Clark's classic observation of the relative paucity of anthropological attention to aging in 1967 (Rubinstein 1990; Cohen 1994). Within the larger inquiries about aging, a central question emerges: How do people cope with the "problems" of aging? The anthropology of aging has examined a wide variety of topics in cross-cultural perspectives, such as the effects of modernization on elders, the analysis of meaning in old age, the influence of age-homogenous environment on elders, and aging and ethnicity. Most of the research focuses exclusively on one extreme—the end of the life course. By integrating two ends of the life spectrum, I attempt to contribute to the inquiry by examining how reengaging the generations may help elders to cope with the "problems" of aging—in this case, loneliness, boredom, loss of status, and loss of *ikigai* ("purpose in life").

By choosing to study an age-integrated facility, I hope further to challenge the traditional ways of age-segregated institutions for elders. There are as yet few studies on institutions for the elderly in non-Western settings (in the case of Japan, there have been only two ethnographic studies of old-age institutions, by Kinoshita and Kiefer [1992] and Bethel [1993]) and none on age-integrated settings before this one.

Why Kotoen?

I first learned about Kotoen in 1989 from a Japanese friend, Kazunori Yamanoi, now a scholar and politician in Kyoto. As an avid advocate for change in the direction of Japan's aging society, he has written an award-winning essay about Kotoen as a model. At that time, I was working on a proposal for my master's thesis on *ikigai* among Okinawan elders. My interest in aging, particularly on *ikigai*, began with my paternal grandfather's admission into a nursing home. I had fond memories of my grandfather, who had always been healthy and full of life until his retirement. His institutionalization aroused my concern about *ikigai* in old age: Why did he deteriorate soon after retirement? Was work his only *ikigai*?

[10]

How can we enhance *ikigai* among elders? Frequent visits to the home also led me to question the alternative to an age-segregated old-age institution; hence, I was particularly intrigued by the vision of Kotoen.

I wanted to study an institutional setting that has frequent and intimate alternate-generation interactions. As I discovered through my preliminary fieldwork in January 1995, most age-integrated institutions have much less contact between the generations than I expected. Some are limited by the frailty of the elders (nursing homes); some have little interaction because the elementary or junior high school children they integrate with are too busy preparing for examinations. In others, administrators cannot find time to initiate more programs.

Kotoen fit my needs perfectly. Elders in its old-age home are relatively mobile, which greatly facilitates their interactions with the children. The children are encouraged to interact with them. Nurseries in general emphasize socialization of values considered to be characteristically Japanese: empathy, gentleness, kindness, cooperation, and harmony (Shigaki 1983). *Fureai* with elders is believed to help inculcate these values in children. I also chose Kotoen because it is the oldest integrated facility in Japan, and its programs are well established.

Via Mr. Yamanoi, I was introduced to Kotoen's administrative director, Mrs. Sugi, who welcomed me to the facility and permitted me to use her name and that of the institution. Names I have given to other staff, residents, and children are fictitious, though, to preserve privacy.

Becoming Part of the Kotoen Family

My research fits the usual picture of participant observation: "some amount of genuinely social interaction in the field with the subjects of the study, some direct observations of relevant events, some formal and a great deal of informal interviewing, some systematic counting, some collection of documents and artifacts, and open-endedness in the direction the study takes" (McCall and Simmons 1969, cited in Jerrome 1992).

From November 1995 to September 1996, I became a morning commuter in Tokyo's complicated and overcrowded subways, traveling one hour to the field site for three to five days a week (for about six hours a day). To have an insider's view of the workings of the institution, I chose to work as a volunteer.

Getting a start at Kotoen was not difficult; it was delayed for almost two months, though, because of a viral epidemic among the elders. Because of it, interactions between the children and the elders were halted for three months.

The first day of my fieldwork coincided with "Open Childcare," a program in which elders and children interact for a day. I was introduced to the crowd as a new teacher helping for the day. The nursery had a part-time Caucasian male teacher assistant from Argentina (a graduate student at a local university), so people had no problem accepting an Asian woman like me who speaks Japanese. However, this "teacher" (*sensei*) identity caused a little confusion among residents when I began to turn up in the old-age home and nursing home.

During my fieldwork, I found my identity switching with different people. I wore a staff uniform, except that my iron-on nametag on the jacket read "volunteer, Tang Ling Ling" and the pin on the nursery nametag on my track pants read "Ling Ling *sensei*." Much like the dual-identity found on my nametags, I was addressed as "*sensei*" by some staff, some elders, and all of the children. Most staff called me Ling Ling-*san* or Tang-*san*. Adding a "-*san*" at the end of a name can mean Mr., Mrs., Miss, or Ms. in Japanese. The directors sometimes jokingly called me Ling Ling-*chan; "-chan*" is normally used for young children and reflects intimacy. Sometimes elders called me "caregiver" (*ryōbo-san*) or Ling Ling-san; a few called me *gakusei-san* ("student"), too. There are always interns at the center, some working for as long as three weeks. It was easy to categorize me as one of them. When a snapshot of me was posted on a board for "Kotoen staff" during the Golden Fair, I was addressed as *kenkyūsei* ("research student").

In general, it was easy to get accepted into the Kotoen "family." When I told them I was a graduate student doing research for my dissertation, they were encouraging and expressed willingness to help me in any way I needed. As I was an ever-ready listener, most elders willingly shared with me their lives, their insights on various matters, and their complaints about the institution. My liminal status as quasi-staff probably encouraged them to confide in me. Miss Tsuji, a new resident at the old-age home, actually told me she felt she could confide in me because I was half-outsider, like her, making the transition from independent to institutional living. I have learned a great deal about various aspects of Japanese society and culture from this "family." As much as I may have been an outlet for Kotoen's residents, they have also been a source of emotional support for my family and me.

My family helped open up conversations. My husband volunteered at the special nursing home on a few occasions in the spring and summer by taking elders in wheelchairs for a stroll. He and our two-year-old son also participated frequently in Kotoen events. We "adopted" our own "grandparents" as we developed close relations. As a family, we also formed friendships with a few staff and their families, were invited to their homes for dinner, and took overnight trips together in the summer. I bonded with the staff as a woman and a mother, as well as a fellow worker.

During the first three months of my fieldwork, I rotated to work in different locations (nursing home, old-age home, and day care service and nursery) to familiarize myself with the setting and its routines. This was a time for laying groundwork. I hung around, not quite sure if what I hoped to see would emerge. Those winter months were quiet; I was beginning to worry about the progress of my research, and then things began to unfold. Either my skill as a participant observer had improved, or the center suddenly burst with activities to observe; the research project became more enjoyable and satisfying. From the fourth month, I gradually focused more on the old-age home. The second-floor caregivers' station soon became my writing station. I participated in all activities that involved both old and young. I attended meetings of the Committee to Promote *Fureai* and residents' meetings with the staff. I also went on shopping trips, outings, and other excursions with them.

I began my fieldwork expecting to discover dyadic pairs between the elders and the children. I soon realized that dyads, if they form, are fluid and change over time. Therefore, I decided to focus on the old-age home elders and to interview them individually. Semi-structured questionnaires for the interview were then drawn, and the interviews were conducted from May to July 1996. They were mostly conducted in the residents' rooms. I tried to maintain a casual atmosphere during the interview, treating it like any other informal conversation. I refrained from using a tape recorder because the residents felt uneasy with it, so I resorted to formal note-taking. Many would talk and then stop to make sure I had correctly recorded what they said. It was quite a learning experience for me: I increased my knowledge of *kanji* (Chinese characters) as a result of it.

Beginning in June 1996, I added videotaping to the data collection. I recorded most events containing interactions between elders and children from June to September. Sometimes I focused on one elder without his or her knowing and followed as events unfolded. David Plath has talked about the increasing expectation (even by the natives) of doing fieldwork with a video camera, particularly in a super high-tech country like Japan (1990). A disadvantage of "writing field notes" with the video

[13]

camera is that people may act unnaturally in front of a lens. Some elders did shy away from me at the beginning, but gradually they felt more at ease.

As I was videotaping others, I was also being filmed by a media crew who came to Kotoen in the summer. The twenty-minute documentary, in which I was introduced as a foreign researcher and was interviewed briefly, was broadcast in Tokyo the week before Respect the Elders Day (September 15). Such were the moments when "fieldwork itself has become a media event" (Plath 1990, 381). As I posed for the film crew, they also became a part of my data collection, providing me with an outsider's portrayal of Kotoen.

Achieving objectivity is a challenge in ethnographic fieldwork. One can rarely study from a neutral position; therefore, we should be as explicit as possible about one's interest and feelings as well as one's position in writing the culture (Rosaldo 1989). I was aware of my possible biases as I see through the lens of a nonnative, a fellow Asian influenced by the same cultural values in Confucianism but trained in Western schools, as a young woman in "the middle" generation situated between caring for the young and the old in the family. However, biases were not always disadvantageous; sometimes they enhanced my sensitivity and consciousness to certain issues. Instead of assuming that one can become totally detached and maintain a distance, I attempted to learn as much as possible about "the other" through maintaining a balance between subjectivity and objectivity.

The viewpoints of various actors are also important in maintaining the balance. I conducted informal interviews with caregiving and nursery staff, volunteers, parents, five-year-old children (at Kotoen), and the interns who were sent from various nursing schools and professional welfare schools. I asked about their impressions of Kotoen and interactions between elders and children.

I left Kotoen "officially" at the end of September 1996. When I went to Tokyo for a conference in mid-November of that year, I returned for a visit. It was both a nostalgic and extremely fruitful visit: I had the unexpected opportunity to conduct an important taped interview with Mrs. Sugi, the administrative director. When I was volunteering at the center, she and I met frequently to talk, but I somehow did not conduct a formal interview. We were under the impression that ten months was a long time; we could wait. I did not even have a chance to express my gratitude to her before I left the field "officially" because she was visiting welfare facilities in Australia. When we finally met this time, before we got down to business, she gave me a farewell gift and apologized for its delay. The interview signifies my true exit from the field, at least for the time being.

Supplementary Data

To gain perspective on young-old generational interactions in other contexts, I collected the following kinds of supplementary data.

1. Two Old-Age Homes That Have No Nursery

I conducted short interviews with twenty-five elders ranging from sixty-five to ninety years old (sixteen females and nine males) in two old-age homes. These old-age homes have a Joint Quoits Meet (a competition for a game played with quoits) with Kotoen. Introductions were made easily through the Kotoen staff. An understanding of the two old-age homes helped me to determine the typicality of Kotoen's old-age home.

2. Two Senior Centers for Community Elders

All wards in Tokyo set up senior centers for elders aged sixty and older living in the community. One of the attractions of these centers is its free baths. Like a neighborhood public bath (*sentō*), these serve as important communication and social centers for the "regular clients" (Clark 1992). These regular clients visit almost every day; after a bath, they gather to relax and interact with one another. Women usually watch television programs, sip tea, and chat, while men play *shogi* and *go,* two traditional Japanese chess games. Old-age clubs in the community may reserve these centers for gathering and classes, too. Senior centers rarely provide opportunities for meeting anybody but other seniors.

I visited two such senior centers in central Tokyo. One was near my apartment, and the other was near my son's nursery. I obtained an introduction through the ward office and interviewed twenty-five elders ranging from sixty-five to ninety-two years old (eighteen females and seven males).

3. Five-Year-Old Children at a Public Nursery

I interviewed one class of eighteen five-year-olds from a public nursery in the same ward as the senior centers. I selected the nursery because my

[15]

son was attending the one-year-old class there, the principal was familiar with me, and he was helpful.

4. *Parents of Five-Year-Old Children*

After an interview with the five-year-olds, I conducted a questionnaire survey of their parents. I received fourteen responses out of the eighteen questionnaires distributed.

5. *A Survey on Children's Perceptions of Elders*

To determine if interactions with elders help to foster a positive image of the aged among children, I did a survey jointly with Kotoen on the nursery graduates. We mailed fifty-five survey forms to graduates who had left three, five and seven years previously. Only eleven responded. At the same time, I also collected responses from ninety-two children in an elementary and a junior high school in the neighborhood.

6. *Interviewing and Visiting Other Age-Integrated Facilities*

I visited and observed five other age-integrated facilities in the Tokyo metropolitan area. During these visits, I interviewed the administrators and recorded participant observations. The visits were brief and done only once (one institution was visited twice)—enough to gather general characteristics. I also conducted telephone interviews with staff at twelve other integrated institutions in Tokyo. The facilities I visited represent a diversity of combinations. They provide a glimpse of the variety of facilities available.

7. *Interviewing Other Welfare-Related Personnel*

To hear the voices of city and ward government agents in integrated programs, I interviewed people in the following offices: the welfare sections in Edogawa Ward and Bunkyo Ward, the Tokyo metropolitan government welfare office, and the Social Welfare Association. I also interviewed welfare officers at the Nara Prefectural Office and the Hakodate City Office to hear voices from outside Tokyo. I inquired about the intergenerational programs available in their respective wards, cities, or prefectures; their interpretations of, and comments about, age-integrated facilities; and their perceptions of the changing social structure in Japan and the future plans and visions of welfare in Japan, particularly those relating to generational reengagement.

Finally, the study was supplemented with statistical data and reports from various agencies and from newspaper and magazine articles, community newsletters, and documentaries.

An Overview

Chapters 2 and 3 look at the physical setting and the actors involved—the staff, elders, and children—and describe Kotoen's temporal structure. Daily activities and seasonal events give spice to what otherwise might become a bland routine.

In Chapters 4 to 7, interactions between elders and children are analyzed in detail. Each chapter begins with a text—a ceremony, a performance, an activity—as a lead in to the analysis. Chapter 4 and 5 discuss the ironies of *fureai* within the *daikazoku* framework. In Chapter 4, I propose the notions of "event grandparent" and "collective grandparenthood" to characterize grandparenting in an institutional context. Chapter 5 juxtaposes the Golden Fair drama with a television documentary on Kotoen and compares the responses of audiences/viewers in this public portrayal of Kotoen. This allows us to compare insider and outsider perceptions of Kotoen as a "Dream Family." Chapter 6 explores the question of how elders perceive and benefit from the exchanges and encounters. This chapter also analyzes the benefits of *fureai* with elders on children. The differences in the perceptions of Kotoen graduates versus commuity schoolchildren help support the assumption that contact with elders changes children's perceptions in a positive way. Factors affecting *fureai*, such as declining health, personal backgrounds, and attitudes, are discussed in Chapter 7. I suggest passive *fureai* as a strategy that helps elders to remain engaged in the face of frailty. This chapter also examines the characteristics of the increasingly more common engagements between male residents and children.

The concluding Chapter 8 has three sections. The first section summarizes generational reengagement in the institutional context and reveals the significance of programming in promoting engagements. In the second section, I step back into the larger society and examine the urgency of generational reengagement in an aging society. The final section provides an overview of intergenerational programming in Japan. The macro level of analysis situates Kotoen as a microcosm of a much broader social phenomenon in Japan and highlights the significance of linking the old and young as we enter the twenty-first century.

[2]

The Place: Staff, Residents, and Children

Kotoen is unusual as a welfare facility integrating the old and young under the *daikazoku* ideal. However, other than its age-integrated nature, Kotoen resembles welfare facilities throughout Japan in terms of its organizational nature, the relationship between the residents and staff, the profile of residents and the relationship among residents in the old-age home, teacher-parent relations, curriculum, and the educational objective in the nursery.

Edogawa Ward

Kotoen is located in Edogawa Ward in Tokyo. Situated west of the Edo River, Edogawa Ward is the most eastern ward of Tokyo's twenty-three wards. Edogawa Ward is traditionally defined as a *shitamachi*, as opposed to *yamanote*, the major divisions in the subcultural geography of Tokyo. As noted by Bestor (1989), *shitamachi* (lit. "downtown"), the old merchant quarter, is a crowded, old-fashioned place, noted for the role self-employed entrepreneurs play in open and informal community life. Among the qualities that characterize a *shitamachi* is *fureai*, which implies generosity, warmth, and neighborliness. A *shitamachi* is also usually occupied by people somewhat in the lower socioeconomic strata. In contrast, *yamanote* (lit. "the foothills") comprises the largely residential areas of western Tokyo, characterized by middle-class, white-collar households and their more "modern," "rational," outwardly affluent, and less community-oriented lifestyles (Bestor 1989, 31). With the developments of large residential complexes in Edogawa Ward, especially during the economic and housing booms in the early and mid-1980s, many parts of the ward now resemble *yamanote*.

Kotoen is located in the ward's *shitamachi* section. Its surrounding is typical of a Tokyo neighborhood: there is a mixture of inexpensive apartments, homes, shops, and small factories; many of these workplaces are also homes to entrepreneurs.

With 49.86 square kilometers and a population of about 580,000, Edogawa Ward is the fourth largest ward in Tokyo. It also tops the twenty-three wards in several demographic aspects: it has the lowest proportion of elders over age 65 (9.7 percent of the population in 1995) and it registers an average annual population growth of about 6,000, whereas all but one of the other wards are experiencing annual declines in population growth. It also has the youngest average age—36.36 years, as compared with 38.75 years in the 23 wards (Tokyo Tokubetsuku Rengōkai 1995). These demographic characteristics are affected by the influx of young families into the ward's newer apartment complexes.

Edogawa Ward is also renowned for its social welfare efforts, particularly those for elders. The ward government defines elders over age sixty-five as *jukunensha* ("ripe-agers")—possibly derived from Erik Erikson's human developmental theory, wherein successful old age is conceptualized as achieving maturity, integrity, and wisdom (1964). Mayor Kiichi Nakazato—himself a ripe-ager in his mid-eighties—has been in office for thirty-two years and is acclaimed as the key motivator for the dynamic welfare programs in Edogawa Ward. Over the years, his efforts to provide a better living for elders has resulted in Edogawa Ward's reputation as one of the best places for retirees.

Edogawa Ward has two old-age homes (*yōgō rōjin hōmu*) and six nursing homes (*tokubetsu yōgō rōjin hōmu*) (see Appendix A).[1] While new nursing homes continue to be constructed throughout the country (the sixth nursing home in Edogawa Ward started operation in June 1996), new old-age homes, which house elders capable of daily functioning, have not been constructed in the ward (nor in Japan) since 1976. With emphasis on measures to keep elders living independently and out of hospitals and residential care facilities, in part to reduce public cost, the Japanese government has ceased funding the construction of new old-

[1] An "old-age home" is officially called Home for Elderly Care in Japan, while a nursing home is called Special Home for Elderly Care. This study uses the term *old-age home* because this is close to the term *rōjin hōmu*—literally, "old-age home" (usually used by the residents themselves in these institutions). *Nursing home* is used because of its functional similarity with nursing homes in the West.

[20]

age homes. However, existing old-age homes continue to receive funding under the 1963 Welfare Law for the Elderly.

As an alternative to living in an old-age home, elders may apply to stay in the "silver pia" (*shiruba pia*) apartments—elderly-friendly apartments—that were built by the Tokyo metropolitan government. Each of these apartments is equipped with buttons in the bathroom and living room that can be pressed to inform the apartment manager of an emergency. In addition, each unit has a warning system that will automatically notify the apartment manager if an elder does not open and shut either the toilet door or the front door over a twelve-hour period. There are currently fifty silver pia units among the government apartments in Edogawa Ward. Although similar housing is being built in other parts of the city, Edogawa Ward has ceased to construct any more silver pia housing projects. The ward officer explained that such housing projects were found to have expanded the demand for nursing homes because they created a larger number of elders who needed to be transferred to a nursing home all at once, when they were too frail to stay alone.

To solve the problem, Edogawa Ward has pioneered several projects to help elders live independently in their own homes. These include the "rental support," "lower loan interest for multigenerational living," and "elder-friendly home renovations support" policies. The "rental support policy" was initiated in 1989 to help bridge the gap between the old and new rents when elders who are staying alone or with their spouse are forced to leave their former apartments for reasons such as apartment redevelopment. Such cases were especially numerous in the late-1980s economic (and housing) boom, when older buildings were torn down and replaced with larger complexes that commanded higher rentals. The "lower loan interest rate for multigenerational living" policy (in effect since 1972) enables families to pay a lower interest rate on loans to renovate their homes to accommodate their elderly members. The "elder-friendly home renovation support" (in effect since 1990), still a unique attempt in Japan, pays the cost of renovating an elder's home (such as lowering the height of the bathtub, or leveling the entrance) unconditionally, without income restrictions or upper limits. Although this is an expensive project (it may cost as much as 4 million yen to renovate a house), the government considers it more economical than supporting an elder in a nursing home, which costs 4.2 million yen per year.[2]

[2] Dollar equivalents in the text have been calculated at U.S. $1 = 110 yen, the approximate rate of exchange during my fieldwork in 1995–96.

Programs such as "home helper service" dispatch caregivers to assist elders at home who need assistance in daily chores. Day service centers provide recreational activities and meals to elders during the day, and in "short stay" programs elders are lodged temporarily (up to one week) to relieve the burden of their family caregivers. In 1995, two "geriatric health facilities" (*rōjin hoken shisetsu*) began operation, offering a maximum three-month stay to elders and those in need of rehabilitation. Such facilities bridge the gap between hospitalization and home care for residents who are expected to return to their homes after rehabilitative care (*Kōhō Edogawa* 1996, 8).

To use limited land efficiently, Edogawa Ward, like other metropolitan areas in Japan, also combines welfare services. There are eight cultural centers for elders (called *Kusunoki karuchā kyōshitsu*) housed in the empty classrooms in elementary schools. In addition, to fully take advantage of the expertise and facilities in the nursing homes, all nursing homes also provide home care services such as short stay, day service, rehabilitation programs, and classes for family caregivers.

Kotoen

Kotoen is one such integrated welfare center in Edogawa Ward, although this facility is unusual because of its age integration. In its three-story building totaling 3,895.4 square meters, it has a 50-bed-capacity nursing home, Riverside Green; a 50-member old-age home, Kotoen; a nursery for 80 children ranging from age one to six, Edogawa Nursery; and a home care service center, *Fureai-no-sato* (lit. "the village of contact") for community elders. Five services are provided under the home care service center: short stay (respite care), a service for bedridden elders in the community who require assistance with bathing, rehabilitation therapy, family caregivers' courses, and a day service center that can accommodate up to twenty elders. Elders attending the day service are usually referred to as "*Fureai* Hall elders" by the staff, following the name of the room where the day service activities are held. In the spring of 1997, short-stay and day service for demented elders in the community (capacity of fifteen) were added to the center.

Kotoen was founded by a philanthropist, Masaharu Shimada (1899–1976), the father-in-law of the present director, Mr. Sugi.[3] It started as a

---

[3] Kotoen is a family enterprise, and Mr. Sugi is the second generation in this family corporation. His wife, the daughter of the founder, is the administrative director who oversees the

two-story wood-frame *yōrōin* (lit. "support house for the aged") in 1962. The *yōrōin* has existed since 1895, primarily to house the childless and indigent. Its origin, coupled with its deviation from the traditional norm of the Confucian ethic of filial piety, has severely stigmatized old-age institutions. Early *yōrōin* were sponsored mainly by Buddhist and Christian organizations. As the need for such facilities increased with postwar poverty, more were developed by the government and by philanthropists such as Mr. Shimada.

When the Welfare Law for the Elderly was implemented in 1963, Kotoen registered to become a nonprofit social welfare corporation (*shakai fukushi hōjin*). It also became the first old-age institution in Edogawa Ward to be licensed by the Ministry of Health and Welfare.[4] The 1963 law shaped the current system of institutional care for elders. Under the new system, the *yōrōin* were reclassified under a new name, Home for Elderly Care. The name change, however, was not particularly successful in elevating the stigma of old-age institutions.

In 1970, Kotoen started the Edogawa Nursery, located next to the old-age home. The nursery was licensed in 1976 to coexist and be managed alongside the old-age home. Longtime residents of Kotoen who used to stay in the two-story building recalled having combined festive celebrations with the nursery children because of their close proximity. Thus old-age home residents have long had contact with children before moving into the new Kotoen.

The new Kotoen, conceptualized by the dynamic Mr. Sugi, was a revolutionary concept in Japanese welfare services at that time. Besides being the first age-integrated facility in Japan, it also added a nursing home and a day service center for community elders—services that are increasingly demanded by an aged society.

The architectural concept of Kotoen further challenges the norm of welfare facilities; Mr. Sugi chose a design that blurs the boundaries of the different services and simulates family living: different facilities share a living hall, kitchen, and bathroom. However, it took much effort to get

---

everyday operations of the center. They hope that their elder son will assume the directorship after they retire, but because he is studying in an entirely different discipline now, it is doubtful whether he is interested. "Any one of the three children is fine [to assume directorship of Kotoen]," said Mrs. Sugi. They have two sons and a daughter.

[4] There are thirty-three old-age homes in Tokyo metropolitan area, four of which are publicly run; the other twenty-nine are managed privately through social welfare corporations, although they may have been built with public funds. All receive subsidies from the national and local governments.

お年寄りと子供の施設

Figure 2.1. Logo of Kotoen. Courtesy of Kotoen.

such a novel idea across to the authorities, who were puzzled with Kotoen's determination to "complicate the whole matter by merging different facilities into one." The new complex was finally completed in April 1987, marking the twenty-fifth anniversary of Kotoen. Construction cost of the complex totaled 958.4 million yen, with funding derived from the Metropolitan (National) Government Fund (51.26 percent), the Edogawa Ward Fund (39.78 percent), the Kotoen Fund (7.87 percent), and private donations (1.1 percent).

The modern, triangular, concrete complex sweeps away the bleak image of an old-age institution. It is painted in cheerful orange-beige and light gray, with a picture of a giraffe eating grass painted on one wall and snails painted on the wall near the entrance. From the far view of the building's east side, the Kotoen logo is visible at the top of the building—a smiling elderly woman in a kimono holding hands and dancing merrily with a bunch of happy children (see Figure 2.1).

The cheerful atmosphere of Kotoen is sustained mainly through the elders' interaction with the nursery children. The interaction can often be seen at the big hall (an open, multipurpose hall) on the first floor as one enters through the main entrance (see Figure 2.2). Like any typical

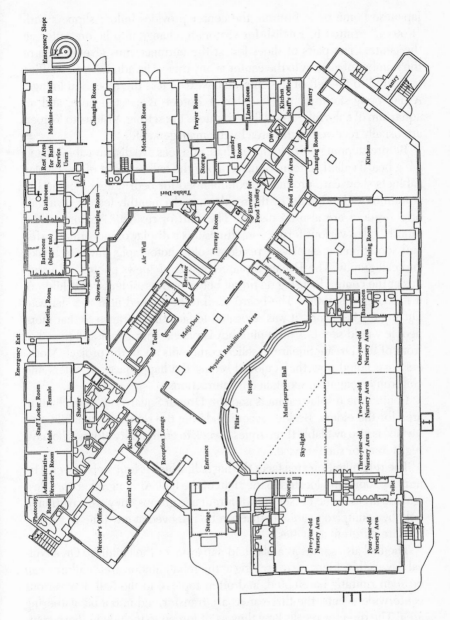

Figure 2.2. First-floor layout. Courtesy of Kotoen.

Japanese home or institution, the center provides indoor slippers with "Kotoen" printed in English for visitors to change into before entering the center. The pairs of shoes left at the entrance thus give an idea of the number of visitors to the center at any time. The administrative office is located to the left of the entrance. Next to it is the reception lounge. A half-body statue of the founder of Kotoen is erected here, and an aquarium of colorful tropical fish brightens the setting. Visitors to Kotoen are usually received in this area by the management.

Before stepping down to the big hall, one sees two display cabinets and a big board called "Dream Square" along the hallway. Part of the display cabinets show care products recommended for bedridden elders in the community. Handicrafts by the residents and a monthly feature on a staff or a resident are also on display. The staff or resident "feature of the month" takes various forms; sometimes it is a display of individual crafts, and sometimes it displays a resident's old photographs, favorite books, and calligraphy. The Dream Square consists of "news photos" of activities at the center, focusing on *fureai* between the residents and children; it is changed monthly. The board used to be located near the stairway. During my fieldwork, it was relocated to face the entrance so that more people would see it. A little pink box is placed with paper and pencil in front of the Dream Square to solicit comments about the project. Mothers have noted how they enjoyed seeing the happy faces of elders and children engaging in spontaneous interactions.

Behind the display cabinets and the Dream Square is a rehabilitation area for the elders. Besides accommodating the residents, rehabilitative service is also available three times a week to community elders who have registered for such service.

The rehabilitation area faces the big hall, which is four steps lower. The nursery rooms are located to the right of the hall. Although there are designated areas in the nursery for different age groups, they are partitioned only by countertop cabinets that can be removed at any time to accommodate different activities.

The hall also serves as a play and nap area for the children. On a typical day, as the elders are exercising at the rehabilitation area, children can be seen running barefooted, and often topless, in the hall. For various centerwide events, the three areas are transformed into a big gathering area. The director recalls how they were forced to include in their architectural plan a mobile wall separating the elders from the children—which they have never put up—in order to obtain approval for construction. Kotoen's idea of an open living concept for both generations was initially frowned on by authorities, who claimed that active children would endanger the elders, and that interaction might also cause the spread of viruses.

Besides the reception lounge, office, nursery, rehabilitation area, and the hall, the first floor houses the dining room, kitchen, bathrooms, laundry room, and staff locker rooms; it also contains a meeting room and a prayer room (a *tatami* room where the *butsudan* or Buddhist altar is located). The dining room, which can accommodate up to eighty people, is also used for residents' meetings. The air duct in the center of the building next to the stairway has been made into a small Japanese-style garden. Because it is too small for one to stroll in, people usually appreciate the garden through the glass door along the corridor.

Rooms for the old-age home and the Riverside Green elders are located on the second and third floor respectively. There are twenty-three double rooms and four single rooms on the second floor, bounded by three hallways (*dōri*) named after the three periods of Japan—Meiji (1868–1912), Taisho (1912–25), and Showa (1926–89), (see Figure 2.3).

If the hallways represent streets, the rooms along them would represent individual houses, where names of the residents are carved on a small strip of wood placed outside the "house." The balcony that each room has, then, would be metaphoric of the back alleys of houses found in the *shitamachi*. Like those back alleys, residents have cultivated potted plants on their balconies, extending their living space beyond the small unit comprised of a bed, a closet, a cabinet, a small round coffee table, and a chair for each resident. Because little space is allocated to each resident, residents are allowed to bring only a minimal number of personal belongings to the home. The wash basin for each resident is located outside the room, and two rooms share a toilet, for which the residents involved are responsible for its upkeep.

Along the "streets," there are also small tables and chairs in which residents may rest or interact. There are three television sets on the second floor. The one in the chatting corner draws the most viewers, as it is surrounded by two long sofas and a settee that can accommodate at least ten people. The other two are located along the Meiji-*dōri* and Taisho-*dōri* and tend to serve residents whose rooms are close by. The administration has deliberately forbidden residents to have television sets in their rooms, hoping this will get them out of their rooms more often to interact with fellow residents. Sharing television sets helps to foster interaction, but sometimes it also causes conflicts over television programs.

Residents also share the refrigerators next to the elevator. Near the

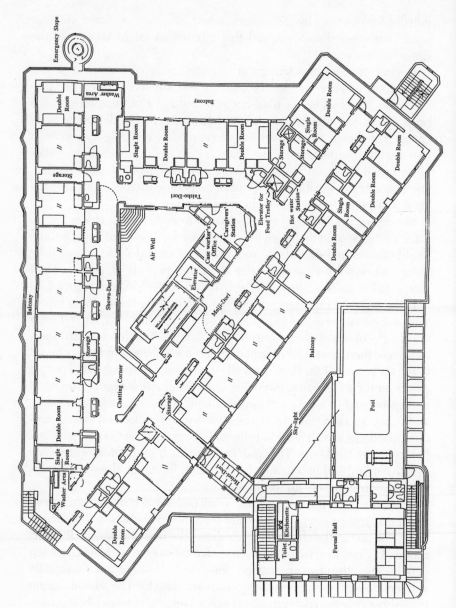

Figure 2.3. Second-floor layout. Courtesy of Kotoen.

elevator, too, are a notice board and a blackboard where activities for the day and upcoming activities are announced. Sometimes a creative staff member will draw caricatures of a fellow staff member or resident on the blackboard to amuse passersby. The public address system is also used frequently to make announcements. The caregivers' station for the home is located next to the notice board. Residents visit the station only when they need to talk to a caregiver, or on designated days of the month to collect a new daily supply of items such as tissues, toilet paper, and toothpaste. Outside the station, a few goldfish swim in a tank whose cloudy water seems to be due to the smoke from the smokers who congregate in that spot.

A walkway overlooking the big hall connects the home with Fureai Hall. Parallel to other hallways, it is named Heisei, after the present period (began in 1989) in Japan. On one end the Fureai Hall has a nine-mat *tatami* raised platform (16.2 square meters) where tea ceremony classes are held. Elders attending day service stay primarily in this room during the five hours in which they have lunch and a snack and participate in cultural activities such as *ikebana* (flower arrangement) and calligraphy. Five different groups of elders attend the day service center here weekly, with transport provided by Kotoen.

Fureai Hall also leads to the outdoor pool that is opened only in summer for the nursery children. Residents whose rooms face the pool particularly enjoy watching the children shouting and jumping in the water.

Across the entrance to the third floor is a bar stating "Cleaning in Process." The bar is placed there permanently to prevent senile elders from wandering down the stairs. The atmosphere between the second and third floor is different despite similar layouts (see Figure 2.4). There are eleven four-bed rooms, two double rooms, and two single rooms in the nursing home; in addition, there are two four-bed rooms with television sets attached to each bed for short-stay services. The nurses' station is also located on the third floor. There are two quiet rooms with five beds for sick residents (including home residents) connected to the nurses' station so that they may be monitored closely. Kotoen has one resident doctor trained in internal medicine who comes regularly to attend primarily to Riverside Green residents. A psychiatrist and a surgeon also visit the nursing home once a month. These doctors provide general health maintenance. Residents are sent to a nearby hospital in cases of serious illness.

Compared with the second floor, the third floor seems more crowded, partly because there are more caregivers on duty there. There are also

[29]

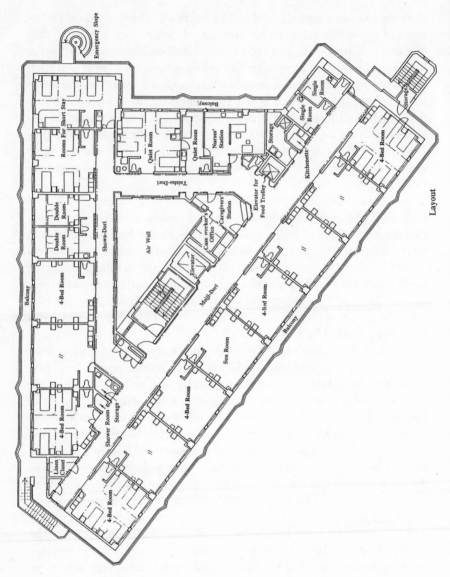

Figure 2.4. Third-floor layout. Courtesy of Kotoen.

more residents sitting along the hallway where the television sets are, although they are not necessarily watching television. As many residents use wheelchairs, it is easier for the caregivers to gather them outside of their rooms. The relatively mobile residents, however, seem to prefer staying in their own rooms. Half of the Riverside Green residents have ascended from the home below, and they sometimes joke about waiting for a passport to the next "promotion"—the "other world."

Staff

Kotoen has a relatively complex administrative structure because of its age-integrated nature. Its seven-member board of directors consists of Mr. Sugi, the director; his brother-in-law (whose father was the founder of Kotoen); a doctor; a company president; and three Buddhist priests from different sects. The priests are usually invited to host memorial services and funerals at Kotoen. There are also two consultants to Kotoen: one is director of a Special Home for Elderly Care, and the other is a priest. This priest has a graveyard in his temple for people who die without family connections (*muenbutsu*); among them are some deceased residents from Kotoen. Discussions about Kotoen owning its own "institutional" graveyard have been ongoing; however, this is complicated by the existence of numerous Buddhist sects in Japan. People who have belonged to other sects may refuse to consent to burial in Kotoen's graveyard for this reason.

All five key administrators at Kotoen hold double positions. Mr. Sugi is both the director for Kotoen and the old-age home. His wife is the administrative director and head of the home care services. Of the three assistant directors, Mr. Hitachi doubles as nursery principal, Mrs. Matsuki is also the case worker for Riverside Green, and Mr. Miki is concurrently the Riverside Green director. Both Mr. Hitachi and Mrs. Matsuki started working at Kotoen as caregivers at least fifteen years ago, while Mr. Miki joined Kotoen only two years ago, after retiring from the civil service. In Japan, the practice of reemployment in another organization after one's first retirement, called *amakudari* (lit. "descending from heaven"), is a common practice among high-ranking officers. When a retired civil servant is transferred to head a welfare institution, it creates a linkage between the institution and the city office, which helps to facilitate dealings between the two bodies.

Mr. and Mrs. Sugi are instrumental in implementing the *daikazoku* ideology at Kotoen. Both in their mid-forties, they are relatively young as directors of welfare institutions. Their youthfulness, positive personalities, and "pioneer spirits" have steered Kotoen toward becoming a special welfare institution. Their efforts are further made possible by a group of dynamic and dedicated staff who are willing to cooperate across departments and devote extra time and energy to program planning and implementation.

There are seventy-seven staff members (sixty-six full time and eleven part time; seventeen men and sixty women) in Kotoen's six departments—nursery (eleven), elder care (thirty-six), nursing (seven), kitchen (fifteen), transportation (four), and administration (four). The professional caregivers (twenty-nine full time and seven part time)—called *ryōbo* or *ryōfu* (lit. "dorm mother or dorm father")—rotate to handle duties in the six separate services for the elders (care home, special nursing home, rehabilitation service, bath service, short stay, and day service). There are four full-time and two part-time men among the caregivers. In recent years there has been an increase in men being employed as professional caregivers, traditionally a female occupation.

According to regulations set by the Ministry of Welfare and Health, the ratio of caregivers to residents must be one-to-ten in an old-age home, one-to-four in a nursing home, and one-to-eight in a day service center. An increasing number of caregivers are graduates of two-year welfare professional schools (*fukushi senmon gakkō*). Although prior knowledge of elderly care is a plus, Kotoen also employs inexperienced staff members who show capability and great interest in elder care. Many of these staff members learn on the job and at some point in their careers obtain the license for social welfare workers (*shakai fukushishi*) or care welfare workers (*kaigo fukushishi*).[5] The staff turnover rate is fairly high at Kotoen because single young female workers who make up the bulk of the staff population have a higher tendency to leave for a change in work environment or because of marriage. During the year of my research, seven resigned and twelve new staff members joined the group, including two part-time men.

There are always five caregivers on duty at the old-age home during

---

[5] A law for the certification of social welfare workers and care welfare workers was passed by the Ministry of Health and Welfare in 1987. Under this law, professional caregivers with a four-year college degree may take the national qualifying examination to be licensed as a "social welfare worker," while those with two-year degrees may take the examination to qualify as a "care welfare worker" (Hamaguchi 1996, 51).

the day. They oversee the daily needs of the residents, help them to adapt to a group living environment, provide a listening ear and sometimes discipline them when necessary. Mr. Yama, the case worker for the home, is also greatly involved in the everyday running of the home, as his office is located next to the caregivers' station because of a shortage of space. In most old-age homes, case workers like Mr. Yama would have a desk in the administrative office, so their relations with residents would be less intimate, and they would be concerned mainly with financial matters. Mr. Yama and the chief caregiver for the home are the two familiar figures that residents see every day. Other caregivers rotate to work an average of two days a month at the old-age home.

The teachers, although they do not take charge of the elders, generally know the names of the residents because of frequent contact with them. It is common to see teachers chatting with the institution's elders.

Each caregiver is also assigned to take charge of four residents—two from Riverside Green and two from the home. The assignment changes every six months with Riverside Green residents and yearly with home residents; this avoids the development of overly intimate relations, which may jeopardize the caregivers' objectivity. Caregivers are expected to be "monitors" of the residents assigned to them; they are expected to spend more time with them and serve as their confidants.

A caregiver works twenty-four days a month, including five days of night duty. He or she usually spends two days at the home and twelve days at Riverside Green, with the other workdays spread among several home care services; this makes the caregiver known, but not particularly close to the elders. Although their official workload is forty-one hours a week, it is usual for caregivers to work overtime, especially before a festival or event. Staff often feel that Kotoen resembles a school with abundant extracurricular activities and events.

Despite complaints that caregivers may have about work burdens and occasionally difficult and demanding residents, the overall work climate is a lively and encouraging one. Compared with other old-age institutions, where the average age of caregivers is between forty and forty-nine (Miwa 1994, 222), an overwhelming number of staff from the elder care and nursery sections are single females under twenty-five. Their vitality helps enhance the institution's lively atmosphere.

A dues-collecting staff union organizes recreational activities such as baseball and bowling to promote interaction among the staff. Staff members also organize their own annual vacation, which is subsidized by the center. However, Kotoen's staff rarely participate in social drinking sessions, which are common among coworkers in Japan. The staff claim that irregular work hours have made getting together difficult; in addition, the administration also discourages such practices, being concerned that any misconduct in public after drinking may affect the Kotoen image. This reflects the concern about image prevalent in Japanese schools.

In the study of the dilemmas faced by nursing homes caregivers in the United States, Nancy Foner (1994) discovered that race, gender, and ethnicity complicate a caregiver's position. In Japan, race and ethnicity do not constitute a factor (at least on the surface) in old-age institutions. As women form the majority of the workforce in these institutions, gender is less of a hurdle in job advancement than is personal capability, unlike the situation found in the typical Japanese company. The power relations between seniors and juniors are also less pronounced here, as compared with the conflicts found among caregivers in Diana Bethel's (1993) study of a Japanese old-age home. A relatively new caregiver at Kotoen found the rumor she has heard about seniors bullying juniors in nursing homes quite irrelevant in this workplace. In general, caregivers at Kotoen are deeply concerned about the residents' welfare and take pride in their work. Ruth Campbell (1984, 89) observes that "in Japan, one does not encounter theft of personal property, endemic in many nursing homes in the United States; nor the scandals about inadequate care and abuses that erupt from time to time in this country." This is certainly true of Kotoen.

In most Japanese old-age institutions, the staff members wear aprons with their nametags pinned on. At Kotoen, however, the usual uniform for all staff (except the kitchen staff) is a T-shirt with the Kotoen logo printed on the back and turquoise track pants (and a turquoise track jacket if it is cold). Their names are written on a piece of cloth ironed onto the track pants and jackets. Because I also wore the same uniform, the residents sometimes conveniently called me *"ryōbo-san"* even when they knew I was only a volunteer.

There are several committees comprised of staff members from different sections. These include the Volunteer Committee, which facilitates volunteer activities at Kotoen; the Fire Prevention Committee, which coordinates with the community during fire-prevention exercises; the Newsletter Committee, in charge of *fureai;* and the Committee to Promote *Fureai,* which facilitates cooperation among different sections in carrying out alternate-generation interactions.[6]

[6] Most volunteers from the community are middle-aged housewives and retirees. They help in the laundry, with bed-sheet-changing for Riverside Green residents, with giving haircuts and

The Committee to Promote *Fureai* meets monthly to plan and discuss events and activities for *fureai*. It adopts an ethnographic approach in recording the extent of *fureai* in the center by placing notebooks referred to as "antenna" in all the staff offices so that staff can record the *fureai* they have observed among different groups, not only among the residents and children but also among the residents and Fureai Hall elders, as well as the home and Riverside Green residents. These anecdotes—the kind of spontaneous interactions most desired by the center—are read during the monthly meetings. The committee also organizes an annual presentation open to all staff. The 1996 presentation featured reports on surveys relating to alternate-generation *fureai* conducted by the elder care and nursery departments. About fifteen staff attended the presentation; many voiced opinions and suggestions on ways to improve *fureai*. Mr. Hitachi, the nursery principal, suggested that the teachers should keep the children informed of their "grandparents'" conditions—for instance, telling them when someone is discharged from the hospital.

Residents

Admission Process

When an elder wishes to enter an old-age home, he or she may apply through the "window" (*madoguchi*) of the ward office's social welfare department.[7] There are four types of institutional care available in Japan (see Appendix A).

In principle, applicants for old-age homes must be sixty-five or over and unable to live independently because of physical, mental, environmental, or economic reasons (physically or mentally disabled individuals may also apply before age sixty-five). An elder's health condition is the main criterion in determining whether he or she should apply to an old-age home or a nursing home. Applicants to old-age homes must have a relatively high level of ADL (activities in daily living) and be able to manage their daily personal care. Economic reasons would determine

---

permanents, and with general maintenance and cleaning. Elementary school children also serve as volunteers to the center on a regular basis.

[7] Kotoen residents are called *riyōsha* (lit. "user"). In this book, as the subjects of the study are mainly residents of the old-age home, *residents* will by default mean old-age home elders unless otherwise specified.

whether one should apply to an old-age home or to other facilities such as care houses or homes with moderate fees. There was no stated income limit for old-age homes in the welfare handbook, but according to the administration (who last inquired about it five years ago), elders who exceed an annual income of 3.8 million yen would be disqualified from applying to an old-age home. The subsidized fee each old-age home resident pays depends on his or her economic status, ranging from zero for elders on welfare to a maximum of 150,000 yen per month. At Kotoen, four residents are on welfare; most pay between 10,000 to 28,000 yen; and the highest monthly payment was 93,000 yen.

With the introduction of care insurance in 2000, the fate of old-age homes has become increasingly uncertain.[8] While nursing home residents would be covered under the new insurance scheme, old-age home residents are excluded from the scheme, as they have already been supported publicly as residents in a welfare institution. Some old-age home administrators anticipate the possible transformation of old-age homes into nursing homes in the future, while others expect changes in future admission criteria such as admitting mentally impaired individuals younger than sixty-five. Kotoen, too, does not rule out the possibility that the old-age home will become some form of care home or even a part of the nursing home in the future.

Edogawa Ward has two old-age homes with a total capacity of 137. An applicant to an old-age home can expect to wait up to three years for a placement because there are so many people on the waiting list. When there is an opening in Kotoen, the case worker informs the ward social welfare department, who will then forward three potential residents on the waiting list to the case worker. These potential residents will then be interviewed by the case workers to evaluate their personality traits and social skills to determine if they are suitable for a group living environment like Kotoen. Because of the unique setting of Kotoen, potential residents are also asked if they like children. Nevertheless, their answers do not jeopardize their chances of entering the home, as the administrator expects diversity among residents even in their opinion on children.

---

[8]The Care Insurance program covers service expenses incurred by individuals age forty and over. In the case of individuals between age forty and sixty-four, the insurance covers care services of those who suffer from age-related illnesses such as stroke or dementia. All persons age forty and over must contribute to the insurance premium. The Care Insurance is financed equally by the premium contributed and general revenue. To cope with conspicuous increase in the insurance payment, the government increased general revenue by raising the consumption tax from 3 percent to 5 percent beginning in April 1997 (Maeda 1996, 111).

When an admission is confirmed, the case worker will brief the residents-to-be on the rules and regulations and on what things to bring to their "final home." This includes a reminder that they are not allowed to preach their religious belief to other residents, although they may practice their own religions in private. Religious altars are also not allowed in their rooms, although their family memorial tablets (*ihai*) may be placed with the institution's Buddhist altar. The few members of new religions among the residents are said to have terminated their membership after entering Kotoen. The staff attributed these residents' withdrawal to their inability to make the financial commitment that their religions required of them. They also claimed that many residents may have terminated their membership in religious sects because they have found a sense of security on entering an old-age home. Perhaps the new religions become less attractive when the biggest worry of care "in this world" has been taken care of.

Reasons for Admission

The decision to apply to an old-age home is inevitably one of the biggest decisions elders make. Unlike residents of private old-age institutions who may still leave their institutions for other living arrangements if they are dissatisfied, elders who enter old-age homes usually have limited financial and social resources. Hence an old-age home is also a final home in this world to most residents. In making the decision, many face the struggle of surrendering their freedom to the regimentation of group life in exchange for shelter and peace of mind as they face frailty in old age.

Many elders have a stigmatized image of old-age homes before entering one. Mr. Okada said he heard only negative things about old-age homes before he entered Kotoen: "Neighbors told me that it is not safe in an old-age home because people will steal your things; your wallet needs to be with you all the time. Then I asked, 'What happens when I take a bath?'" He found Kotoen much better than what he had thought and heard.

Mr. Ishii shared his feelings, too. He expressed his initial fear when entering Kotoen: "I was feeling uneasy about entering an old-age home. Why must I end up in such a place? I was depressed with myself. When people knew that I was moving into an old-age home, they gave me that look and exclaimed, 'What? Old-age home?'"

Mr. Ishii is among the thirty-two (twenty-four women and eight men) residents who were living alone before entering Kotoen, either because they were divorced, childless, widowed, or never married. Like most of them, he applied for admission because of anxieties over weakening health.

Although a resident of the silver pia that was designed for convenient old-age living, Mrs. Kita opted to enter Kotoen after thirteen years of widowhood: "The ward welfare office staff suggested that I should consider entering an old-age home rather than staying alone. I thought it was a good idea. Although there are emergency buttons in public apartments, doors are always closed there. What if I fainted in the room? Nobody would know."

Given their circumstances, residents in general see the old-age home as a safe haven where they are provided three meals a day, medical attention, heat in winter, and a cooler environment in summer. However, the social stigma that Japanese society has placed on old-age institutions has made elders' situation paradoxical: on the one hand, they are thankful for the presence of such an alternative, but on the other, they feel that it is a socially less desirable alternative to staying with one's children.

An overwhelming majority of Kotoen elders agree that the ideal place to live out one's old age is with one's children. The eighty-three-year-old Miss Onuki, who has never married, expressed this most emotionally: "The best blessing in life is a family. In this world, it is considered the highest blessing if one could take one's three meals in a family."

Eighty-five-year-old Mrs. Hara entered Kotoen eleven years ago, after her husband's death. She thinks that old-age homes should be places for people like her who have no children to support them in old age. Thus she is sometimes cynical about those who are parents: "Some people have as many as eight children; I wonder what they are doing here?" She is one of the childless (including the never married) residents (comprising 60 percent of the residents) who often idealize parenthood: "If only I had a child, I wouldn't be here," she said. However, those who used to live with their children prior to admission may think otherwise.

Environmental reasons such as conflicts with their sons, daughters, daughters-in-law, or sons-in-law; cramped living space; and a lack of caregivers at home are the main reasons cited by elders with children who applied to enter old-age homes. Ninety-year-old Mrs. Chiba entered Kotoen seventeen years ago. She was living with one of her six daughters but decided to apply to an old-age home because she was not comfortable living with her son-in-law. She applied without the knowledge of the children. When she announced this to her children on the eve of her move to Kotoen, they were surprised and objected vigorously to her "stubborn action."

As Edogawa Ward has two old-age homes, what made residents decide on Kotoen? Some residents had no preferences and entered simply because there was a space. Two residents have friends in Kotoen who told them Kotoen is a good place. About half of the residents, however, made comparisons between the two homes before they decided on Kotoen. Location was one attraction for some residents. Kotoen is only a two-minute walk from the bus stop and a twelve-minute walk to the subway station, which takes one directly to Shinjuku in little more than thirty minutes. The immediate neighborhood offers a shopping street with a variety of stores that cater to all daily needs. The building, size, and newness of Kotoen are other well-cited reasons. Kotoen is among the thirty-three old-age homes in the Tokyo metropolitan area and has one of the smallest capacities (50 persons); the old-age home with the largest capacity accommodates 920 people. Mr. Yokohira, who chose Kotoen because of the size factor, thinks that fewer people would mean fewer conflicts and less congestion. Built in 1987, Kotoen is also relatively new; its rooms are double-occupancy (the ward's other old-age home has four persons to a room) and its beds are more comfortable for the back and legs (the other old-age home provides futons).

The presence of an on-site nursing home also attracts applicants. Kotoen gives priority to residents in placement to the nursing home on the third floor. Few old-age homes offer their frail residents priority placement in a nursing home on the same premises, even with the same managing organization. Residents of an old-age home in a neighboring ward I visited had lower chances of being admitted to one of the two adjacent nursing homes on the premises than did elders in the community. The home's case worker explained that this is because elders in the community are thought to need nursing home care more urgently than the old-age home elders already institutionalized. As a result, the old-age home must stretch its resources to devote additional medical attention approaching that of nursing home care to about 15 percent of its residents who are on the waiting list (men usually wait about 18 months and women about 3 years).

Eleven residents were at Kotoen before the new facility was built. Of the remaining thirty-nine residents, more than half were unaware of the nursery's existence until they entered, and many were surprised at the

[39]

combination of age groups at the facility. Miss Murakami, however, is one of the few who elected to enter here because of the nursery: "I have seen Kotoen on TV and in the newspapers and learned that this is a place where elders and children interact. That is why I wanted to enter only this place, and waited two years for it."

Regardless of whether the nursery had influenced the residents' initial decision to enter Kotoen, all (except two) claim that the presence of children has made Kotoen a better place for elders. Most think that children make an old-age home lively and help maintain elders' health. As Miss Tanaka claims: "It is definitely good to have children around instead of only groups of elders clustering together and talking about nothing but their pains and aches."

Profile of the Residents

The demographic characteristics of Kotoen's elders mirror those of elders in most welfare institutions: There are more women than men; most residents are widowed, divorced, or never married; and few residents have more than six years of elementary school education.

Sex and Age Structure

Kotoen has 15 men and 35 women, and the average age is 80.32 years. Men (age range from 67 to 89) have a lower average age of 75.53, as compared with women's average age of 82.37 (an age range from 67 to 91). More than half (58 percent) of the residents are over 80, which is above the average life expectancy of Japanese. One 82-year-old woman who has been a resident for 11 years is proud that she has never visited the doctor since she entered Kotoen; she jokingly claims that the vitality of the children must have been a factor.

As the youngest and the oldest in the home have an age difference of twenty-four years, Mr. Asada, the youngest man, found several of the women here the same age as his mother, and he feels a generational gap between them: "It must be due to generational differences, but I hate to watch period drama [historical drama] [on television]. But here all three TV sets are tuned to the same program; I can't watch my favorite sports program. . . . Also, the older residents use different words [*kotoba*]; sometimes I don't understand what they are saying."

Mr. Asada entered Kotoen when he turned sixty-five. He had applied

Table 2.1
Resident Age and Sex Structure

Age Group	Male (%)	Female (%)	Total (%)
65–69	2 (13.3)	1 (2.9)	3 (6)
70–74	6 (40.0)	3 (8.6)	9 (18)
75–79	3 (20.0)	4 (11.4)	7 (14)
80–84	3 (20.0)	12 (34.4)	15 (30)
85–89	1 (6.7)	13 (37.1)	14 (28)
90+	0	2 (5.7)	2 (4)
			50 (100)

for admission prior to the minimum eligible age because he was told that there was a seven-year waiting period. He was shocked when informed of his placement several months later and was hesitant because he was still working then. After much contemplation, he decided to quit his job to secure a place in the home. He and several others in their sixties or early seventies are termed the *Showa-mono* (people born between 1926 and 1988) by the staff, as compared with the *Taisho-mono* (people born between 1912 and 1925) and *Meiji-mono* (people born before 1912). These demarcations roughly coincided with the demographic divisions of the elders as young-old (sixty-five to seventy-four years old), old-old (seventy-five to eighty-four years old), and oldest-old (above eighty-five years old).

Generational differences expressed by Mr. Asada are often felt among the residents. Referring to Mrs. Matsuda's age, eighty-eight-year-old Mrs. Hoya says that "she finally received the silver pass last month!"[9] This implies that Mrs. Matsuda is much younger than Mrs. Hoya. The difference in attitudes between the two women is distinct: While Mrs. Hoya dresses and behaves like an elderly person, Mrs. Matsuda is still conscientious about her appearance and dresses like a middle-age woman. The differences reveal the former's resignation to old age and the latter's resistance of it.

Until recently, the *Meiji-mono* and the *Taisho-mono* have dominated the old-age homes. These elders, many having undergone hardship in their youth, are said to complain less, demand less, and be more appreciative. The emerging *Showa-mono*, however, are more demanding and individualistic and are characterized as more highly educated and more vocal, which makes them harder to please.

[9] Japanese over age seventy may apply for a "silver pass" that entitles them to free rides on public transportation.

Table 2.2
Marital Status

	Male (%)	Female (%)	Total (%)
Single	2 (13.3)	6 (17.1)	8 (16)
Married	0	1 (2.9)	1 (2)
Widowed	2 (13.3)	20 (57.1)	22 (44)
Divorced	9 (56.0)	8 (22.9)	18 (36)
Others	2 (13.4)	0	2 (4)
			50 (100)

Marital Status

It is not surprising that many women have outlived their husbands by the time they turn eighty. Some widows place the photograph of their deceased husband in the display cabinet near the entrance of their room; it represents their family memorial tablets, near which they present a cup of tea and pray every day. Others place their family memorial tablets in the prayer room on the first floor, where they pray and burn incense. Only one resident is still married, but her husband stays in the nursing home on the third floor.

A greater number of men are divorced, which helps explain why most were staying alone and applied to enter the institution at an earlier age. Japan's family-centric culture has placed a stigma on divorce, which makes it more difficult to remarry than is the case in the West (Sugimoto 1997, 159).

Educational Background

Because of poverty, the war, and limited access to higher education, few Japanese elders, particularly women eighty and over, attended school beyond the compulsory six years of elementary education. This is also reflected in the educational background of the residents. Two-thirds (thirty-four) have four to six years of compulsory school education. Several women have additional schooling beyond that; the most highly educated among the women had attended two years at a prefectural girls' high school (about thirteen years of schooling). Among the men, one graduated from high school under the old system (the equivalent to today's university education), and the other had withdrawn from a university to enlist in the army during the war.

Educational level contributes to class differences felt among the residents. Several more educated residents often complained about the oth-

Table 2.3
Educational Level Attained

	Male	Female	Total
None	0	2	2
Old primary school (4 years)	4	17	21
Primary school (6 years)	6	7	13
Middle school (boys)	3	0	3
Middle school (girls)	0	7	7
Vocational school	0	1	1
High school	2	1	3
			50

ers being unrefined (*hin ga nai*): "Don't even know the proper etiquette," "Does not dress appropriately," and "Don't know the proper way of speech" are some of the commonly heard comments by these residents.

Old and New Residents

Although class differences perceived among the residents sometimes cause conflicts among them, old-timers and newcomers are also a constant source of friction. Old-timers complain that the newcomers are arrogant and "do not even greet us properly." One old-timer commented, "Why are the newcomers getting so rude now? They should know that past status is no longer significant and that it doesn't serve to identify them here. Once here, we are all the same."

Greeting is particularly important to older Japanese, who see a greeting—usually a bow and a few polite words—not returned as a great humiliation (Kinoshita and Kiefer 1992, 180). Greetings play an even more important role in closed settings like an old-age home, where limited resources among its residents make it one of the few significant "resources" for reciprocal exchange.

Similarly, the newcomers are bitter about the seniors here. Miss Tanaka, an outspoken woman who had been at Kotoen for a year, recalled: "When I first came, there were some who had been here longer trying to boss me around, but I didn't care. I think by staying here a long time, they have lost touch with the outside world. So those of us who came in later know more about the changes in the outside world. The world is changing so fast now."

Many residents believe that entering the home isolates one from the outside world. The oldest male resident, Mr. Koyano, tries to keep abreast of the outside world by visiting his friend downtown every

[43]

morning. A woman maintains that she likes to interact with the elders who come for rehabilitation as a way to learn about the recent happenings outside.

One way to demarcate old and new residents is to differentiate whether they entered before or after the new Kotoen was built. Eleven residents are considered old residents by this criterion. When asked about how they would compare the past and the present Kotoen, they are usually nostalgic about the past. One thirteen-year resident commented, "The past was better; we were closer, as four persons shared a Japanese-style *tatami* room. It was more family-like, and the caregivers were more understanding, too; most of them were older."

However, this resident sees the presence of children as the major merit of the present Kotoen: "Children are lively; they also help increase our activities." Indeed, the presence of children has expanded the number of events that residents celebrate each year, which have made both residents and the caregivers fairly busy, particularly in "high seasons." Kotoen having too many events is perhaps one of the few things that both the staff and the residents agreed on unanimously.

Residents and Staff

The conflicts and complaints residents have of the staff and vice versa are typical of any "total institution" of which an old-age institution is part (Goffman 1961; Shield 1988; Bethel 1993). As in most old-age institutions, residents often complain to one another about the food, the staff, the facility, and the recent measures implemented. They often complain about the staff's indifferent attitude to their needs. In much the same way as mothers-in-law complain about their daughters-in-law at home, staff members also feel that the residents are too dependent and misunderstand their good intentions.

The annual changing of rooms is one of the biggest events for both the staff and the residents. The home adopts this regulation to be fair to all residents and "also as a way to force them to clean up and discard unwanted stuff," said Mr. Yama. Most residents prefer south-facing and single rooms; hence every annual change of rooms is a disappointment to some and a joy to others. Their newly assigned roommate is another great concern to the residents. To avoid problems, prior to room allocation, residents are asked to submit the names of three residents, if there are any, whom they definitely wish to avoid as roommates. This has helped the staff a little in their efforts to pair off the residents without friction, although after room changing in the spring of 1996, curtains between the two beds were drawn permanently in two rooms, signifying hostile relations and thus an unexpected mistake in pairing.

The O-157 incident is another recent episode that has caused widespread dissatisfaction among the residents. The outbreak of the deadly O-157 *E. coli* food poisoning, particularly in Osaka, during the summer of 1996 caused alarm nationwide, especially among nurseries, grade schools, and old-age institutions, as children and elders are said to be most vulnerable to the infection. To avoid possible contamination caused by uncontrolled purchase of food from outside, the Kotoen management announced in mid-July that they were curbing all food brought from outside by the residents, because as long as a single case of food poisoning is found in an institution (even when its residents are not contaminated by the home's food), the kitchen would have to cease operation. Many residents were upset when the food they kept in the refrigerator and in their rooms was disposed of. For a while, the topic of food dominated the residents' conversations; many complained that the curb had deprived them of their favorite food. Most residents thought the curbing of pickled plum (*umebōshi*)—their version of healthy food—unreasonable. It is a custom for many Japanese elders to eat pickled plum with rice, or even to just eat it as a snack.

Mrs. Shibuya was especially disturbed by this regulation and couldn't stop sulking. When she saw me, she pulled me aside and protested: "I want to live only for another few more years; why are they doing this to me?" She said she was deprived of eating cheese and other supplements she needed to put on weight. She was going to have an eye operation in two months and had been asked by the doctor to gain some weight before that. She thought this was now impossible with the food curb. I suggested that she should eat more then, but she gave a sour face and complained that the food at Kotoen was not tasty at all.

Though there is no resident association here, Mrs. Shibuya could have aired her grievances at the monthly meetings arranged by management. Most of such meetings are devoted to announcements and reports by the center's various departments. In a typical meeting, the chief caregiver will comment on last month's aim for the residents before an appointed resident representative discusses and decides on the aim for the following month. Both the nursing home and old-age home maintain an "aim for the month" in the form of slogan, such as "Striving for Better Health," "Let's Have More Smiles and Interact More with the Children" or "Let's Defeat the Cold Season."

[45]

After the aim of the month is decided, the chief caregiver addresses some housekeeping matters before the residents are asked if they have any comments. Some residents take this opportunity to air their grievances. During the meeting held just after the annual change of rooms in 1996, one resident complained that someone always got south-facing rooms while others didn't. On the whole, few complaints are aired during these meetings. On the one hand, it suggests that the residents are generally satisfied with institutional living; on the other hand, it implies that they feel constraint by their position as "institutional beings"; as one resident has commented, "We are all being taken care of [*osewa ni naru*], and this makes it extremely difficult to demand anything."

Although residents in the home generally try to avoid causing inconvenience or trouble to others (*meiwaku o kakenai*) and to the staff, the staff still has to frequently tackle the problems of alcoholism, quarrels, and conflicts between residents. Sometimes problematic residents can cause difficult moments for the staff. Mr. Yama, the home's case worker, often has a problem trying to curb Mr. Shimizu from drinking before the 3 P.M. curfew. One day, he asked him to his office and blew up at him. The caregivers and I were in the staff office then; we overheard Mr. Shimizu promising that he would not do it anymore. Mr. Yama continued in a stern voice, reprimanding him for breaking his promise over and over again; it was like a schoolmaster chiding his student. After a while, the door opened, and Mr. Shimizu walked out. When he saw the chief caregiver, Miss Matsu, he suddenly shouted at her, "It's all because of you that everyone knows that I drink!" Then he held her shoulders and shook them violently while continuing to shout at the top of his lungs, "You are a smart person; go get married formally! I will be your matchmaker! Don't keep saying you have a boyfriend . . . get married and have children; do not be like me. My children are gone and I am all alone; this is lonely!"

We were all stunned and dumbfounded. Miss Matsu was so taken aback by his fierce attitude that she struggled to pull away and started weeping. Miss Matsu is single and in her mid-twenties; she has been working here for five years. An attractive young woman with tanned skin, she is lively, responsible, and capable, the kind of staff person that any care institution would find itself blessed to have. Later Mr. Yama demanded that Mr. Shimizu apologize to Miss Matsu for what he had done and said, but Mr. Shimizu refused to admit that he was wrong. "I am telling the truth, and I am advising her," he claimed.

This was not the first time that a caregiver had been confronted by a resident. This incident reveals how residents view the staff—single, young, and lacking experience in life. It also implies that the residents see marriage and having children as a societal norm; in their view, life is not complete without these accomplishments.

In general, staff members feel that the residents are too pampered and dependent. They always wish for the same treatments that Riverside Green residents are accorded, such as being able to use the center's transport (which is available only to nursing home residents) for hospital visits. During the year of my fieldwork, Mr. Yama introduced a new project called Fifty People, Fifty Voices, in which the residents were asked about their dreams and desires. The management hopes to fulfill residents' wishes as much as possible. Despite the conflicts and tensions that may arise among the residents and the staff, both try to maintain harmonious relationships to make living bearable, if not an enjoyable experience to all. Although the residents seldom praise the staff, the teasing, joking, and caring that are part of the daily interactions with the staff show that they do appreciate their efforts in providing for their physical and emotional needs. Mr. Yama often sighs and says that it is a more difficult task to take care of the second floor residents than those on the third floor: "Problems of the heart [*kokoro no mondai*] are harder to tackle than the care of everyday living, such as changing diapers, feeding, and bathing."

The Second Floor and the Third Floor

The old-age home and nursing home residents at Kotoen are generally addressed as second-floor and third-floor residents, respectively. The differentiation between the second floor and the third floor is distinctive, particularly among the residents themselves. The administration sees the differences as a "continuum of care" in which each resident can receive an appropriate level of care depending on his or her physical conditions without being transferred to an unfamiliar setting. However, the distinction goes beyond physical differences. Although many considered themselves making an exit from the outside world once they were institutionalized, when compared with the third-floor residents—many of whom use wheelchairs, are demented, or are bedridden—they are in an intermediate space, at the boundary between the outside world and full institutionalization. To be a second-floor resident means that one is still mobile, has the freedom to go out, and has more contact with the children.

[47]

Being a second-floor resident can in itself be a source of great satisfaction to many Kotoen residents. Very few second-floor residents seem comfortable with the idea that they will eventually be transferred to the third floor with ailing health. "I will not go to the third floor; I will just die *pokkuri* [drop dead]" and "I want to stay on the second floor as long as possible" are some of the common responses when conversations about the third floor arise.

Although half of the third-floor residents were originally from the second floor, once they ascended, contacts with second-floor residents were reduced significantly. Residents of the different floors usually greet one another only when they meet occasionally at the cafeteria, or when the second-floor residents visit the third-floor nurses' station. Some second-floor residents feel that they don't need much contact with the third-floor residents because they have their own daily life rhythm and that third-floor residents should spend more time interacting with their fellow residents there.

Mrs. Ishimura, who, according to the staff, would be ascending to the third floor once a space was available, was the only one who got to stay in the same room during room changing. She seemed glad to stay constant while others were busy rearranging their belongings, which had been hauled to them from their former rooms. "I like this room, and I want to stay here till I die," she said. Her ADL level was already declining as she experienced increasing difficulty walking and carrying out daily tasks such as doing laundry and cleaning. However, she seemed determined to hang on in the second floor—I even saw her becoming more active with exercising.

To my surprise, Mrs. Ishimura was transferred to the third floor three weeks later. Mr. Yama said she was supposed to move up a year ago, but she had turned down the move twice. This time, she consented to the move because her frailness and incapability to carry out cleaning tasks had inconvenienced the other residents. "Many actually feel relieved to move up because they can relax," he said.

When I met Mrs. Ishimura two weeks later at a garden barbecue party organized for all residents, she was in a wheelchair, looking happy. I asked, "Isn't it better on the third floor now?" I assumed she was feeling good, but she turned furious instead: "I am already old; how long can I live? I said I wanted to stay on the second floor until I die, but they just moved me up like a piece of baggage; I was not even informed beforehand!"

[48]

"Mrs. Ishimura says different things to different people," Mr. Yama commented when I told him about the incident. The staff are often troubled by residents like Mrs. Ishimura who resent the reality of their physical conditions. There have been cases of second-floor residents who resisted going to the third floor so strongly that they were finally allowed to remain on the second floor in the last days of their lives. To many, to be asked to move to the third floor publicly announces that one is deteriorated and no longer fit for independent living. It also means forced disengagement, as residents' social world shrinks with "upward mobility."

Seventy-four-year-old Mr. Yokohira, a six-year resident, however, was quite candid about it. He is one of the healthier and younger second-floor residents: "It is natural that we have to go to the third floor when the time comes. Look at those who have ascended to the third floor from here. I think they have become healthier and happier because they have less stress than on the second floor. I will be happy to go if I need to."

When I asked two former second-floor residents how they felt about the nursing home, apart from structural differences such as four to a room and more help from the caregivers, they said it was pretty much the same. Except for reduced contact with children, they can continue with the same club activities they participated in before. For third-floor residents, personal challenges are transformed to another level—the semimobile residents striving to improve or at least maintain their physical conditions, trying not to become senile or bedridden "like the rest."

As Mr. Yama and Mr. Hira have observed, after their initial resistance, former second-floor residents do feel better about being transferred to the next level of care when second-floor care is no longer sufficient for them. By accepting their status as third-floor residents, the elders are also coming to terms with aging by accepting their weakening physical state.

Children

To most elders in Kotoen, the presence of children has made their institutional experience unique. Many see the children as a collective group who are always there, except that older children graduate and are in turn replaced by the incoming group of tiny toddlers each spring.

The nursery at Kotoen has a capacity of eighty children. In the school year from April 1996 to March 1997, the eighty children in five age groups named after flowers were distributed as follows:

[49]

Cherry group (one-year-olds)	10
Violet group (two-year-olds)	18
Dandelion group (three-year-olds)	18
Rose group (four-year-olds)	14
Lily group (five-year-olds)	20

Nursery is one of the two forms of pre-elementary education available in Japan. The other form, kindergarten or preschool, differs from the former in both hours of operation and the administrative umbrella under which they function. Nurseries operate longer hours than kindergarten. Kotoen, for example, operates from 8:30 A.M. to 4:30 P.M. for normal childcare and until 6 P.M. for extended childcare. Most kindergartens operate only from 8:30 A.M. to 2:00 P.M. Nurseries come under the jurisdiction of the Ministry of Health and Welfare, whereas kindergartens are administrated by the Ministry of Education. Lois Peak (1991) has observed that most children in nurseries tend to be drawn from somewhat lower socioeconomic strata than children who are enrolled in kindergartens because nurseries strictly enforce an eligibility criterion that the mother must be employed or otherwise incapable of caring for the child. This may be true to a certain extent in *shitamachi* locations like Kotoen; however, in recent years, as more mothers are being employed full time as professionals, my assumption is that the socioeconomic background of parents of the nursery children has become more diversified.

In the Kotoen nursery, a quarter of the children's fathers are self-employed, while the rest are company employees. Among the mothers, half of them work part-time, and eight families were single-mother households. Although nurseries were established to serve working mothers, many mothers can only work part time because they are restricted by the hours of childcare availability. Even with hours extended to 6 P.M., many mothers still could not engage in full-time employment, which usually ends at 5:00 to 5:30 P.M. but may sometimes require overtime. A few mothers wished for the childcare hours to be extended an hour so that they could transfer from part-time to full-time employment in the same company. One mother hoped that the hours could extend beyond 7 P.M. so that her husband could come to pick up the child, too. Several families engaged in small businesses also expressed a wish for longer childcare hours.

The parents of the nursery children are generally supportive of the age-integrated nature of Kotoen. It is worth noting that Kotoen's neighborhood contains two other nurseries (one is ward-run, and the other is operated by a temple). Thus parents who have chosen to send their children here are already a self-selected group who believe that their children will benefit from alternate-generation interaction.

However, the idea of "merging" the children with the elders was not wholeheartedly embraced by the parents in the first few years of its experimentation. As Mr. Oka, the nursery supervisor, recalled:

> Now we have no problem at all. But during the first two years, to be honest, the parents did respond with *e*- [he tilted his hand to the side, implying that the parents were uncertain or doubtful]. I am really being honest here. But now, the children are here because their parents deliberately want them to attend this nursery. They have come to know about this nursery as one where elders coexist with the children. They have seen the pamphlet and understand the structure and philosophy before they decided to send their children here.

The actors in interaction—the little children—however, seem happy with the extra attention they are receiving from the residents. Because many stay in nuclear households, they experience constant *fureai* with elders only while in the nursery.

Other than the addition of elders, the Kotoen nursery operates as a fairly typical Japanese nursery (Tobin et al. 1989; Peak 1991; Ben-Ari 1997). It follows the goals of the official nursery curriculum, which emphasizes group life, basic self-sufficiency, and personal management skills (Peak 1991, 39). The nursery aims to inculcate empathy, gentleness, and honesty in the children. Like most nurseries, it does not teach reading or writing skills. Most children, however, are taught by their mothers at home to read and write by the time they turn five.

As in a typical Japanese nursery, children take afternoon naps on futons, except that in Kotoen, all eighty of them sleep together in the big hall. There are regulations for major daily activities, such as fixed phrases and songs for morning greeting, morning exercises, snack time, lunchtime, and going home. The children are trained in proper table manners from one year of age. They are required to sit quietly, wait to be served, and begin eating only after the proper phrases and songs are performed. Those who have finished eating must sit and wait for others to finish and say the after-the-meal phrase together before leaving their seats. Children are sometimes chided for bad table manners. They have nursery uniforms and caps, although the uniforms—white T-shirts and blue shorts—are worn only during formal occasions and outings. All children wear the same canvas shoes when they visit other parts of Kotoen—

the teacher calls them "shoes to go to visit the grandpas and grandmas." It is also common for different age groups to play together. In the monthly Open Childcare, they play freely with different age groups of children, as well as with elders in the activities they choose.

Some aspects of the nursery differ from those of a typical public nursery: Children are encouraged to stay topless both indoors and outdoors throughout the four seasons, and they run or jog around the block every day. There are some innovative activities, such as the annual summertime overnight stay at the nursery and a summer day at sea. Moreover, the nursery supervisor and vice head teacher are men (they were formerly teachers themselves), an uncommon situation in nurseries. The presence of both men and elders in the nursery challenges the official view of nurseries as compensating for the absence of mothers by showing one to be compensating for the absence of fathers and grandparents.

Kotoen also engages people from different nationalities to play with the children and teach them simple English conversation once a week. Through contact with "non-Japanese," Kotoen hopes to expose the children to "internationalization." This desire to develop children with "international feeling" coexists with practices to cultivate children who embrace such Japanese characteristics as group-centeredness and interdependence. Under the balance of the two, Kotoen seems to have succeeded in cultivating a group of lively and energetic children who are at the same time rule-abiding, respectful, gentle, kind, and open to people of other nationalities.

This chapter has established the study's physical context and has introduced the actors—the staff, elders, and children—who will become familiar figures to the reader. What these groups do in the course of a day and the programs and activities that promote *fureai* between the elders and the children are discussed in Chapter 3.

[3]

Rhythms of Reencounters

The rhythm of life at Kotoen flows with the seasons. Life in the winter moves at a slower pace, and activities gradually intensify as cherry blossoms and spring arrive. Summer and autumn are the busiest seasons. During these months, "(I'm) so busy!" becomes the most common greeting at Kotoen.

When I first attempted to interview Miss Tsuji (the newcomer) an afternoon before the overnight hot springs tour, she was resting on the bed saying, "Again? [The staff had just conducted short interviews for the project called 'Fifty People, Fifty Voices,' asking what residents liked.] Didn't the caregivers say we should rest before going on the tour tomorrow? But there are so many things to do!" That summer day had been particularly busy. Miss Tsuji had morning exercise with the children; then the children, visited the elders for a forty-minute activity session, after which there was a stretching exercise club to attend before lunch. In the afternoon, Miss Tsuji went for a calligraphy class, then listened to a volunteer performance of *rakugo* (a comic monologue); afterwards she had to take a bath before the bathing time ended at 6 P.M.

The tempo at Kotoen combines that of a school, a community center, and a traditional family as club activities, festivals, concerts, and the observance of all cultural and seasonal events are added to the daily timetable.

A description of the various activities offered in an old-age institution serves two purposes. First, it aims to dispute the stereotypical perception of an old-age home as a dull place where elders sit doing nothing. Second, it proposes to illustrate how the various activities and programs are intended for promoting *fureai*. I show that Kotoen is concerned with *fureai* with and between different groups, including *fureai* with the community and *fureai* between different groups of elders within the facility. Nonetheless, the focus of *fureai* in Kotoen (and this work) is on the alternate generations.

Daily Schedule

A glimpse at the daily timetable of the home depicts a temporal structure typical of old-age homes (Table 3.1). However, this is only a basic schedule; at the beginning of every month a "monthly program" sheet is given to all residents, informing them of the upcoming events and the dates of specific club activities. The program sheet also includes the names and ages of the residents whose birthdays fall in that month and the slogan of the month's aim. Some events, such as children's visits to the elders' quarters, however, are not included in the program sheet but are often announced through the PA system minutes prior to these visits. Miss Tsuji complains about such announcements because she finds they disrupt her daily rhythm and plans for the day. Her complaint may reflect her newness to the environment—to other residents, the announcements have become a part of group living at Kotoen.

Except for the nursery children and teachers, all residents and staff take their meals in the dining room on the first floor. The Riverside Green residents use the dining room for about half an hour from 11:45 A.M., although those who are unwell may stay in the sunroom or their own rooms on the third floor for meals. The home residents dine thirty minutes later. Mealtimes are announced over the PA system by the caregivers. Residents are discouraged from crowding around the dining room before the announcement because this would jam up the dining room's entrance and make it difficult for those who leave with their wheelchairs. Instead, residents wait near the elevator on the second floor. Once the announcement "Meal is ready!" (*gohan dayō*) is heard, they start pressing the button of the elevator waiting for a ride downstairs. Some elders take the stairs instead because the elevator is often crowded at this time with Riverside Green residents returning to the third floor.

The menu for the day is posted on a board opposite the entrance of the dining room. Menus often reflect the seasons. Cold noodles, for example, are served during the summer, while *oden,* a dish for cold weather, is usually served in the winter. During mealtime, residents first collect their

Table 3.1
Daily Time Table

6:00 A.M.	Wake up
7:10 A.M.	Breakfast
	Cleaning tasks
9:30–10:00 A.M.	Morning exercises
10:30–11:40 A.M.	Club activities
12:15 P.M.	Lunch
1:45–2:30 P.M.	Club activities
2:30–6:00 P.M.	Bath
6:00–7:00 P.M.	Dinner
9:00 P.M.	TV turns off

trays, which are labeled with their name, from the food trolley. The tray holds the main dish and appetizer. Then they receive bowls of rice and soup from a staff member. On three Tuesdays a month, the kitchen serves a buffet lunch. During special occasions such as the monthly birthday celebrations, residents are treated to special food. On such occasions, they can have their choice of a bottle of beer or *sake* (rice wine).

Residents have permanently designated seats in the dining room; four to six people share a table. After each meal, they rinse and deposit their utensils in the receptacles next to the sink. Residents may leave the dining room once they finish eating. The average mealtime is thirty minutes, although some fast eaters return to the second floor in fewer than ten minutes.

Every morning after breakfast, residents can be seen doing their cleaning duty either in the dining room or along the second-floor hallways and the stairs. Residents are divided into seven groups (called *han*); each group is responsible for cleaning one of the two areas for a one-week period. In addition, residents are responsible for cleaning the toilets shared by every two rooms. A group member needs to make arrangements with the others if one is unable to carry out the duty being delegated on certain mornings. Members in a group will usually cover for the unwell members; however, if this becomes frequent, dissatisfaction can arise. The monthly program also assigns different days for residents to clean their own rooms, balconies, wash basins, and cabinets. The staff hopes that this will help the residents to establish a routine for cleaning their immediate living space.

There are three bathing rooms for residents. A special bathing room with two machine-aided bathtubs is used by some Riverside Green residents and by bedridden elders in the community who have registered for bath service. The other two bathing rooms can each accommodate at least four people at one time. Because there are more female residents, they always use the room with the larger tub. A caregiver is stationed at each of the bathing rooms to help the residents, such as by scrubbing their backs for them. The home residents have a designated bathing time of 2:30 to 6:00 P.M. on every Monday and Wednesday and 5 to 8:30 P.M. on Friday. Tuesdays and Thursdays are reserved for the Riverside Green residents. Bathing seems to be a significant activity, especially for the Riverside Green residents. They are absent during morning exercises on bath days. Caregivers in charge of bathing keep a record of attendance, and if a resident is noted to have been absent from the bath for a few days, he or she is particularly reminded to take one. Although there is no order as to who will take a bath first, the residents seem to develop an order among themselves. Four to five women normally get ready with their small plastic basins and towels ahead of time and head toward the bathroom once an announcement is made. In a family, it is usually the head of the household and guests who are the first to enjoy the clean, hot water; it is no wonder some residents are dismayed at these "early bathers" who have unofficially reserved the best bathing time.

A couple of men regularly attend the free ward-operated public bath (*sentō*) for elders, which is about a fifteen-minute walk from the center. Besides providing a bigger bathing place, it also provides opportunities for social interaction with other elders in the community. Miss Tsuji sometimes visits the fee-charging public bathing house "to relax." Regulated bathing hours and the feeling that one has to bathe in a hurry to make room for the next person contribute to the uneasiness she feels in a group living situation to which she is still trying to adjust.

Other than regulated time in meals, cleaning, and bathing, residents are pretty much free to do what they want during the day. They spend time watching TV, playing board games, chatting, or (if they are women) doing craft work in their rooms or at the small tables along the hallways. A checkout log is placed outside the caregivers' station for residents to sign out when they go out. Some residents, however, do not sign out when they go for a short stroll. One claims that "I don't want other people to think that I go out all the time." Many residents go out at least once a day, either to the doctor, for a walk, or to go shopping or even to a movie. However, with the different kinds of club activities and events lined up for the residents, there really isn't much free time that the elders can spare if they dutifully attend everything the center offers—especially in the busy summer and autumn months.

[56]

Club Activities

All group-oriented hobby activities are regarded as "club activities" (*kurabu katsudō*) at Kotoen (Table 3.2). Calling them "club activities" brings to mind the club activities in schools. However, these club activities are more similar in content to the hobby classes held at community culture centers. Many residents have attended hobby classes at the community culture centers before entering Kotoen, and they mention the opportunity to join clubs in the home as one advantage of institutional living.

There are sixteen hobby clubs residents may choose to participate in, ranging from traditional Japanese hobbies to an English conversation club (*Ingurishii rekueshon;* lit. "English recreation"). Eight of the clubs also include Fureai Hall elders as members. These are basically traditional Japanese hobbies and exercise clubs, and all employ qualified instructors from outside Kotoen. Some Riverside Green residents also participate in these clubs, particularly for rehabilitation exercise, stretching exercise, *ikebana* (flower arrangement), and calligraphy. Another seven clubs were formed mainly for the home residents. Two or three Riverside Green residents also join in the English conversation club. On the other hand, a couple of home residents are members of the "karaoke chorus club," organized mainly for Riverside Green residents.

In general, residents are encouraged to participate in as many clubs as they like. Club membership is informal, and residents do not need to sign up for a place, but they tend to be loyal to the club they join and see it as a commitment. A club usually has a membership of three to nine second-floor residents. With the exception of the gardening club, most have an overwhelming number of female participants. Eighty-nine-year-old Mr. Koyano is an exception among the men; he enjoys learning and participates in five hobby clubs. He thinks he is fortunate, noting how much it would have cost to join in such activities outside Kotoen.

Only half of the residents belong to one or more clubs. Of the other half, most had been active club participants in the past but quit as their health declined.

Traditional Japanese hobbies are the most popular activity, and most women join one of these hobby clubs at some time. Many of them had taken up these hobbies only after entering the home, although a few of them, particularly the better educated ones, had been taking these lessons before coming to Kotoen. Eighty-five-year-old Mrs. Hara had learned tea ceremony and *ikebana* when she was young, which is typical of women from the upper middle class. She continues to participate in the

Table 3.2
Club Activities

Club Names	Meeting Time	Meeting Frequency
Bonsai art[†]	Mon. P.M.[‡]	weekly
Flower arranging[†]	Tues. P.M.	weekly
Calligraphy[†]	Wed. P.M.	weekly
Haiga (watercolor painting)[†]	Thurs. P.M.	weekly
Tea ceremony[†]	Fri. P.M.	weekly
Uta Samisen (traditional ballad with samisen)[†]	Thurs. P.M.	weekly
Stretching exercise[†]	Mon./Wed. A.M.	twice weekly
Rehabilitation exercise	Fri. A.M.	weekly
English conversation	Thurs. P.M.	weekly
Folk dancing	Sat. A.M.	weekly
Handicrafts	Sat. P.M.	weekly
Othello (board game)	Tues. P.M.	semimonthly
Go (Japanese chess)	Wed. P.M.	monthly
Gardening	Tues. A.M.	semimonthly
Omatsuri Waiwai (gateball, quoits, and other games)	Sun. A.M.	weekly
Karaoke chorus	Fri. P.M.	weekly

[†]Clubs at the day service center.
[‡]Afternoon activities usually start around 1:40 P.M. and last for 45 minutes to 1.5 hours; morning activities usually start around 10:30 A.M. and end around 11:15 A.M. The exercises run from 11:15 to 11:45 A.M.

tea ceremony club now, but she quit the *ikebana* club after a brief participation. She repeatedly emphasizes that she had taken lessons from a great *ikebana* master from Kyoto when she was young, and claims the school of teaching here is different; her school is superior, she insists.

Participation in traditional Japanese hobbies may not be an obvious indication of class differences among the residents. Subtle class and educational differences are shown, though, among the members of the English conversation club, of which Mrs. Hara is one. The club is held every Thursday afternoon between 1:30 and 2:00 P.M. and is taught by Kotoen's part-time Argentine nursery teacher. During my research period, I volunteered to relieve him in the English class when he was away for a month.

There are five regular second-floor residents in the English conversation club. All of them had some exposure to English in their pre-Kotoen days. They are also the more highly educated ones among the residents. Mr. Koyano's educational level is comparable to that of a university graduate of today; Mrs. Hara, Mrs. Noyama, and the younger Mrs. Matsuda graduated from girls' middle school; the last member, an eighty-five-year-old female resident who graduated from a six-year primary school, worked as an English typist until her retirement.

Although the staff members wish that more residents would join the various clubs offered to them, residents are not obliged to do so. With the variety of activities designated as "events" under the monthly program handout, residents sometimes find themselves fairly busy even without any club commitments.

Events

The monthly program handout contains a column marked "Events" (*gyōji*), which announces the various special activities for the month. Participation is voluntary but strongly encouraged. These events fall into several types: events connected to the community, events joined with other groups of elders at Kotoen, events celebrated with the children, and events exclusively for second-floor residents.

Only a few events are organized exclusively for second-floor residents. One of these events is called "day's outing" (*odekake kai*), which is for small groups of about five residents at a time. Started two years ago, this event aims to let residents enjoy the activities they have missed, such as eating out at a restaurant or going to a show. Two staff and one of the directors join them for the event. This is also a social time for residents and staff to interact. Residents signs up according to the cuisine they wish to eat (such as sushi, *yakiniku* [barbecued meat], Japanese traditional, or Chinese). Residents are sponsored for one outing a year; if they wish to go for another trip within the year, they must pay for it themselves.

Residents also go on sponsored group shopping trips twice a year at a big department store in the neighboring city. Much like the summer and winter bonuses that employees receive annually, each resident receives 8,000 yen in the summer and 10,000 yen in the winter from the administration for these shopping trips. Most spend their money on clothing. Miss Tsuji was so excited over her first upcoming summer shopping trip that she went to the store one day before the actual trip to preselect the items she would buy, afraid that the one-hour shopping time was not enough for her.

Three times a year, the residents also go on picnics. Sometimes they eat out; other times they bring box lunches (*obentō*) prepared by the kitchen. In April, the theme of the picnic is "cherry blossom viewing" (*ohanami*) at a park in the neighboring ward; in January, it is *hatsumōde*, the first prayer for the new year at a Shinto shrine. It is a Japanese tradition to visit the shrine on New Year's Day and pray for a safe and healthy year ahead. Both the Fureai Hall elders and Riverside Green residents also go on similar trips separately, usually to a nearer location. During the year of my research, the staff—for the first time ever—planned a July trip to the

[59]

Tokyo Disneyland for the residents. Because of the costly admissions and the experimental nature of the excursion, only twenty spaces were available. Once it was announced over the PA system for signing up at the notice board (by circling one's name on the name list), the spaces were soon filled. Miss Matsu was anxious before the trip, worrying that the residents might find such excursions too exhausting. She was relieved when the residents returned with favorable feedback. It was certainly an exciting change from the expected venues for elders, such as parks and temples.

Once a year, the administration also organizes an overnight hot springs tour for all elders at Kotoen. Hot springs (*onsen*), which are abundant in geothermally active Japan, are attractive sites for vacations, especially among elders, because waters from the hot springs are believed to have healing powers for a variety of illnesses. Social bathing associated with hot springs (as well as *sentō*) is also regarded as a part of Japanese cultural identity: It is even seen as a way to understand the Japanese "heart" (Clark 1992, 103).

This year, residents went to the Nagaoka hot springs resort on the Izu peninsula, about a three-hour trip to the west of Tokyo. Fifty elders (twenty-five from the second floor, seven from the third floor, and eighteen from Fureai Hall), twenty-five staff members, and two family members of the elders (one from Fureai Hall and one from Riverside Green) went on the trip. They visited a safari zoo nearby before they returned to Tokyo the next day. Both the residents and the staff claimed they had a good time. A number of teachers also went as helpers, contributing to the sense of family at Kotoen, whereby different departments provide extra hands in time of need.

Various events inside the center are also organized for elders. Every May, a garden barbecue party is held in the courtyard for all elders at the center. Once a month, the home residents interact with the Fureai Hall elders during a forty-five-minute session called "*fureai* meeting," at which they bowl (using empty drink bottles) and play board games. Riverside Green and home residents also have a joint snack time monthly and a *homu kissa* ("coffeehouse in the home") with *izakaya* (a Japanese bar) twice monthly on Saturday afternoons. The *homu kissa* tries to resemble a coffeehouse: The menu is also somewhat similar, but prices are a quarter of what they are at the usual coffeehouse.

A regular event for all the elders at Kotoen is the joint birthday party, for which the big hall is turned into a large dining hall.

One hour before the party, caregivers on the second floor start to urge the residents to dress up for the occasion, particularly the birthday celebrants. Many male residents put on coats, while women change into nice clothes, not forgetting to take off their aprons, which many wear while in the premise. Sometimes a birthday celebrant wears a kimono for the occasion, the formal traditional attire for special events in Japan.

This particular month, there are five celebrants from the home and three from Riverside Green. Fureai Hall elders also celebrate with the residents on this day. All birthday celebrants of the month have their pictures posted on the notice board beside the Kotoen "big family" photograph opposite the stairway on the first floor.

Thirty minutes before the hour, another announcement sends the residents moving downstairs to the hall. Because residents may sit freely during such occasions, the women and men usually group separately at different tables. Soon the hall is filled as the Riverside Green residents and the Fureai Hall elders gradually join the crowd. The birthday people take their seats on the stage. Their names, age, and birth dates are written in calligraphy on a big piece of paper placed on the left side of the stage.

Around noon, the party begins. It starts with speeches by the center director, Mr. Sugi, and the director of Riverside Green, Mr. Miki. Mr. Sugi is a friendly and humorous person; he jokes with the elders and reminds them to keep healthy and active: "Unless, of course if you wish to die early; then you may do as you please." His speeches always bring chuckles to the elders and staff.

After the speeches, the staff emcee passes the microphone to an appointed resident-emcee, either from the second or third floor. Mrs. Koyama is the emcee for this party. She sits by the emcee stand with a large-type script that has been prepared for her. With clear articulation, she first asks everyone to give a hand in appreciation of Mr. Furuya, who had written the birthday list displayed on stage. Then she introduces each birthday celebrant, who gives a brief thank-you message to the audience. The staff expresses thanks on behalf of some Riverside Green elders who have problems with speech.

Next, a group of nursery children comes on stage to present their gifts to the elders. These are handmade cards and gifts made jointly by the teachers and children. These children usually come in pajamas, as it is immediately before their nap time. After their gift presentation, they line up to sing a song for the audience (Figure 3.1). Throughout the event, other nursery children continue their daily activities in the nursery area, which is separated from the big hall only by moveable cabinets. While the director is giving a speech, the sounds of children saying thank-you after lunch and the noise made while cleaning up can be heard clearly.

[61]

Figure 3.1. Five-year-olds in pajamas stand in front of the birthday celebrants on stage to sing a song.

Mr. Furuya, the children's favorite "grandpa," likes to sit just next to the nursery areas so that he can switch his attention to the children occasionally. During such times, when the big hall is occupied at noon, the children will take their naps in the enclosed nursery rooms for the four- and five-year-olds.

The Edogawa Ward government gives gifts of appreciation to the "ripe-agers" living in the ward who turn *kiju* (seventy-seven years old), *beiju* (eighty years old), and *hyakusai* (a hundred years old) on their birthdays and on the annual Respect the Elders Day. Acting on behalf of the ward, the director presents the gifts and flower bouquets to those residents at this time, before they return to their seats at the front tables. When the birthday elders are seated, the light is dimmed, and a caregiver comes on stage to conduct the birthday song. This is followed by the ritual of blowing out the candles on small pieces of cake given to each celebrant.

Before the dining begins, Mrs. Sugi, the administrative director, makes a toast to the health and longevity of the birthday elders. Then the nutritionist introduces the menu for the day. More expensive food and *sekihan* (red bean rice for celebrations) are usually served during these special events. A little after the dining begins, the curtain on the stage opens for entertainment provided by the Fureai Hall elders (a song), the staff (a sketch, comedy, or imitation of a TV quiz show), and sometimes the residents (a dance or songs). Dance troupes from the community sometimes volunteer to perform during these events.

Community-Related Events

In addition to events organized by the administration, residents in the home are often invited to events in the community. There are various such events throughout the year; some may restrict attendance to only a handful, while others are open to all, depending on their nature.

All residents are encouraged to attend the concerts or shows performed by volunteer entertainers at the center. These events are held in the big hall. There are as many as twelve performances a year by different groups, including performances of traditional ballads, *rakugo* (comic monologue), and classical dances. Residents are notified about these events through the monthly program sheets. The staff classifies these visits as *imon* ("consolation" or "condolence"), which has the connotation of visits to the less fortunate (such as the emperor's visit to earthquake victims). Hence, referring to these events as *imon* implies that they serve to comfort or console the elders. Although American nursing home residents may find such a term offensive, Kotoen residents seem to think this is appropriate, as they are staying in a welfare institution. Some *imon* are more welcomed than others, especially when they come in the form of donations of delicacies such as visits by sushi chefs to make sushi on the spot for the residents.

At community-organized events, which residents attend on an invitation basis, space is sometimes limited. The caregivers will announce the event at the home and put up an attendance sheet on the notice board so that residents can sign up on a voluntary basis. At Riverside Green, though, the caregivers decide who will go. Some events are more popular than others; for example, residents immediately fill up spaces available for the annual *pachinko* (pinball machine) parlor excursion to celebrate Respect the Elders Day and for the trip to see a professional sumo wrestling match. For events that have difficulty drawing enough residents (for example, sports meets and talent shows for ripe-agers organized by the ward office), caregivers may appoint residents to attend.

Making invitation events available to residents and accepting *imon* to the centers are some of the ways that Kotoen attempts to promote *fureai* with other community members. The monthly volunteer activity of sweeping the neighborhood street by the residents is also a part of Kotoen's *fureai* with the community. On the tenth, twentieth, and thirtieth of every month, the caregivers lead the second-floor residents, provided with brooms and dustpans, to sweep the immediate shopping street or the marathon route the children take (they clean the first floor of the center when it rains). Sometimes shopkeepers and residents come out to say *gokurōsamadeshita* ("many thanks for your trouble") as the residents pass by, appreciating their efforts to help keep the vicinity clean.

Fureai with the community also takes the form of craft exhibitions at which works by Kotoen children and elders are displayed in neighborhood elementary schools and in the lobby of a financial institution for a limited period annually.

Elementary schools in the community maintain frequent contact with Kotoen. Besides providing space for craft displays, they also invite residents to their school's annual sports meet. Students from four elementary schools volunteer at Kotoen.

Kotoen also organizes events with invitations extended to the community. This includes the fund-raising bazaar (held once every two years), the summer festival, the Golden Fair to celebrate Respect the Elders Day, and the Cultural Festival. These are major annual events for which the community is notified through banners, posters, and announcements in the ward newsletters. These events also solicit help from the community in various forms, such as donations of unwanted goods to sell in the bazaar and volunteers to help out during the events. These events have kept the residents busy as well. Prior to these events, they help with decorations; make sales items for the bazaar, such as candy boxes constructed with colorful rice paper; and rehearse for the summer festival dancing and stage performance at the Golden Fair.

Twice a year, in June and December, three old-age homes rotate to organize a Joint Quoits Meet. In June 1996, this event was held at Kotoen. All of the home residents (except those who were unwell) and half of the Riverside Green residents attended. They were all dressed in lilac track suits, the Kotoen sports outfit. Children from the Lily group also participated: Four children participated as contestants, while the rest attended as supporters, cheering for their "grandparents" and classmates. The children's cheering added gaiety to the atmosphere. Kotoen has always taken the last place in the competitions. One reason is that Kotoen has the least number of residents among the three participating institutions: The old-age home in the same ward has 87 residents, and the old-age home

Figure 3.2. Children challenge a sumo wrestler during a Sumo Meet. A "grandpa" serves as a referee.

in the neighboring ward has 140 residents, which increases the probability of their having good players. The other reason, as the director Mr. Sugi playfully commented when he gave away the first prize to the 140-capacity old-age home residents, is that "our residents are too busy here with a line-up of activities. You must be too free there and practice quoits the whole day (to win)!"

Events with the Children

All traditional cultural events celebrated at the center include both the children and the residents. The residents make *kabuto* (helmets) from newspapers for the children during the Children's Day celebration in May; they tie their wishes on bamboo branches and celebrate *Tanabata* (Stars of the Vegas) day together in July. They gather for the *yusuzumi taikai* (lit. "cooling evening event"), when the children stay overnight at the nursery to enjoy the summer evening by eating watermelon and playing with fireworks. Some events include the parents, such as the Christmas concert, the rice cake–making ceremony, the Sports Day, and the Sumo Meet (Figure 3.2).

Figure 3.3. The five-year-olds burn incense and put their palms together to pay respect to Kotoen's deceased "grandparents" during the memorial ceremony. The rehabilitation area has been transformed into a stage for the Buddhist altar.

Besides cultural events, Kotoen residents and children also participate jointly in events such as the biannual traffic safety talks held by police officers and the monthly fire safety drills. Children in the older age groups participate in more events with the residents. They attend the *hatsugama,* the first tea ceremony held during the new year, and the annual memorial service for deceased elders (Figure 3.3).

Every month, an appointed group of residents attends the children's birthday party held in the big hall. It is often an enjoyable event for the residents; they are entertained by songs performed by each age group and interesting storytelling by the teachers. The residents also go on stage to deliver their handmade presents to the birthday children. In 1995, all children received a bar of soap and a birthday card from the residents (prepared by the staff) during their birthdays. In 1996, they received letter racks made from rice paper (*washi*) (Figure 3.4).

For these joint events, the elders usually sit separately from the children, maintaining a distance, although they are experiencing the events together. *Fureai* between the residents and children in such formal meetings is alternated with more informal interactions on a daily basis,

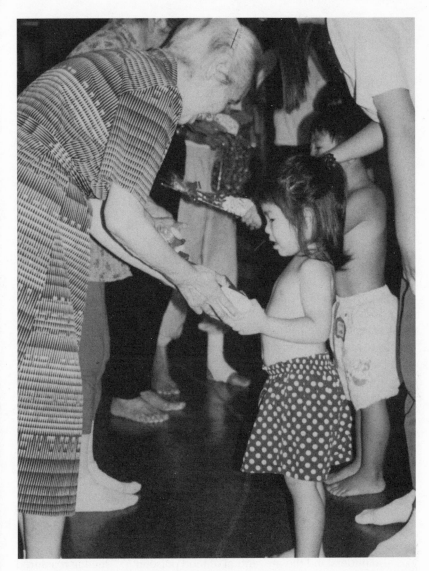

Figure 3.4. A birthday girl receives a present (a letter rack) from a "grandma" during the monthly birthday party for children.

more closely resembling spontaneous interactions between grandparents and grandchildren at home.

Activities with Children

Residents may interact with the children daily (except on weekends and public holidays) during the morning exercise and the afternoon changing of clothes after the children rise from their naps. They are also welcome to play with the children during their free playtime before they go home. During the year of my fieldwork, Mr. Furuya was the only resident who played with the children regularly during this hour. His relations with the children are discussed again in the later chapters.

Daily Morning Exercises

The morning exercises epitomize the elders' and children's *fureai,* and images of morning exercises are most often used by the media to introduce Kotoen. Morning exercises are held in the courtyard during fine weather and in the hall on rainy days. Around 9:30 A.M., the PA system begins to play a marching tune, signaling the assembly for exercise. About twenty residents regularly join the morning exercise. Usually about ten or more Riverside Green residents are present as well on the non–bath days. Most children and all male staff attend the morning exercises with their shirts off; they do so even on chilly winter mornings, as a challenge to beat the cold.

There are always two teachers in charge at the morning exercises— one from the nursery and the other a "teacher of the grandpas and grandmas" (a caregiver). They both address the children and elders, taking the opportunity to announce some messages or concerns. During the *E. coli* epidemic, the head teacher constantly reminded both the children and the elders of personal hygiene. After getting an affirmation from the children, he would turn to the elders and ask, "Do the grandmas and grandpas also understand the prevention of food poisoning?," feeling reassured only after hearing an affirmative "Yes" from them. Exercise begins after lively greetings from the children: "Grandpas and grandmas, how are you?" This is returned with the gestures of *banzai* and the response from the elders, "We are fine!" Then everyone turns toward the office, bows and shouts, "*Recorda-san onegaishimasu*" ("Mr. Recorder, please").

The elders, children, and staff exercise to two pieces of music every-

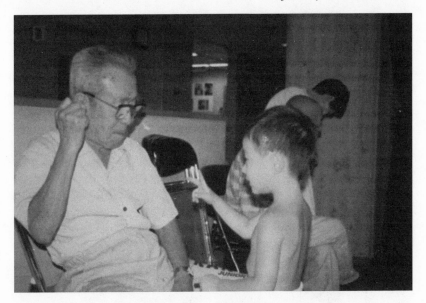

Figure 3.5. A "grandpa" plays *jan-ken-pon* with a boy after morning exercises.

day. The first is a lively and fast-paced children's song called "Please Place Your Hope in Us." The teachers have come together to decide on the actions, which includes some kung fu–like kicks. This piece of exercise song is supposed to change biannually, but this song has remained for the past two years because the teachers could not find time to plan a new song. The second piece of music is called "radio exercise" (*rajio taisō*), a decades-old morning exercise rhythm dating from late Taisho. Some residents feel that the tempo of the first song is too fast, and many modify the actions themselves so that they may exercise while sitting down.

After the exercises, the children wait for the cue from the teacher for the routine *fureai* with the elders. Some children have favorite elders to whom they run every morning for a hug and a swing. Others are led by their teachers to make rounds of greetings. Conversations are sometimes exchanged as they shake hands and play *jan-ken-pon* ("paper, scissors, stones," the hand and finger game) (Figure 3.5). Mr. Furuya and the other healthier "grandpas" often have a queue in front of them as the children wait for their turns to be carried up for a swing. The morning exercise usually ends with a mini marathon or stroll in the neighborhood. Some elders join the children, holding hands with them and chatting during the walk.

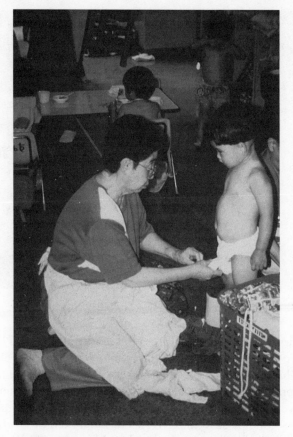

Figure 3.6. A "grandma" changes a two-year-old's clothes before the afternoon snack time.

Daily Help to Dress the Children

All children take afternoon naps at 12:30 P.M., and most are awake by about 2:40 P.M. The black curtains are then opened, and the teachers start to put away the futons and wake those who still refuse to leave their futons. Some children follow a teacher to the office to make an announcement to the elders: "Grandpas and grandmas, friends have woken up; please come down to help us get dressed."

Interested elders on the second floor head for the entrance to go downstairs. Usually about five residents come to help the one- and two-year-olds who are still too young to dress themselves (Figure 3.6). They make small talk with the children while dressing them. Some children, still sleepy, prefer to remain lying on the elders' laps after they have been changed. When everyone is done, the teacher leads the children to say "thank you very much, grandpas and grandmas," after which residents return to the second floor while the children sit down for their snack. The elders join them only for snacks during the monthly Open Childcare program.

Open Childcare

Once a month, about twelve residents are invited to join the children for a day. Each resident gets to attend the Open Childcare program once every four months, as the fifty residents are divided into four groups. The program begins at about 10:30 A.M. with an hour of free play. Children of all age groups may play with the elders in any of these areas: origami (paper folding), coloring, *otedama* (a game played with little beanbags), quoits, and making things with newspapers. It is an informal play session, and teachers sit around with the elders and the children. It is as much a *fureai* between the elders and the staff as it is with the children, because as the elders color or teach the children to play *otedama,* they often chat with the staff, too. They have a buffet lunch after the free play. Buffets are served only on special occasions such as during "open childcare" and the children's monthly birthday celebration (Figure 3.7). There are usually two elders at each long table with eight children from different age groups. When everyone is seated, the daily rotating monitors (*otōban*) first distribute the plates and chopsticks before the teachers place the dishes to share on each table, usually food with colorful combinations to attract the children. After everything is in place, the teacher plays the piano and the children sing the lunch song. Elders try to follow the tune and imitate the actions of the children sitting beside them. After singing, everyone puts his or her palms together, bows, and says *itadakimasu* (an expression used before eating). Elders sometimes help the teachers to serve the children. Children seem to enjoy the buffets because they can eat whatever they like and as much as they like. Most elders said they enjoy eating with the children; a handful of them, though, say they couldn't eat enough during these meals, as they are too reserved to take more for themselves.

Although the children have been told to eat silently, they chat and repeatedly request the food they like when they can't get it themselves. It

Figure 3.7. A "grandma" lunches with a child during the monthly Open Childcare program.

is fairly noisy until the teacher on duty stands in front to ask if everyone has finished eating. The room quiets down, and everyone puts his or her palms together again to say *gochisōsamadeshita* ("thank you for the food"). Songs and greetings are integral to every transition in the nursery. Except for the presence of elders, the scene is much the same during mealtime in a Japanese nursery (Ben-Ari 1997, 97–98).

After lunch, the elders help children to change into pajamas. They take a two-hour rest as the children sleep and join them again for snacks later. Like indulgent grandparents, the elders sometimes pass their snacks to the children sitting beside them, often secretly in case the teachers disapprove of it.

Children's Visits to the Elders' Quarters

While Open Childcare is regarded as an event for the residents under the "event" column of the monthly program handout, the forty-minute visits by the children every other day or so take place on a more ad hoc basis. These visits may occur whenever the elders and children are free, although they usually follow the schedule decided by the nursery at the beginning of each week.

Residents are informed of the visits just before the children arrive. Another announcement is made by the children after they arrive to urge the elders to join them in their activity of the day. This ranges from drawing, to origami, to clay building, to making things with newspapers, to *garakuta asobi* (building from unwanted items), to *kami shibai* (paper drama). There are usually twelve to twenty resident participants. The activities, held either outside the caregivers' station or at the chatting corner, provide good opportunities for *fureai*.

Other than the children visiting the elders for joint activities, nursery teachers sometimes bring their class for a walk in the center. The children walk on the "streets" of different floors and wave at the elders who stick their heads out of their rooms as they hear children's noises along the hallway.

Narashi *Childcare (Beginning Childcare)*

Every April, the residents are invited to help in babysitting the new one-year-old toddlers in the nursery. The presence of the elders greatly helps to calm the otherwise panicky toddlers, who are trying to get used to institutional living. Within a few days, one elder gradually becomes the main caregiver of a particular toddler as he or she becomes attached to the child. This is soon recognized by the other residents, and when they come by to visit, they refer to the toddlers by whose "grandchildren" they are.

Many who are single, childless, or who have severed their ties with their families find *fureai* with children a novel experience. Miss Tsuji claimed that she was taken aback to be addressed as "Grandma" here for the first time. She had lived alone for most of her adult life and felt uneasy about becoming a grandmother all of a sudden.

To many, "grandparenthood" is a new identity. As an elder enters an old-age home, he or she may feel strongly about making an exit from normal social life into a shelter. However, a look at the temporal structure in the home shows that *fureai* with the society does not end with one's proclaimed exit. It is not unusual for elders who were living alone to realize that their contacts with the community have in fact increased after they moved into the institution with new identities as both Kotoen resident and "grandparents."

Staff members are instrumental in the planning and implementation of various activities and programs that enhance *fureai* and help integrate the elders into their newly acquired roles.

Through his or her identification with these roles, an elder emerges as part of the family that the administration strives to create. In the tapestry of Kotoen living, the concept of *daikazoku* serves as a thread weaving together the different generations, including the staff. In the following two chapters, the *daikazoku* ideal in Kotoen and its implications are discussed.

[4]

The Goal: A Big Family Eating
from the Same Rice Pot

When describing the setting in Chapter 2, I mentioned the logo of Kotoen painted on the east side of the building: a smiling elderly woman in kimono holding hands and dancing merrily with a bunch of happy children. The logo, which spells out the *daikazoku* ideology of Kotoen candidly, also appears on the staff's name cards and T-shirts and on Kotoen's van and coach. All staff answer telephone calls from outside with "This is Kotoen, facility for elders and children."

Kotoen has worked hard to portray its *daikazoku* ideological framework since the merging of the old and young services a decade ago. An explicit illustration of this is represented by a "family" picture depicting more than 250 members ranging from 1 to 96 years old, which is posted on the board facing the stairway on the first floor.

The physical layout at the center is also devoted to the creation of the *daikazoku* ideal, where different generations share the same living space. All food for the center is prepared in one kitchen. Mr. Sugi often mentions this fact to support the *daikazoku* concept of Kotoen: "We are one big family; well, we all eat from the same rice pot" (*onaji kama no meishi o kū*), he quotes from a Japanese proverb.

However, physical structure alone only sets the stage for the goal. How do various events and activities attempt to inculcate and reinforce the desired goal? In this chapter, I describe one of these events—the nursery graduation ceremony.

A ceremony can be perceived as a drama. As Clifford Geertz (1973) points out, besides reflecting on the society, it also shapes and constructs the society. Hence I argue that the graduation ceremony is not merely a mirror; instead, I shall call it "participant drama," a performance in which the residents, together with the parents of the nursery children who make up the audience of the ceremony, are drawn into becoming participants in the whole act directed by the staff. Note in the description how the drama is an idealistic projection of grandparent-grandchildren relationships—one in which exchanges of appreciation are duly performed, and continuity is encouraged by the repeated invitations for the children to visit the residents.

Taking the graduation ceremony as a point of departure, I follow by exploring the ironies revealed in *fureai* in an institutional setting that embraces the *daikazoku* ideal. I introduce notions such as "event grandparent" and "collective grandparenting" to characterize *fureai* and suggest that the gap between ideal and practice (reality) exists because of the elders' and children's attitudes toward *fureai,* and also because of the constraints of the administrative practices, which in turn influence the elders' behaviors.

The Graduation Ceremony

The annual graduation ceremony is one of the most important events at Kotoen. Although this could have been solely an event for the nursery, the management has extended it to include the residents, some of whom were as busy preparing for this day as the graduates themselves. Preparation began two months prior to the ceremony, with residents rehearsing the song they would present during the ceremony and the handicraft club making presents for the graduating children.

On the day of the ceremony, the elders were encouraged to dress up for the occasion. "You are attending your grandchildren's graduation ceremony," they were told. Men wore suits, but Mr. Yokohira looked the smartest, wearing traditional black Japanese formalwear that is normally worn only during celebrations such as weddings and graduations. Women came with pretty dresses and makeup.

It was to be a solemn ceremony. The big hall, rehabilitation area, and nursery areas were transformed into a ceremonial hall for the event. Fabric with broad red and white vertical stripes lined the sides, delineating the event's boundaries. The stage, a rehabilitation area on normal days, had a black backdrop and two large flags hung up side by side: a Japanese national flag of the rising sun on the left, and the Edogawa nursery flag on the right. The Edogawa nursery flag features a boy in a red one-piece suit, shouldering an ax. On his suit is the Chinese character *kin* (lit. "gold"). A Japanese would easily identify this character as the famous heroic folk character Kintaro, a strong, courageous, and kind boy who is well-loved by Japanese children. The Kotoen organizational flag stood on the left front of the stage. Mr. Sugi (center director), Mrs. Sugi (administrative director), Mr. Hitachi (nursery principal), and Mr. Miki (Riverside Green director), the four key administrators, were seated near the flag. The three guests of honor were seated opposite them on the right side of the stage behind the table of presents.

All the female teachers, not only the teacher of the graduating class, were dressed in *hakama,* a kimono that is traditionally worn by Japanese women during graduation ceremonies. The teachers had spent many hours preparing and rehearsing for this special occasion.

The ceremony was similar to a high school or college graduation ceremony. When the ceremony began at 9:30 A.M., the emcee, the head teacher of the nursery, announced the entrance of the graduating children. Twenty of them—twelve boys and eight girls—marched out on the red carpet to piano music when their names were announced. Embarking on their first graduation ceremony in life, the children looked nervous. They wore the Edogawa nursery uniform dress code—blue shorts, white T-shirts, knee-length white socks, and white canvas socks, with a colorful paper brooch attached on the left side of the chest. Their names were written on blue plastic tags in the shape of an elephant and attached to the left side of their shorts. As the spotlight of the day, they were ironically the most casually dressed.

After they were seated in front of the stage, a series of speeches followed. The first speech was made by Mr. Sugi. In his usual humorous tone, he urged the graduates to visit Kotoen often. "The grandpas and grandmas sitting behind would definitely feel sad and lonely as you graduate," he said.

The next speech made by the nursery principal reinforced the relationship as he addressed the elders. "Grandpas and grandmas from the second and third floors, you have brought up your twenty grandchildren, and the things you have imparted to them are far beyond what we staff can ever teach them."

The three speeches by the guests of honor that followed continued on the same theme. A city council member spoke about the phenomenon of declining childbirth in Japan and praised Edogawa Ward for having the highest birth rate in Tokyo. He further congratulated the children at the nursery on having gone through such a unique experience of co-living with elders, which he urged them to treasure and be proud of.

A mother-representative from the Rose group next gave a speech to the graduating Lily group. She ended with this advice: "Even when you have gone to the elementary school, please don't forget the nursery, grandpas, and grannies. And please work hard."

Then it was the elders' turn to address the children. Mr. Okada, one of the two home residents who had received a college education, was selected to represent the elders. He walked on stage with Miss Matsu. As he stood at the lectern, he spread before him the script that the staff had transcribed for him in large characters. In a precise and steady manner, he delivered the speech to the graduating children:

> Do you remember? When you first entered the nursery, you cried in such loud voices. . . . We always looked forward to seeing your smiling faces every morning. Your smiles have brought strength to us. . . . Friends [referring to the children] who announced over the public address system, "Please help us to get dressed," are today already capable of doing so on their own. From April, you are going to be brand-new first graders. We do feel sad at the thought of not being able to see you every day; do visit us sometimes and show us your cheerful faces. . . . Please be cheerful, kind, and considerate always. Grandpas and grandmas are looking forward to the days when we meet again. Thank you very much for all you have done.

A song presentation—which the emcee announced as the elders' present to the children—followed the speech. With a caregiver as a conductor, all elderly residents at Kotoen held the lyrics in front of them and sang "Today we bid farewell" (*Kyō no hi wa sayōnara*). They sang the first verse and hummed the second verse while one Riverside Green resident recited a short speech, inviting the children to come and visit them at any time. It was an emotional speech; some residents were seen wiping tears from their eyes.

After a round of messages to the graduates, the moment most significant to the children arrived: the time to receive their graduation certificates. The children had rehearsed for this moment and took their places well. When their names were called, they marched up to the stage and faced the principal, who read the content of the certificate aloud (but only for the first graduate). When the principal had finished reading, they bowed, received the certificate, shook hands with the principal, and then came the part which most interested the audience: Each graduate turned toward the audience to tell of his or her ambitions for the future. There was applause and laughter after each child's public announcement of his or her ambitions. The elders were particularly intrigued by the children's imaginations and chuckled and whispered to each other as some children described unexpected ambitions.

Out of the twenty graduates, four wanted to become athletes in baseball, badminton, tennis, and sumo wrestling. Three wanted to become train conductors or airplane pilots. Seven wanted to engage in some kind of service trade, ranging from florist, dairy supplier, painting shopkeeper, candy vendor, and electrician. Of the rest, their ambitions included police officer, cartoonist, robotics engineer, nurse, and nursery teacher. Their ambitions reflected the fact that most of the children came from the small entrepreneurial class. Many were interested in becoming the grownups they encountered every day, such as the florist or candy vendor; no one thought of becoming a lawyer, a doctor, or even a salaried professional. The children's choices also revealed the occupations that children in Japan (and other countries) regard as "cool" (such as baseball player and a sumo wrestler), reflecting the influence of the mass media. A series of formal speeches again followed the lighthearted tone of the graduates' ambitions. The message on gratitude toward Kotoen and the elders was next delivered by the mother of one of the graduates, also a member of the Mothers' Association, the PTA for the nursery. The ceremonial presentation of a token of gratitude by the families of the Lily group to Kotoen concluded the ritual of appreciation "for nurturing our children."

Most mothers have limited contacts with the residents. They sometimes make small talk at chance meetings during dropping-off or picking-up time. But during such ceremonies and events, mothers become, collectively, along with the staff, the middle generation between the children and the elders in the Kotoen *daikazoku*.

The children were the last to give speeches. The only other group of children present for the ceremony was the four-year-old Rose group, who sat behind the graduates, also in their nursery formalwear. In this session of "farewell speeches," both groups stood up to face one another. The Rose group first recited a memorized speech (prepared by the teacher) that offered congratulations to their elder brothers and sisters of the Lily group and recalled the events they had enjoyed together. The speech ended with "Please do not forget the grandpas and grandmas."

The graduates' thank-you speech (prepared by the teacher) that followed was the last in the succession of speeches throughout the ceremony. They narrated their speech in unison: "Everyone present, grand-pas and grandmas, we thank you for attending our graduation ceremony today." Their speech, like that of the Rose group, recalled memories of events they had participated in together, such as a summer outing and sports meets. "Grandparents" were being mentioned before they ended the speech: "We will not forget the time we spent with other young children (from the nursery) and grandpas and grandmas. . . . Grandpas and grandmas, please be healthy always."

Song presentations by the Rose group and the graduating class followed. The Rose group sang "We Are All Friends," while the graduates presented "The Graduation Song" and "When I Become a First-Grader." I saw Mrs. Sugi sitting on stage touching her eyes with a handkerchief.

Another high point was the flower presentation ceremony. The appointed graduates presented bouquets to the teachers and special guests. Designating a time for flower presentation is one of the routines in Japanese ceremonies. This is done not only during graduation ceremonies to thank the teachers for their guidance, but also during wedding ceremonies to the parents of both the bride and the groom in the same sentiment—in appreciation for nurturing the marriage couple (Edwards 1989). The emcee then announced that the presents on the table by the stage were to be given to the children after the ceremony. These included presents from the elders and Edogawa Ward. The ceremony came to a close with the exit of the graduates on announcement of their names. Their march was accompanied by songs sung by the Rose group and the audience's applause. The whole ceremony was a grand experience for the children, who had played their roles well, thanks to the rehearsals and meticulous efforts of the teachers.

The exchange of presents and gratitude continued between the grandparents and the children (specifically the mothers) after the ceremony. Elders from Riverside Green, most of them in wheelchairs, were requested to line up along the corridor. When the teacher led the graduating children and their mothers to them, the elders presented each graduate with a set of five hand-sewn hand towels. A representative of the parents reciprocated with a box of red and white *manjū* (a traditional dumpling given during celebrations). A similar exchange occurred with the residents on the second floor. On both occasions, the children and their mothers bowed to the elders and said politely, "Thank you very much," a gesture that symbolize an end to their relationships. "Please come again" or "congratulations" were the most usual replies. When the children were leaving, a smiling Mrs. Tanaka held the hands of a girl and said, "Do come again!" The girl's mother turned around to reply, "We'll come again!" When I asked Mrs. Tanaka if she felt sad, she said, "New children will come in; I am not sad at all."

Not all of the elders were as optimistic as Mrs. Tanaka, though. Mr. Ishii, who had been a resident for only six months, refused to attend the graduation ceremony. When I asked him why, he said it would be embarrassing because he knew he would definitely cry. Several months later, Mrs. Michihata, who had wept during the ceremony, still couldn't hold back her tears when we talked about the event, even though she did not know the names of any of the graduates.

One would expect the children to be the central focus in a graduation ceremony for nursery children. However, the text reveals that at Kotoen, the residents were equally central to the drama. Every speech in the ceremony mentioned the "grandpas and grandmas." As much as the children were congratulated, the residents were also repeatedly reminded of their roles in the children's experience.

In Japan, it is common for elders to be referred to as "grandparents" by children and their parents even if they are not actually related. Joy Hendry (1986, 161) explains that children make sense of the overlap in the use of terminology by a clear distinction between people associated with the inside and outside of the house. Frequent mention of grandparents in the ceremony implies efforts to distinguish Kotoen grandparents from other elders living in the neighborhood. This encourages the development of a familylike familiarity among the children with the residents.

Such "participant dramas" are repeated in various forms throughout the year. Every January, for instance, there is the annual *omochitsuki taikai* (rice cake ceremony), when the children, their parents, the elders, and the staff gather to make *omochi*. In July, when the annual memorial service for deceased elders is held, the Lily group were allocated seats immediately in front of the elaborate Buddhist altar; they also lined up to offer incense like the adults.

One characteristic of the age-integrated facility is the children's frequent encounter with the death of nursing home residents. When asked how children face death, the head teacher said that the Kotoen staff think children should learn about death as a natural process in life. Sometimes the teachers lead the children to pay respect to deceased elders at the prayer room when they go on a stroll in the building. One teacher said because Kotoen is not affiliated with any religion, she talks about the deceased residents as grandparents who have ascended to heaven, adding remarks such as "the grandpas and grandmas are up above looking at all

[81]

of you; they are watching to see if you are being good children." Like family ancestors, the deceased elders play a guarding role to the children in symbolic ways.

The Grandparent Obligation

When I saw Mr. Okada on stage delivering his speech during the graduation ceremony, he reaffirmed my impression of him as someone who is very fond of children. He seemed like a loving grandfather; I have often observed him chatting with the children after morning exercises and playing with them during joint activities.

However, when I interviewed him some months later and asked how he felt about combining old-age institutions with childcare services, he claimed that it had been a great mistake to have come to such an old-age home (*shippaishita*). Although he agreed that such integration is good in principle, he thought that an age-segregated setting would suit him better. He had never had much contact with children before. After staying in Kotoen for two years, he still thought he was poor at communicating with them. He made the speech during the ceremony only because he was appointed to do so.

Participating out of obligation is also echoed in Miss Tsuji's case during the Tanabata celebration in early July. The thirty-minute in-house celebration for the elders and the children at the big hall included a sketch performed by both caregivers and a teacher on the legend of Tanabata, a reading of some wishes written on paper streamers hung on the bamboo leaves, and a question-and-answer session at which children asked a female elder about the origin of Tanabata. Miss Tsuji was informed a few days before the event that she was to represent the elders. When the emcees—a caregiver and a teacher—announced "Grandma Tsuji," she came forward to sit beside them. Then three children who had also been appointed beforehand came forward to sit with her and began to ask questions; "Grandma Tsuji" answered them in order, reading from a piece of paper prepared by the staff. The whole session was indeed another performance in the program. Miss Tsuji, portrayed as the child-loving and patient "granny" in the performance, however, often confessed to me that she was not particularly fond of children.

These conflicting images of Mr. Okada and Miss Tsuji as the "good old grandparents" on stage and their confessed lack of interest in children off stage reveal that many residents see their "grandparent" status as an obligation. Fortunately, most enjoy this obligatory role and are thankful for the opportunity. The minority who claim that they dislike children do not display resistance but perform whatever task they are asked to do.

I first thought it was curious that the staff should select Mr. Okada and Miss Tsuji as representatives of the elders. They may, however, have intentionally organized this in the hope that increased public recognition of their status as "grandparents" would in time modify their attitudes. During the period of my research, I did, in fact, find Mr. Okada and Miss Tsuji behaving more positively toward the children than their interviews would have suggested.

"Event Grandparenthood"

Because the residents associate the grandparent role with an obligation they must fulfill at Kotoen, the phenomenon of what I refer to as "event grandparenthood" emerges among some residents. One morning, I was in Mrs. Nakada's room conducting an informal interview. She said she had never held a baby and was afraid to do so. "When the baby cries, I feel like crying with it," she said. She even found changing the children's clothes a difficult task. Being childless, she sees herself as having no "luck" (*en*) with children. As we were talking, there was an announcement reminding the residents that the children would come up soon for clay modeling activity. She said, "Oh, I have to go; I need to attend the event" (*gyōji*). She quickly left the room as if on-call to attend to urgent business—in this case, the "business" of being a "grandparent" during an activity she refers to as an "event."

The staff's concern in delineating an activity or event within a definitive frame contributes to this phenomenon. During an activity session, greeting in unison by the children marks the beginning of their *fureai* and casts the residents immediately as "grandpas" and "grandmas." This role is relinquished at the end of the activity, when the children bow and say, "Thank you, grandpas and grandmas." After the children leave, the residents then go back to the daily routine of an old-age home.

Children are also socialized to become aware of the *fureai* context. Besides the commonsense rules that forbid shouting and running in the presence of elders, children are required to mark the transition when they visit the elders or move through other parts of the center by changing into white canvas shoes. Visits to the elders' quarters were suspended for five months in 1996 because the white canvas shoes had not arrived.

[83]

This is but one instance where opportunities for more actual *fureai* were hindered by concerns about formalities.

Terms of address by the staff also signify a transformation of the residents' status within the activity frame. All residents are addressed by their family name followed by *"san."* When asked why, the staff explained that this is deliberately used to show respect. Besides, as the residents are not blood-related to the staff, they should not be called by kinship terms. In the presence of the children, however, the staff instantly switch to addressing the residents as "grandpas" or "grandmas." Takie Sugiyama Lebra (1976) refers to this teknonymic usage as "vicarious kin" terminology in which the addresser takes the child's point of view. Such a shift in the term of address also implies an effort to inculcate the *daikazoku* ideology within the framework of *fureai.*

As one will notice in the various discussions of *fureai* throughout this study, most elders operate within the rationale of "event grandparenthood," although some do become more emotionally involved with the children. I found that newer residents tended to belong to the latter category. Perhaps one measure of adaptation into the Kotoen *daikazoku* is the extent in which a resident has become an "event grandparent."

One way to analyze "event grandparents" and the more emotionally involved "grandparents" among the residents is to draw on Kinoshita and Kiefer's (1992, 160) discussion of the concepts of "situational specificity" and "additional significance." "Event grandparenthood" can be explained by "situational specificity," where interactions are specific and bound only to particular social situations such as activities or events. Additional significance—a concept similar to "functional diffuseness" (Levy 1952, cited in Kinoshita and Kiefer 1992, 160), wherein other meanings are derived from the functionally specific situations—on the other hand, denotes circumstances in which the residents take their grandparenthood role more seriously. Rather than institutional arrangements favoring the development of "situational specificity," it might be thought that the development of additional significance in *fureai* would contribute more effectively to the achievement of the *daikazoku* ideal at Kotoen.

"Please Come Again"

One indicator of the development of additional significance is the frequency with which graduates return to visit their "grandpas" and "grandmas" at Kotoen. "Please come again" (*mata kite ne*), heard repeatedly in the speeches made during the graduation ceremony, signifies the center's wish that the bonds cultivated between the elders and the children will continue as the children exit the institution.

Sometimes graduates do make surprise visits to Kotoen elders. This may happen with fresh graduates during their first few weeks as first-graders. Once a graduate brought two of her classmates along to visit the elders. They came to visit them in general since this graduate was not close to anyone in particular. As they sat at the chatting corner, four women whose rooms were nearby came forward to meet them. It turned out to be a meaningful exchange: The girls brought *otedama* (small bean-bags) to play with the "grandmas"; they also chatted about what they learned in school and compared it with what the elders learned in the prewar educational system. Mrs. Sugi was excited that the girls had come of their own volition, and she kept reminding them that they were welcome to visit at any time. This was, however, an isolated instance. With new friends and new school commitments, graduates soon left Kotoen behind them.

Some graduates volunteer at Kotoen through their schools. They come to work on cleaning tasks, keeping very much to their own school group and having little interaction with the elders. The graduates seem to lack the urge to meet the elders, although they said they could still remember some of their names. Though there are a few who maintain contact with the residents through New Year greetings (often written by their mothers), most graduates leave Kotoen without fostering intimate relations with any residents. It is therefore difficult for them to identify with any elders.

It also appears that most children view their Kotoen "grandparents" as part of the memories of their nursery life—a chapter that closes as they advance to the next stage of schooling. One spring morning, a group of first graders from a neighboring elementary school visited the home residents. They presented some plants they had cultivated during the "social education" class; the pots were accompanied by letters. One of the letters was by a Kotoen graduate: "Dear grandpas and grandmas, how are you? I am a graduate from Kotoen. Please get well soon and play with the present children. Please play with them in harmony. If I have time, let's play together, too."

Identifying themselves as the children of the past group and urging the elders to interact more with the present children shows that with graduation, the nursery children have passed the baton of *fureai* to the next group of nursery children and relinquished their own membership. Even the present group of five-year-olds, when asked if they would like to return to meet the grandparents after they graduate, said they were not sure if they could, as they would no more belong to Kotoen. Just as the elders have become "event grandparents," the children, too, seem to have developed a group identity among themselves in perceiving their interaction with the elders. This raises the question of whether deliberate efforts to reengage the children and the elders would automatically mean a merging of the two groups. To what extent can *fureai* continue beyond programming? The emphasis on interactions on a group basis may have constrained the development of more meaningful and long-lasting relations between the old and the young.

"Collective Grandparenting"

The emphasis on interacting as a group appears to be one of the reasons why there is little ongoing contact between the graduates and the elderly. I refer to this as "collective grandparenting." It is an unwritten rule, but the center expects elders and children to interact on a group basis and discourages the favoritism that may arise from intimate interaction in pairs. Miss Tsuji, a new resident at the old-age home, found this out only after she had unintentionally violated the "rule."

Miss Tsuji replaced Mrs. Ishimura (mentioned in Chapter 2), who claimed she was forced to move to Riverside Green. Miss Tsuji is unmarried and has lived on her own for the past thirty years or so. She repeatedly claims that she does not really fancy children because she has never even held one before. However, she had developed a special liking for Judy, an American-Japanese girl in the Lily group. Miss Tsuji's newcomer status had prompted her to feel attached to Judy in the new environment. Judy was responsive, too; after a while, they seemed to have paired up, and they usually stayed with each other to play *jan-ken-pon* right after morning exercises. I was happy for Miss Tsuji and hoped that the relationship would help ease her transformation into institutional living.

When Miss Tsuji attended her first Open Childcare, she played exclusively with Judy. She taught her how to play *otedama*, sat beside her during meals, and looked lovingly at her as if she were her favorite grandchild. While I was sitting at the same table with them, I could hear the teachers at the next table talking about them. The teachers seemed worried that Miss Tsuji had ignored other children with her passion for Judy.

The teachers' disapproving attitude toward the pairing-up became clear in the following incident. On the afternoon of the Open Childcare, Miss Tsuji came back with a present for Judy. It was a simple mask she had made from used newspaper. She wanted to give her a little gift to show her affection for her like a loving grandmother would. But her gesture was objected to by the teacher, who said she was not supposed to show favoritism to a certain child, as this would be unfair to others. Miss Tsuji was taken aback by the refusal and appeared disappointed, murmuring to herself, "I was not aware of such rules [of prohibiting gifts to a child]."

It is common for a nursery to set rules like this, but it seems contradictory to impose it so strictly in a setting that aims to encourage *fureai*.

The teachers' concern about "collective grandparenting" and their opposition to indulgent "grandparent-grandchildren" relations reflect the preference for group or collective interaction at Kotoen. This illustrates the prevalence of "group orientation" or "group consciousness" (*shūdan seikatsu, shūdan ishiki*) in Japanese society and explains the Japanese preschools' efforts to socialize children into a collective identity (Hendry 1986; Tobin et al. 1989; Ben-Ari 1997). Children's and elders' individual identities also become less significant when collectivity is juxtaposed with the *daikazoku* framework. In this way, people are valued more highly for their roles within the framework than for their individual selves. As individuals leave Kotoen, the "grandparent" and "grandchildren" roles will be assumed by the generations that succeed them.

The emphasis on group interaction is also clearly reflected in the sending of midsummer greetings. In Japan, it is common to send greeting cards to inquire about the health of the addressee during the summer heat (*shocchū omimai*). At Kotoen, all home residents and some Riverside Green elders were asked to send summer greeting cards to the nursery children. The caregivers prepared eighty handmade cards complete with hand-drawn stamps. Then each resident was given a card on which they wrote summer greetings and signed their names. As they were not told to which child their cards would be given, most wrote in a general manner using simple Japanese and addressed the children as a group. Mr. Ishii, for instance, wrote that "it is a joy to look at all of your cute faces," although his card would be addressed to only one child. A few of them wrote in formal Japanese style, which was obviously directed toward the children's parents.

Because of the emphasis on group interaction, elders and children do not often remember one another's names. When the children meet a Kotoen resident on the street, they usually greet him or her as "grandpa or grandma of Kotoen." Some parents have requested that the nursery teach the children the elders' names, so that they may call their names when they meet on the street. Even though the teachers try to address the residents by their names plus *obāchan/ojīchan* (for example, Ishii *no ojīchan*, meaning "Grandpa Ishii"), only the more popular elders' names are remembered by the children.

Similarly, most residents related to the collective identity of the children, and many are really fond of them as a group. Like any proud grandparents, they sing the children's praises, describing them as cute, smart, and well behaved. One resident said that she though the excellent guidance of the teachers, the spaciousness of the building, the sunlight, and the clean air have contributed to the quality of their children. She probably feels that the presence of the elders plays a significant part as well but was too humble to say so.

The sense that "our grandchildren are the best" was especially strong during the annual Six Nurseries Sumo Competition held at the end of May at another nursery. Eight residents who signed up for the event formed the Kotoen cheering team. Of course, Kotoen children were the only ones in the competition accompanied by a bunch of elders in bright red or blue *happi* (cotton kimono overcoats) with "Kotoen" printed on the back. They were energetic, shouting and cheering to their hearts' content when the Kotoen children appeared in the ring. An elder later commented that he felt as passionate as a family member while cheering for the children.

When the team returned, several elders from Riverside Green and the home were already lining up along the driveway to welcome the participants and cheering team. They had received the news that the girls had won. When the champion team appeared, it was like a victory homecoming parade, with the leading girl in the line wearing the paper crown, the girl behind her holding the winning certificate, followed by the rest of the team, who waved to the elders applauding at them as they marched past. The boys who followed were encouraged to try harder the next year; they had not made it to the top three positions this time.

After the children had proceeded into the courtyard, the teacher led them to bow and say thank you to the grandparents. The waist-high gate behind them was then closed, signifying the end of the event. As the residents walked back into the building, their conversations centered on the strength of the girls. Mrs. Kondo, a Riverside Green resident in wheelchair, was still by the gate, and I stayed behind to accompany her. Compared with the second-floor residents, the Riverside Green residents are identified in a more collective way, sometimes as "grandpas and grandmas in wheelchairs." Their frailty has restricted their contacts with the children; although their *fureai* with the children seems peripheral when compared with that of the home residents, many display a fondness for the children.

Mrs. Kondo had wept as she greeted the children, and when I mentioned the children, her eyes were flooded with tears again. Was she emotionally touched by the children's victory? Mrs. Kondo used to be pessimistic and refrained from interacting with the children, claiming that children wouldn't come to her because she was disabled (stroke paralyzed). However, her attitudes had changed recently. On the morning of the sumo competition, she took the initiative to wave to a girl during the routine *fureai*. The girl ran to her; then they shook hands and played *jan-ken-pon*. Her presence at the welcome parade was another indication of her changing positive attitude toward children.

Fureai in the Kotoen *Daikazoku*

Age integration at Kotoen is founded on the ideal of *fureai* in a *daikazoku*. To what extent has the dream been inculcated and fulfilled?

The graduation ceremony successfully evoked the "grandparent" identity among the residents. The children whose names were still unfamiliar to them had merged to become a collective group of "grandchildren" under the Kotoen family. Kotoen emphasizes an image of *fureai* resembling a multigenerational family. However, it is ironic that instead of the familial dyadic pairing and the image of a family in which children and elders interact any time of the day, *fureai* at Kotoen has become a contradictory juxtaposition of spontaneity and emotional involvement, with rules and regulations that may inhibit that involvement. On the one hand, the old and the young are separated as they are classified collectively in different age grades; on the other, they are sentimentally linked in the image of loving grandparents and grandchildren.

In this chapter, I have suggested the notions of "event grandparenthood" and "collective grandparenting." These are useful notions that will help my analysis of the concepts of *fureai* and *daikazoku* in the following chapters.

[5]

The Vision: Dream Family

In Kotoen, the administration holds the vision of the place as a multi-generational facility where dreams, love, and mutual care are enlivened by generations in touch. The events organized throughout the year are designed to position everyone—elders, staff, and children—within this *daikazoku* ideal.

The graduation ceremony described in Chapter 4 is a ritual intended to reinforce the status of the residents as "grandparents" to the graduating children. It is a drama for the residents themselves, staged by the staff and participated in by residents, children, and parents.

In this chapter, I present two more instances of performances—the Golden Fair and the making of a documentary about Kotoen by a Tokyo television station. Compared with the graduation ceremony, these are public appearances: The former is an annual event opened to the community, while the latter had a wide viewership. They are interpretive depictions of Kotoen's vision of the "dream family." Following the theme pursued in the previous chapter, I continue to examine the gap between ideal and practice in alternate-generation *fureai*. This chapter also discusses outsiders' perceptions of Kotoen in particular and age-integrated facilities in general. Finally, I expand the discussion to address the larger relevance of the "dream family" to changes in family institutions and family alternatives in the future.

The Golden Fair

"Sit tight; you're on board a flight through the past into the future of the Kotoen *daikazoku.*" This is the sensation you are supposed to experience on entering Kotoen during its tenth Longevous Kotoen Golden Fair (*Chōju Kotoen Goruden Fea*). This is Kotoen's own celebration of Respect the Elders Day.

The Golden Fair was first held in 1987. Being the tenth year, 1997 was significant, providing a good occasion for the institution to reflect on the past and to set goals for the future. The designation of themes for the annual Golden Fair began in the third year of the celebration. Past themes were *Tobidasu, seishun, daikazoku!* ("Fly, youth, big family!": 1989, 1990), *Wasshoi!* ("Heave-ho!": 1991), *A, Fureru ai* ("Ah, love in touch": 1992), "Smile of Rainbow" (named in English: 1993), *Fureai noshoku kaju 100%* ("Contact concentrated juice 100%": 1993), and *Sumairu ressha, fureai go* ("Smile train, number *fureai*": 1994). The theme of the tenth Golden Fair was *Jūnen yume hikō* ("Ten years' dream flight")—a flight where one embarks on the Kotoen rocket "loaded with fuel, filled with happy memories of the past and hopes for tomorrow." To make the flight realistic, the whole center was transformed into a fantasyland: The first stretch of the first floor corridor was covered with paper leaves and branches. Looking out from the window into the central porch, one could see a huge giraffe, monkey, and alligator, all made from cardboard painted in cheerful colors. This stretch was named "the Earth" (*daichi*).

The conference room on this corridor was converted into a rest area for visitors. It was also a photographic gallery in which a montage of photographs depicting Kotoen over the past ten years filled three walls. Two of the walls, entitled "One Day at Kotoen," featured activities going on at different times of the day in the center. Another wall, titled "Kotoen *Daikazoku*," had an interesting combination of photographs depicting multigenerational interactions. Covers of past issues of *Fureai*, the center's newsletter, filled the fourth wall of the room.

At the end of "the earth," one encountered a bunch of blue and white balloons floating above, symbolizing the blue sky and the floating clouds. This corner was termed "the sky" (*sora*). Turning right along the corridor from "the sky," one passed through a curtain of black paper streamers to enter "space" (*uchū*). Here colorful stars sparkled against the black backdrop. Accompanied by relaxing music, a stroll through "space" was hoped to engage one in the fantasy of a dream flight. Returning from "space," one entered the cafeteria named "glitter star" (*guriru stā*). One could purchase lunches here from staff who had several glittering stars attached to their T-shirts. Like the cafeteria, the game corners in the nursery area also had "starry" names—"Cassiopia gate" (*kashiopia gēto*) for the indoor game area and "Orion gate" (*Orion gēto*) for the outdoor game corner.

The marvelous transformation of the hallways into a fantasyland reflected the hours of hard work put in by the staff beyond their regular duties. Most staff worked overtime the week before the event. Three days before the event, I met a young female caregiver who appeared exhausted. "How is the preparation?" I asked her, knowing that she was with the photographic gallery work group. She said, "Did you see the bags under my eyes? I have not been getting enough sleep for the past few days because of the event!" The residents and children also rehearsed hard for the stage performances.

The tenth Longevous Kotoen Golden Fair began at 9:50 A.M. on a Sunday morning in September. It commenced with the Edogawa Ward song broadcast over the speakers. The audience was encouraged to sing along, as the lyrics were provided on the program sheet. In the fifteen-minute ceremony that followed, speeches were given by a member of the Kotoen board of directors, an officer representing Mayor Nakazato of Edogawa Ward, and a guest of honor who is a member of the Diet. All three speeches mentioned the cooperation Kotoen had received from members of the community and from volunteers. The Diet member also released the latest statistics on the aged population in Japan: 14.3 million persons over the age of 70 and 6,378 centenarians. "With the extended life span today, being seventy years of age is still *mada mada* [still young]," said the guest of honor; "therefore seniors should engage in more activities and do what they like." He continued to say that it is a fantastic thing (*subarashii koto*) for Kotoen elders to have frequent contact with the children, members of the community, and volunteers (mainly students). "*Shitamachi* is great!" he exclaimed. Focusing on Kotoen, he recalled his visit here during the time when elders were helping the children in changing. One resident told him she felt happy with the children, and that their presence had made her wish for longevity. "The ideal of co-living is realized in Kotoen," the speaker claimed; with this he also honored Kotoen as the "model of welfare society."

The Golden Fair speeches had a different focus from those of the graduation ceremony. Here the focus was on Kotoen as it is presented to the public: an ideal and model of welfare society, an integration with the larger society receiving support from the community. The audience included members from the town associations (*chōkai*) and women's associations (*fujinkai*); then there were the residents themselves, the staff, the children and their parents, graduated children, and relatives of the residents.

The Golden Fair mobilized numerous volunteers in comparison to other events at Kotoen. Before the fair, fourteen students from two junior high schools volunteered to draw a poster each for the event. Intern students from a nursery teacher-training school also contributed three big posters. On the actual day, there were about seventy volunteers, most of them students from junior high schools and the interns. Regular volunteers at Kotoen and members of a women's association also helped out. Participation by the volunteers extended *fureai* beyond different generations within the institution to a larger context in the community.

The highlight of the Golden Fair was a fifty-five-minute song and dance performance. The lights dimmed, and a young caregiver in a formal staff uniform stood at the side of the stage as the show's emcee and narrator. She began with a slide presentation of the memory lane of the past ten years. As the memories unfolded with slides of activities at Kotoen, the narration took its own course; significant events that happened each year in Japan were juxtaposed with Kotoen's events in the past decade:

Showa 62 years [1987], Kotoen began as an integrated institution allowing interaction between elders and children. With this, the Longevous Kotoen Golden Fair celebrates its tenth anniversary. During these ten years, many things happened in Japan as well as in Kotoen. Here, let's take a brief look into the past.

Ten years ago in 1986, the average life expectancy in Japan was 75.23 years for men, and 80.93 years for women. Now, it is 76.36 years for men and 82.84 years for women. Japan has become the world's most long-lived nation. In Kotoen, too, we celebrated the 100th birthday of Mr. Tsuda.

In 1987, JNR [Japan National Railway] was privatized. In 1988, *Sekan* tunnel [the tunnel connecting Aomori in Honshu and Hakodate in Hokkaido] opened, bringing to a close the eighty-year history of the *Sekan* ferry [*Sekan renrakusen*].

It was in 1989 when the Showa emperor passed away, and we changed from the Showa to the Heisei period. During this year, the well-beloved singer, Misora Hibari also left this world. In Kotoen, the Committee to Promote *Fureai* was initiated, which further activated elders' contact with the children.

As we entered the Heisei period, in 1992, the famous Takahanada [now called Takanohana] received his first victory [in sumo wrestling].[1] This year,

---

[1] Takanohana is a famous sumo wrestler in Japan. In 1996, he achieved his fourth straight year of victory.

astronaut Mori Mamoru-*san*, after experiencing an eight-day space flight, returned to lecture about his experience to the children in Japan. During this year, too, Kotoen celebrated the thirtieth anniversary of its establishment.

In 1993 Crown Price Naruhito married Kowada Masako-san.

The winter of 1995 may still linger in your memory. Hanshin earthquake happened. During this year, *Fureai*, the Kotoen newsletter, received the *Yomigotae* Prize in the national institutional newsletter contest organized by the welfare center [*Fukushi Kōsei Sentā*].

This year, 1996, Arimori Yuko-san received a bronze medal in the women's marathon at the Atlanta Olympics.

Next year in 1997, Kotoen will have new facilities added; it will be another year of flight.[2]

With this, Kotoen's Everyday History—Ten Years' Dream Flight sets off!

The curtain opened for two dances from a community dance troupe. Then the main attraction of the day began. When the curtains reopened, an elderly woman walked on stage with three children. Mrs. Noyama was selected to play the lead. She is one of the newer residents in the old-age home, having entered only ten months before. However, her positive disposition and articulateness made her the perfect choice as "Grandma Kotoen."

Grandma: It was very good dancing indeed!
Child 1: That was really good!
Child 2: Ah, I enjoyed myself.
Child 3: Over here, we have lots of happy things!
Child 1: Granny, which is the most enjoyable?
Grandma: Well, talking about enjoyable things, I could recall many.
Child 2: What are they?
Child 3: Tell us, tell us!
Grandma: Hmm, in that case, bring the album over here for me.

As they sat down in front of the stage flipping through the album, the curtains drew and the spotlight landed on Mrs. Noyama and the children.

[2] A new wing—a four-story building across the courtyard—was under construction during the celebration. Completed in 1997, the wing provides day service for demented elders in the community. The construction began in June 1996.

It was a heartwarming scene, the dream scene of a harmonious interaction between elder and children. A closer look at the conception would
remind one of its replication of the logo of Kotoen; yes, the drama is pre-
senting to the audience the ideal of Kotoen.

In the background, the narration began: "The Kotoen Golden Fair is
celebrating its tenth anniversary this year. For Grandma, too, it is her
tenth year at Kotoen. Well, what happy memories does she have? Shall
we follow her to look back on the past?"

Grandma: Talking about enjoyable things, I think everything is enjoyable.
For example, every morning, doing exercises with you all, shaking hands
and playing *jan-ken-pon*. They help Granny to feel good, to feel that
Grandma should hang in there!

After Grandma's lines, the familiar morning exercise music could be
heard in the background: "At Kotoen, every morning, the three generations of the elders, small friends, and staff get together to exercise joy-
fully." Then the curtains opened. It was a performance of the morning
exercise scene. There were greetings, exercises, handshaking, and the
playing of *jan-ken-pon*. The narration began: "They surely looked very
happy. It is said that this moment in the morning is the source of energy
for the elders. But this is not all; there are more heartening scenes in
a day."

The curtains opened again. Several children were standing on stage
in colorful pajamas. They shouted toward the backstage, "Grandpa,
grandma, please help us with changing!" There were responses from the
side of "Hai!" and five elders came out. What followed was a replay of
the everyday clothes-changing scene, as described by the narration: "To
the children, grandpa and grandma are a dependable existence. To the
grandpa and grandma, too, *fureai* with the children becomes a source
of their *ikigai*. They treasure them like their real family and grandchildren."

Slowly the curtains closed, and the focus returned to Mrs. Noyama and
the children:

Children: Is there anything else?
Grandma: Well, there are also various other events.

Here the screen moved in front of the audience, and as the children recited the host of annual events, such as the rice cake ceremony, doll's day,

[95]

Figure 5.1. The multigenerational *taiko* performance during the Golden Fair.

the garden party, and the sumo wrestling meet, corresponding slides were shown. When a slide of a performance at a past Golden Fair was shown, Grandma commented:

> Grandma: Oh, yes, talking about the Golden Fair, there is the famous Kotoen three-generation *taiko* [Japanese drums] performance. Granny, too, participated in the performance once, a long time ago. That was enjoyable. I was nervous. Look, [pointing at a picture in the album] this is the photo taken then.
> Children: Show me, show me! [The children buried their faces in the album.] Grandma was cool!

The curtains opened and the famous Kotoen three-generation *taiko* performance began (Figure 5.1). It was indeed an impressive performance—three children, two elder women, and three male staff beating in unison. After the performance, they trooped down to the front of the stage, beating the small gongs and chimes. The audience applauded heartily with the emcee's introduction of their names. As they retreated backstage, a narration followed, one that expressed explicitly the ideal of Kotoen:

As you have seen, in Kotoen you can see very natural *fureai* scenes going on every day. Grandpas, grandmas, the children, and the staff—we are all a big family (*daikazoku*). In our daily life, we sometimes encounter pains and sorrows. During such times, we stand firm, encourage and cheer each other up. Next, let's sing cheerfully as we step toward the future of Kotoen!

The curtains opened again; all performers were now on stage swaying to the melody that just came on. The song was titled "A March of 365 Steps": "Happiness does not walk to you; therefore, you have to walk to it. One step a day, three steps three days, three steps forward and two steps back."

At the end of the performance, the names of all of the performers—young and old—were announced. One after another, they lifted up their hands when their names were called and said "Yes!" firmly before marching backstage. Before the last performer (a staff member) left the stage, she brought a chair covered with a cloth to the middle of the stage. When the cloth was flipped back, a huge photograph portraying the Kotoen "big family" appeared, the photograph from the board on the first floor.

The stage lights were dimmed, until finally there was only a spotlight zooming in on the photograph. The music in the background continued, yet the audience hall was silent. It was after the light finally went off that applause was heard.

The stage show is another participant drama; it is also a document, or a report card, to the audience, including the residents themselves, on their achievements of realizing the *daikazoku* ideal. This is a profound moment of *communitas*.[3] In the silence, when the spotlight focused on the big family photograph, many in the audience, the elders, the staff, and even the administrative director were moved to tears. They were drawn in to being a part of the *communitas*. The performance had brought them closer to one another. The Golden Fair, though meant as a celebration to honor the aged, was in essence a celebration of the *communitas* of *daikazoku* at Kotoen.

As this part of the show ended, floor activities resumed. Long tables were set up for lunch, and residents exchanged for box lunches one of the tickets they were given. They had each been given games, food, and

[3] The term *communitas* was developed by Victor Turner (1974) to refer to the potential fullness of human encounters, both within and beyond the social group. "Both cerebral and heartfelt, *communitas* allows thought to shape feeling and feeling to inform thought. In its full plenitude, *communitas* encompasses the turbulence of human life as well as the warmth of friendly fellow feeling" (Rosaldo, Lavie and Narayan 1993, 2).

[97]

drinks tickets that were hung on their chests with a ribbon. After lunch, staff and volunteers pushed some of the residents in wheelchairs around for games or crafts at the "Cassiopia gate" or for a "cruise" in "space." There was also a traditional rope-making demonstration, and some residents and visitors joined in for a hands-on experience.

I asked a few residents for their impressions of the event. No one, though, mentioned that they had been moved by the performance. Miss Tsuji, experiencing this for the first time, wanted me to take a picture of her with a junior high school volunteer. Unlike the "old-timer" residents, Miss Tsuji was concerned that I take pictures and develop them for her, reflecting the novelty of the Kotoen experience to her. Mrs. Tanaka, who was experiencing this for the third time, simply noted that there were fewer visitors this year. The staff also gave the same comment. According to newspaper clippings about past Golden Fairs, the event was celebrated on a much larger scale in the past, involving more community efforts, such as the setting up of a mini-zoo and handicraft sale. There had been close to one thousand people in attendance in previous years, twice the number present this year. Perhaps the construction outside had limited the number of outdoors activities, thus resulting in fewer visitors.

The last stage performance, "The Finale Stage," began at 1:20 P.M. There was a smaller audience for this show as compared with the one in the morning. When the final performance began, a staff member, dressed in a spacesuit, came on stage: "Ladies and Gentlemen, did you have a relaxing time strolling in space today? Right now, a rocket that will fly high up to space is ready on stage. Riding on all our happy memories for today and hopes for tomorrow, let's open the curtains for the finale!"

The curtain opened and a rocket made of cardboard covered with shiny blue paper stood in the middle of the stage. The backdrop was a blue sky and clusters of clouds at the bottom and dark space with the Earth on the right side covering the rest of the wall. The narration continued: "Riding on the fuel made of everyone's happy memories and hopes for tomorrow, let the rocket set off! Let's wish for a better tomorrow. . . . Shall we count down to the launching of the rocket? . . . Let's do it together: three, two, one, zero!"

With the countdown, the rocket "flew" gradually into "space": "Look! Now the rocket is flying toward the sky; it will soon fly through the atmosphere. Wow, it is now flying in space!" As the rocket lifted off, a lot of balloons rose, too; these were given away as finale gifts to the audience. The tenth Golden Fair ended on a hopeful note; one staff member exclaimed emotionally as the rocket left the ground, "I am so touched!"

What specific symbols were deployed in the Dream Flight? If the residents were given a dream that could come true, would they choose a "flight" out of institutionalization instead? Within the institution, though, the staff would continue to pilot the rocket, while the residents and the children sit tight as the passengers onboard. Where do they go after these ten years? As a pioneer in Japan, Kotoen has no ready model to follow; the rocket seems to symbolize uncertainty; they must grope into the unknown much like the astronauts' expedition into space.

I later learned that Kotoen's vision for the next decade is to extend its *fureai* to the community. It hopes to provide more community-based services and aims to become the focus of the community in the future. This vision was, however, not emphasized in the Dream Flight or the television documentary, as Kotoen remains unique and famous for its decade-old *daikazoku* ideal.

The Making of a Television Documentary on Kotoen

Kotoen, the *daikazoku*, has received much publicity in the past decade. Frequent visits by the media and others have trained the residents, staff, and children to remain fairly at ease before the camera. They have also been introduced to foreign readers twice through *Japan Pictorial*, a semi-official pictorial magazine on Japan published in different foreign languages. Mrs. Sugi also recalled filming by a television station from France a few years back. Of course, almost all the Tokyo television stations have at one time or another reported on Kotoen. The most extensive media coverage Kotoen has received so far was a forty-five-minute documentary by NHK titled "A Big Family with Eighty Grandchildren," which was shown during prime time (between 8:00 and 8:45 P.M.) in April of 1989. Even now, residents who were present during the filming (which lasted from winter through early spring of that year) could still fondly recall moments when they were unexpectedly caught in action and appeared on television.

One morning in July, when I arrived at Kotoen, I saw a film crew setting up their camera and lighting equipment on the steps of the big hall. This was not particularly surprising, as the morning exercise scene was the most representative of the elder-children *fureai* at Kotoen, and visitors are advised not to miss this daily event.

However, these were no ordinary visitors; they were from a Tokyo television station and were here to make a twenty-minute documentary on

Kotoen to be broadcast sometime near Respect the Elders Day. The documentary turned out to be the second most extensive media coverage Kotoen has had to date, after the NHK documentary. The documentary director was a mainland Chinese who has stayed to work in Japan after his graduate study here. We identified with each other easily (as *gaijin* [foreigners] in Japan) and spoke in Mandarin instantly.

When I asked the director why he had chosen to feature Kotoen, he said that although he had visited more spacious, well equipped, and modern old-age homes, they lack the "software" that has made Kotoen "alive." He attributed this to the special qualities of the director, who is not only relatively young but also innovative, flexible, and committed to uplifting the negative stereotypical image of old-age homes. He commented that the other facilities he had visited are run by directors who are retired civil servants; they are more complacent and lack the spirit to initiate changes.

The director wanted to make a documentary on Kotoen to show the *fureai* of the old and young and how this had affected the elders in a positive way. In addition, they would also interview me to show Kotoen's enthusiasm in interacting not only across age, but also across nationalities. To dramatize the scope of Kotoen, it was arranged for several nursery graduates to visit Kotoen so that a reunion with the elders could be shown.

The crew completed the project in three days during the summer. On the first day, they filmed the monthly Open Childcare. Because of the filming, Mr. Furuya and Mrs. Noyama were added to the list of twelve residents scheduled to attend during that month. They are the two most active elders among the home residents. Mr. Furuya was strongly recommended by the staff as a subject for interviews. However, the director found it difficult to highlight him because he seldom speaks, which made interviewing difficult. Instead, he "discovered" the more articulate Mrs. Noyama and focused more on her. Activities in the Open Childcare carried on as usual, and no one seemed bothered by the working camera crew. In the latter part of that day, the arranged reunion was filmed.

The six graduates who were asked to return had left Kotoen five to seven years ago. Four of them were returning for the first time since graduating. They joined several residents at the chatting corner for the filming. Both the children and the elders were a bit shy at first and were not able to recall each other's names. Nevertheless, they found each other while flipping through the photo albums provided by the teachers. It turned out to be a heartwarming reunion; there was laughter and tears as they recalled the things they had done together.

The second filming took place a week later. That was a warm morning, and after the morning exercise, the Lily group and a few residents were requested to go outside the building so that the camera crew could film a jogging scene. The camera followed as the children were led by their teacher to run up and down the driveway in front of the building. Mr. Furuya and Mr. Yokohira, the healthier elders from the home, followed behind them while the other elders (including two Riverside Green residents) stayed at the side accompanied by the staff. They were asked to cheer and clap as the children passed by. Although it was an apparently simple scene, it was repeated several times before the director was satisfied.

The highlight for the second filming was the monthly joint birthday party for the elders. The camera focused on Mrs. Otake, one of the three birthday celebrants from the old-age home, during the event. She was a petite lady with a quick temper. At eighty-three, she was radiant-looking on that day, with her makeup applied by a caregiver. In the afternoon, after the celebration, the director requested that she pray at the Buddhist altar on the first floor for filming. She consented and went to the prayer room with them. As she sat down to pray, she asked the director, "What should I say?" "Perhaps your gratitude and your wish for the future on your birthday," the director suggested. "Today is my birthday; please bless me with good health." She put her palms together and rubbed them lightly up and down as she closed her eyes and prayed; when she was done she struck the "bell" in front of her (a gesture done after a prayer); then she turned around and asked if she had said enough. "Oh, yes, it's all right, but you don't need to ask that," the director answered, and we couldn't help grinning. The sequence had to be repeated because of her question. The memorial tablets enshrined here commemorate deceased residents without family connections and family tablets of the residents. Because she had not placed her own family memorial tablet here, she was actually praying to a collective body of deities related to Kotoen. When this segment was broadcast, Mrs. Otake was narrated as "reporting at the Buddhist altar," mirroring Robert Smith's observations on the Japanese custom of reporting events to their ancestors (1974, 143).

After the prayer sequence, the crew set up an interview with Mrs. Otake. It was held at the big hall, now empty and quiet. "How did you feel when you received the birthday present from the children today?" the director asked, referring to the party when children presented gifts to the birthday celebrants. With a smile she replied, "I felt happy to receive the hand-made present from the little children. It was like receiving it from

[101]

my grandchildren." I saw in her the image of the happy "grandma" from the Kotoen logo. Because she had not been actively interacting with the children, her answer may have seemed superficial, yet the reply may also have reflected what she hopes to be.

The last filming was devoted to the annual summer festival (*natsu matsuri*). The festival was divided into two sessions: a *mikoshi* (elaborate palanquin shrine) procession in the morning and *bon* dancing in the evening. Parallel to the Citizens' Festival described by Jennifer Robertson (1991), the summer festival was derived from the Shinto shrine-centered festivals.

Summer festivals are common throughout Japan, ranging from local, small-scale festivals organized by town associations (*chōkai*) to huge, well-publicized events sponsored by city governments and big businesses. The highlights of the large-scale festivals, besides *mikoshi* and *bon* dancing, are usually fireworks displays and a string of food and game stalls.[4] It is rare, though, for a welfare institution to stage a summer festival on the scale of Kotoen's. Kotoen's intention in organizing a summer festival is not only to celebrate the summer in a traditional way but also to foster a community spirit, or more appropriately, to revive the *shitamachi* spirit of *fureai* and mutual help through festivals.

During the *mikoshi* procession, the streets around the block were closed temporarily, and a timber yard around the corner was "borrowed" as a rest station during the procession. During the *bon* dancing, members from the community dance troupe and *taiko* troupe were invited guests. In addition, everyone in the neighborhood was invited. Like the Golden Fair, the summer festival extends outside the four walls of the institution to *fureai* with the community. There were six *mikoshi* in the procession. Each age group in the nursery carried its own *mikoshi* made from cardboard, milk boxes, and other recycled materials painted in bright colors. Some were fashioned into popular cartoon characters such as Thomas the tank engine, which was made by the Lily group; others were cute animal characters, such as the red octopus made by the Rose group and the blue elephant made for the Cherry group. The elephant *mikoshi* was more like a float in which all the toddlers rode inside, pulled by the teachers. All the children wore *happi* and orange nursery caps.

---

[4]The *bon* dance was formerly an essential part of the public communal celebrations held during *bon,* a rite directed to the collectivity of ancestors in mid-August (Smith 1974). Today *bon* dancing has become a kind of amusement during the summer festival and has departed from its religious significance.

While they were either pushing or carrying their *mikoshi,* their parents (mostly mothers) followed beside to photograph or videotape the event, sometimes shouting *"wasshoi, wasshoi"* ("heave-ho, heave-ho") with the children.

The *mikoshi* shouldered jointly by the staff and the residents in *happi* and headbands headed the procession.[5] In a shrine festival, a *mikoshi*— the temporary abode of a given shrine's deity—is carried through the parish territory so that the mobilized deity can purify the area (Robertson 1991, 65). Although the Kotoen festival is devoid of religious significance, a bench serving as a temporary altar was still placed in front of where the *mikoshi* was parked; two sake bottles (filled with Calpis soft drinks instead), fruits, vegetables, and dried seafood were carefully displayed on it. These are items used during Shinto purification rituals. They were displayed even though no Shinto priest was engaged to conduct a purification ritual.

Kotoen residents not involved as *mikoshi* bearers stayed with the staff in a designated area along the parade route as spectators. Some of them carried huge fans with the character of "festival" (*matsuri*) written on them, and they fanned the *mikoshi* bearers and shouted *"wasshoi"* as they paraded past them. To stir up the ambience of festivity, some staff prepared buckets of water and splashed them on the perspiring bearers, much to the delight of the spectators. Besides the members of Kotoen, neighborhood residents, including shopkeepers, also formed part of the crowd. The camera crew mingled with the crowd, busy with their own assignment. The director interviewed a few bystanders, who claimed that the idea of age integration at Kotoen is great. One said, "I wish to put my grandchildren in the nursery when I have any!"

Although the *mikoshi* procession was a joint event, children and elders stayed separate in their own groups throughout. Even during the interval, children stayed within their own groups to eat watermelon apart from the elders. They were side by side, but not interacting. The director, who was waiting for scenes of intimate *fureai,* eventually realized that it was not going to happen. After Mr. Furuya ended the *mikoshi* procession (already drenched with sweat and water), the director quickly asked him to

---

[5] This *mikoshi* was in fact a children's *mikoshi* donated to Kotoen two years earlier. It is miniature in size, weighing about 20 kilograms. The *mikoshi* seen in usual festivals can weigh up to a few hundred kilograms and must be carried by thirty to forty people (see Bestor 1989). Nevertheless, it was constructed elaborately with lacquered wood and shiny metal fittings, and it was topped with a golden phoenix, in the style of an Edo *mikoshi.* It was carried on a framework of poles by eight bearers.

help push the *mikoshi* of the Cherry group to create the *fureai* scenes he needed. Similar arrangements for filming also had to be made during the *bon* dancing in the evening.

In previous years, *bon* dancing had been held in the open courtyard surrounded by dim lantern lights. This year, the event was held at the big hall instead, because of the construction. It was the Japanese version of a summer carnival, with dancing and *taiko* performances by both professionals and the children themselves. The elders were all dressed up in *yukata* (summer kimonos)—female residents from the home were all wearing the same green *yukata;* male residents and third-floor elders wore blue *yukata.* Parents of the children participated, and most children came in colorful traditional summer costumes for boys and girls. Because it was an open event with no arranged interaction, the children and the elders were clearly segregated. The elders joined in the dancing occasionally; some elders in wheelchairs were pushed by the staff in the dance circle. Most elders, however, sat around watching the dance while children stayed with their parents who also danced occasionally. Interaction was minimal; even Mr. Furuya and Mrs. Noyama had to be requested by the director to join the children and parents so that the crew could film some form of *fureai* pertaining to their theme.

After spending three days filming Kotoen, the director commented that he sensed a lack of open or spontaneous interactions between the children and the residents despite cohabitation. He felt it was especially difficult to try to show effectively how elders were influenced by the presence of the children. Nevertheless, he still presented an idealized image of Kotoen.

In the same program, he introduced Kotoen alongside a nursing home in which residents interact with pets. Some old-age institutions are experimenting with pet therapy, as pets are said to provide unconditional loyalty and affection as a replacement for no-longer-available human bonding. Placing Kotoen in the same documentary with the nursing home with pets implies that the children, like pets, replace the lost human bonding significant to the elders.

The documentary was broadcast from 9:00 to 9:30 A.M. the week after the Golden Fair. As both are portrayals of Kotoen to an outside audience, it is appropriate to juxtapose the two texts when reading them. Do they reinforce the *daikazoku* images effectively? Because one is a performance and the other a documentary of daily life at the center, can they be seen as a mirror to each other?

Both texts portray the ideal of the Kotoen "big family." They are retellings of Kotoen's uniqueness—that this is not just an old-age home but one in which elders live happily with children. Both run in similar sequence: They both present a synopsis of alternate-generation interaction between the elders and children at Kotoen. The classic morning exercises and clothes-changing scenes were highlighted. The Golden Fair used slides to reveal a series of events at Kotoen, while the documentary reported on two events—the monthly joint birthday party of elders and the summer festival. Both texts freeze the time frame of interactions, assuming that such interactions will remain constant through time.

By its depiction of the ideal, the documentary can be seen as collaborating with the Golden Fair to create Kotoen's dream of *fureai* in a *daikazoku*. The Golden Fair portrays the dream through the symbol of the dancing "grandma" and children. This image, taken from the logo (see Figure 2.1), also appeared in various comical forms on the covers of the newsletter to symbolize the happy encounters of the old with the young (see Figure 5.2).

Its mode of presentation made the documentary more convincing than the Golden Fair in delivering this dream to the public. The former was able to pull together different segments across time and space through editing, creating a coherent and realistic image of the dream. Positive feedback about Kotoen was also solicited by interviewing the parents, the staff, the women in the neighborhood, and the ethnographer in the documentary to support the claim that Kotoen is successful in building the dream.

The documentary amplified the dream and made it more real. In the documentary, the actors seemed more "real"; Mr. Furuya and Mrs. Noyama, for example, represented themselves before the camera; their names were printed on the screen, and their voices heard. In contrast, they were merged with others in a collective identity of Kotoen "grandparents" in the Golden Fair drama. Compared with that of the documentary, the staff's presence was felt more in the drama. Similar to a three-generation family in which the elder generation is aged and retired, the staff represents the middle generation in control.

Both the Golden Fair and the documentary were narrations of the same place, one being the insider's and the other the outsider's version. Both were attempts to convey to the audience/viewers that at Kotoen the dream of *daikazoku* exists. How did the audience/viewers respond to their projections?

Figure 5.2. Images superimposed on the Kotoen logo. Courtesy of Kotoen.

Response from the Audience

Most of the audience at the Golden Fair were people who have some connection with Kotoen, either as parents, relatives of the residents, volunteers, or members of neighborhood associations. They have, in a sense, taken part in the making of Kotoen in the past decade; many have attended other events held by Kotoen and could identify the various events and activities mentioned in the drama of "everyday history."

To elicit responses from people who were previously entirely unaware of Kotoen, I took the opportunity to interview two friends who attended the Golden Fair and had heard about Kotoen for the first time. Mr. and Mrs. Ishida, both in their thirties, have two children of nursery age; they are a fairly typical salaryman family, where the husband works in a big company and the wife is a homemaker. Mrs. Ishida speaks good English; before she became a mother, she had traveled widely as a flight attendant with an American airline. They have a stereotypical image of old-age institutions as bleak and hopeless, and they resemble the public who view entering an old-age home as the equivalent of *obasuteyama* (lit., "granny-abandoning mountain").[6]

Equipped with such stereotypical images, they were disturbed by the carnival atmosphere of the Golden Fair and were critical of what they saw. The young and energetic staff in uniform track pants and T-shirts among the elders seemed unreal to them. Mr. Ishida commented, "Why would a young girl spend Sunday morning in an old-age home doing a 'holy' job? This looks like some kind of new religious movement!" They felt uneasy with the whole atmosphere, and thought it was like entering a different planet (incidentally, the Golden Fair included a "space walk," quite similar to their metaphor).

Mrs. Ishida's comments on the stage show further reflected her comparison of Kotoen to a new religious movement:

> At Kotoen, it seems like everyone has to do the same thing. The elders look like they are forced to participate, forcing old people not to stay in bed and encouraging them to be active. I feel the initiative should have come from the elders themselves. I have visited retirement homes in Canada and Swe-

---

[6] *Obasuteyama* refers to a legend about the ethic of filial piety and describes the dilemma of a man who must bring his aging parent to die in the mountains. There are many versions of this story (see Bethel 1993). The name of the legend, *Obasuteyama*, has become a label for old-age institutions, implying that residents have been abandoned by their families. The label also expresses the children's violation of the Confucian ethic of filial piety.

den; my impressions there were that the staff are always playing the supportive roles while old people are the main focus. But in Kotoen, the staff is taking leadership. When I first saw old people playing instruments, I felt that they were forced to play, and they did not seem to enjoy it fully. In the end when they have to say *"Hai,"* I feel pitiful for them because they are treated like little children. In a normal musical concert, no one does that—it doesn't seem natural at all. When the picture was shown at the end, it made the whole thing look like some kind of religion.

On the general feeling of the place, she said,

Kotoen looks more like a hospital to me; it didn't feel cheerful. It looks like an abnormal world, like going into a cancer ward. It is serious and you can't make jokes since everyone is trying their best to support the elders. I feel that old people should have more control; for example, the emcee should be an elder and not the staff. . . . I have expected elders to play with children like natural grandparents, but they seem disabled here. They look different from old people out on the street; those old people are more alive—the difference can be seen from their eyes.

However, when I asked if she would enroll her children in such an age-integrated facility if there were one near her place, she said, "Yes, on the whole, I think this idea is good. If there are more such places, I hope the management could improve and become better, more spontaneous." The main criticism they had, apparently, was their perception of the performance as too regimented and imposed on the elders—so much so that everything looked unnatural. I have suggested in Chapter 4 that *fureai* in Kotoen is a contradictory blend of spontaneity and emotional involvement with rules and regulations. Mr. and Mrs. Ishida emphasized regimentation to the extreme (that is, that everyone is doing the same thing) in their skeptical view of Kotoen.

I believe that Mr. and Mrs. Ishida preconceived negative image of old-age homes attributed to their negative perception of Kotoen. Through these preconceptions, they viewed institutionalized elders as pitiful and incapable, that they were left at the mercy of the staff after being abandoned by society.

I agree that the whole production might appear to be too much of a "drama" that the elders and children were appointed to perform. But instead of perceiving the elders as being manipulated, I would argue that the process of working together across generations has provided opportunities for *fureai* and helped to construct the *daikazoku* ideal in an institutional setting. I find Mr. and Mrs. Ishida's metaphor of a new religion interesting. Besides the negative overtones (the whole thing is too perfect to be true), I suggest that Kotoen does emulate various positive aspects of a new religious movement, such as the management and staff's ardent efforts to present their dream to the public. Like some new religions, which have provided meaning to many people who were distressed by a lack of human fellowship in the modern mass society, Kotoen, too, attempts to reinforce the disintegrating generational ties in contemporary society by dramatizing its vision through the *daikazoku* setting.

Response from the Viewers

I obtained some viewer responses to the documentary from the director. As a program director, he was given ten representative responses to the program by the television station's feedback unit. Out of the ten, nine viewers rated the documentary as "very good" and one rated it "good" (on the scale of very good, good, neutral, and bad). Because it was broadcast in the morning, the respondents were housewives in their thirties and forties. Comments gathered from them included "When I get old, I hope to enter such an old-age home," "I would feel at peace if my parents could enter such an old-age home," "I would like to send my children to such a nursery," "Kotoen is lively, very different from the image of an old-age home that I have."

These responses are similar to those received by the NHK documentary on Kotoen in 1989. NHK was able to solicit viewers from more varied backgrounds, as the program was broadcast during prime time. Its feedback unit reported that they had started to receive phone calls in the middle of the broadcast inquiring about admission procedures and the location of Kotoen. Here are some of the responses:

I was deeply moved. Please repeat the program again. (not identified)

It was a very good program. It expressed well where elders should belong. (a seventy-five-year-old woman who was sobbing at the same time she talked)

Both the program and the attempts by Kotoen are fabulous. I want to initiate it at my own place. (a kindergarten principal)

[109]

I would like to propose the Kotoen model to my city mayor. (a city assemblyman in his fifties)

I was moved to tears when I saw their *fureai*. Please build more such age-integrated facilities in the nation. (not identified)

Some viewers wrote lengthy letters to NHK. Here is one such letter:

When I saw the program, I couldn't help shedding tears of joy. It was a joy to know that such a wonderful place exists. . . . These elders were said to be people who had to enter the home either because they were not able to stay with their own children and grandchildren, or because they had no family and relatives to stay with. However, they do not seem unfortunate at all. This is because they have little children to support them. . . . In the world today where families are experiencing the process of nuclearization, parent-child relations, and also grandparent-grandchildren relations are becoming distant. In times such as these, even a congregation of strangers can be a big family, don't you think [*tanin dōshi demo daikazoku nan desu ne*]? In this way, to the elders, it is a joyful thing to live long, to the children too; they can develop to become someone who loves and treasures the elders. . . . I hope there will be more of such age-integrated facilities nationwide. We, too, will get old one day. Although we don't know what is in the future for us, I think we all hope to live a long life, and hope to die thinking that we have been blessed (with a good life). I have the feeling that all the elders in this old-age home are leading a life in which they don't feel lonely.

These favorable viewer responses contrast with Mr. and Mrs. Ishida's comments. The different mode of presentation of the text, through which the documentary was able to capture (or create) more spontaneous interactions, probably impressed the viewers. Mr. and Mrs. Ishida, on the contrary, highlighted the organizational limitations through their visit during a particular event. Although Mr. and Mrs. Ishida represent an extreme in opinions, they, nevertheless, agreed with the viewers that age-integrated facilities are good and should be introduced widely.

Perceptions of Outsiders

Do you favor age-integrated facilities? I asked the question to different groups outside Kotoen, including (1) twenty-five elders in an old-age home, (2) twenty-five elders in the community, (3) eighteen five-year-olds from a public nursery, and (4) fourteen of their parents (see Chapter 1).

This question has different implications to the different groups of respondents. To the elders, it means whether they like having children around, while to the children and parents, it means whether they see the presence of elders as being beneficial to the children.

About 70 percent of the respondents in the first three groups favor the idea of age-integrated facilities. Of those who answered "not sure," some said they did not know about such facilities, while some others said they could not visualize such interactions. The latter reason reflects many elders' rare opportunities to interact with the young. Among the Group 2 elders who said they disliked the idea, one felt that children are too active, and that the elders may not be able to catch up with them. Another feared that with such a gap in age, they would have nothing in common. Both replies were more concerned with whether older persons could fit into the environment; they were not expressing opposition to the idea of such combinations.

In contrast, only slightly more than half of the parents (eight out of fourteen in Group 4) answered positively to the question. Among those who replied positively, they gave these reasons: "It will be a great merit to bring children and elders in contact in today's nuclearization"; "Children can learn about empathy and kindness from the elders—learning something different from contact with their peers"; and "There are elders who are lonely, so it will make them happy to interact with children who are like their grandchildren." Those who responded negatively questioned the spontaneity of deliberate attempts to link the old and the young and emphasized interaction with the children's own grandparents instead. One commented, "It is all right to have age-integrated facilities, but I don't think it will benefit those who are involved. To the nursery children, the most important thing now is for them to play among their own peers freely. I think the *fureai* between elders and children is very important, but, if possible, the children, parents, and grandparents should interact among themselves and cultivate the sense of empathy to elders in the children this way."

In general, all the different texts—the Golden Fair drama, the documentary, the responses from audience and viewers, the perceptions from the others through survey and interviews, as well as my own field observations—have converged on the same idea: believing that alternate-generation interaction is good, and that frequent contact between the old and the young is beneficial to both. At the same time, they lead us to rethink the concept of the family. What is the Japanese ideal of a family? Is Kotoen conveying a dream that is equally held by Japanese in general?

[111]

From *Obasuteyama* to *Daikazoku*

Old-Age Institutions as Obasuteyama

In emphasizing *daikazoku,* Kotoen attempts to destigmatize old-age institutions by removing the negative label of *obasuteyama.* A magazine titled its report on Kotoen "There Is Human-like Life Here—Old-Age Home and Nursery Coming Together" (*Ōjima Shinbun,* August 27, 1989). This title portrays the stereotypical image of elders in an old-age home as without family and therefore not human. Such stereotypes persist among the Japanese. Mrs. Ishida repeatedly claimed that almost everyone feels that it is sorrowful to have to go to an old-age institution. However, as she spoke of someone she knows who lives in an old-age home now, she began to express ambiguity:

> My neighbor's mother is living in an old-age home. She has three children, and at first she was living in an apartment paid for by her eldest son. But since she was living alone, she did not eat proper meals, which was bad for her health. Moreover, it was expensive; she had to pay 100,000 yen for monthly rental in addition to food and other expenses. So both the children and she decided that she should move to an old-age home. But her son feels so guilty, and the mother, too, has to lie to relatives and friends that she is now staying with another daughter outside of Tokyo. It was a feeling of shame for the whole family. Sometimes, she comes to stay overnight with my neighbor, and she said she wants to take a bath for as long as she likes, not having to rush because of a time limit. She said old-age homes have fixed bathing time and no choices in food. Her daughter felt very guilty when she heard this and she almost broke down into tears. However, her mother's life has become busier and less boring now, compared to when she was living alone in an apartment. She has picked up hobbies she had missed at home, such as calligraphy and folk dancing. She doesn't need to worry about skipping meals anymore, and she also pays less now. But when she becomes frail, she will have to move out of the place because it is only for relatively healthy elders. This is the only worry for her and her family now.

In fact, the ambiguity (rather than a totally negative image) about old-age institutions is common among Japanese. Although many are aware that the nursing homes and old-age homes may be a better alternative than a hospital for their parents who need long-term care, many still opt for a hospital stay, sometimes referred to as "social hospitalization" because of the stigma attached to being a resident of an old-age institution

(Yamanoi 1995). To conform to the *seken* (the society standard) has caused many children to refrain from placing their parents in old-age institutions for fear of being ridiculed as unfilial. This is especially felt by the eldest son in the family, who is traditionally responsible for his parents' care.

The elders, too, being brought up in the cultural and social background of Confucian ethics, expect their children to provide for them and honor them in old age. It is only when all else has failed that entrance to an old-age institution is considered. Despite Kotoen's *daikazoku* ideology, to the public, Kotoen is after all still a social welfare institution for the aged; thus it is equally affected by the negative connotation of *obasuteyama*.

Obasuteyama *and Family Connections*

Although it is common to regard one's entrance into an old-age institution as an announcement of abandonment by the family, Kotoen tries hard to educate residents' family members that old-age institutions are not a dumping ground for their unwanted aged relatives. Instead, it holds the principle that family should share the responsibility with the institution in caring for the elders. Despite Kotoen's efforts to create among the residents the sense of family belonging, it also realizes that many residents enter old-age homes as a last alternative; hence their desire to live with their own families should not be overlooked.

To encourage contact with family members, separate family associations are formed for the second- and third-floor residents. It was difficult to get all family members to join the associations because some residents maintain no ties with their family at all. As members are required to pay monthly dues of 2,000 yen, a few residents joined the association without participating family members and pay the dues themselves. At present, the family association for the old-age home (second floor) has forty-six members.

Mr. Yama, the social case worker for the home, reports to the family members about their aged relative through an annual letter during the month of the resident's birthday. He strives to keep all family members informed of the center's activities by sending them a monthly program sheet and the newsletter *Fureai* regularly. They are encouraged to attend events at Kotoen, particularly the birthday celebrations of their own relatives, although very few did. When the contents of the Fifty People, Fifty Voices survey (names were not mentioned) were published in the newsletter, Mr. Yama highlighted the wish of the appropriate resident before sending the newsletter to his or her family. Staff members were thrilled when the family of Mrs. Kita responded promptly by bringing her out to dinner after reading in the newsletter her wish to eat formal Japanese cuisine (*kaiseki ryōri*). Mrs. Kita was quite an exception among the residents because of her close relations with her daughter. The home also approaches the family members to help in transporting the elders to hospital visits, but only Mrs. Kita's daughter came to help her mother.

Kotoen also encourages family members to visit their elders more frequently and to invite them home for short stays, particularly during festive seasons. Except for Mrs. Matsuda, who stays frequently at her daughter's home whenever her son-in-law goes on business trips, very few elders leave for short stays. A female resident whose daughter visits her regularly once told a caregiver, "My daughter asks me to visit with them sometimes, but it's too tiring, and I don't like it." When the caregiver encouraged her to go, she then spelled out her uneasiness with her identity as an old-age home resident: "I don't feel relaxed at her house because her husband's people are also living there. Besides, they will feel awkward with me around since they all know that I am in such a place. There are many reasons to consider, aren't there?"

Sometimes the residents turn down their relatives' offers to accommodate them. After the widowed and childless Mrs. Kojima was discharged from the hospital, she was invited by her niece and nephew in Miyagi prefecture to stay with them. She turned down their offer, assuring them that she was living well at Kotoen. When asked about her decision, she said, "Miyagi has many hot springs that are good for one's health, but there is no bed in the country, and besides, people may get tired of living with me after some time. Over here, the living conditions are better, and people here do not particularly wish that I die early; they always respond when I need help."

Mrs. Kojima's choice to stay within an institution is echoed in Diana Bethel's (1993) study of an old-age home in Hokkaido: She found that the residents were willing to stay within the *obasuteyama* because it offered them more attractive advantages such as an independent lifestyle, which is difficult to achieve in a family setting.

In general, residents at Kotoen have come to identify themselves with the social world constructed by the staff and the media. The performances and the television programs of which they are a part have in turn shaped their perceptions. Many agree that they are a "big family," citing the photograph of "Kotoen *daikazoku*" shown in the drama as evidence. Some elders see the term as symbolizing the group life here. Mrs. Hoya emphasized that this is the only family she has. As many are aware that this is their "final home" and often their only family, they do cooperate and pitch in to help make it a better place for all.

Daikazoku: *Dream Family*

The dream of Kotoen, as we have learned, is to achieve *fureai* across the generations symbolizing a *daikazoku*. Its image of a "happy home" (*ikka danran*) has been repeatedly publicized in the media. Its acceptance by the media and television viewers indicates that the dream is not simply a private one but also a dream endorsed by the public.

Statistics have shown that the proportion of three-generation families is declining in Japan. However, this does not imply that the dream of three-generation families is dwindling. Advocates for traditional family arrangement emphasize its merits: It provides elders with financial, spiritual, and physical stability. Elders often become a valuable resource to the family; they help in taking care of the grandchildren, cooking, doing laundry, and cleaning; they make it possible for more women to work outside in the family business or farm or elsewhere (Yuzawa 1991). Although more Japanese elders are nowadays living independently from their children, many are still expecting to live with and receive care from them when they become weak. My interviews with community elders reveal similar expectations. When asked their ideal living arrangement, most said multigenerational living; of those who preferred to live alone, they hope to live with a child when they become frail.

By locating *fureai* within the *daikazoku* framework, Kotoen hence addresses the dream of Japanese (especially the older Japanese) for a traditional multigenerational family. Moreover, the "dream family" context also leads us to rethink the larger issues of changes in the family institution and family alternatives in the future.

Familial relations in Japan are characterized by the concept of *uchi* (insider) as opposed to *soto* (outsider, others) (Nakane 1970). This helps explain the skepticism among Japanese regarding the spontaneity of alternate-generation interaction outside the familial context. When I told a government official from a Japanese welfare office about Kotoen, his reaction was, "Oh, it's like a drama family" (*engeki kazoku*), implying that such relations sound unreal. In sum, this group of Japanese is asking "How can a congregation of *tanin* [strangers] be a family?"

Contrary to people's doubts, the changes in modern family forms have prompted postmodernists to ask whether family types not based on mar-

[115]

riage or biological links could emerge. Such a tendency is not impossible. The letter to NHK in which the viewer wrote, "In such a time, even a congregation of *tanin* is also a big family," offers a glimpse of the possibility of diverse family forms, beyond biological bindings, to satisfy the human needs to connect.

Kotoen may have fallen short of its goal of being a place where you would find a "dancing grandma and children," as the gap that exists between the dream image and actual practices suggests. However, such a goal (or ideal or dream) is at the same time a driving force that inspires the staff to engage in providing more opportunities for *fureai*. These programs and activities are held within the limits of the institutional setting; nonetheless, as the following chapter shows, both the old and the young do benefit significantly from the opportunities to reengage.

[6]

Fureai: Encounters and Exchanges

Kotoen has been envisioned as a *daikazoku,* epitomizing the good old multigenerational family prevalent in the traditional Japanese social system. Nevertheless, the *daikazoku* framework does not exist simply as a convenient template to position all members within the institution. Underlying the framework are the assumption and belief that *fureai* is beneficial to both generations, and that it may even prove to be a solution to the dilemma of an increasingly aging society.

The advantages of alternate-generation interactions have been recognized in numerous cross-disciplinary and cross-cultural studies (see, for example, Newman and Brummel 1989). Studies have also shown that, although sporadic and occasional contact with various age groups can provide stimulation to both children and institutionalized elders, it is consistent, frequent interaction that fosters positive attitudes and increases self-esteem and self-confidence within close relationships (Kocarnik and Ponzetti 1991). At Kotoen, frequent interactions between elders and children are made possible through various programs. As outlined in Chapter 3, morning exercise sessions and elders' help in dressing the children after their afternoon naps promote daily contact. However, *fureai* is most evident during the monthly Open Childcare and regular joint activities conducted when the children visit the elders in their living quarters. These activities constitute the essence of interactions within the overarching framework of the Kotoen *daikazoku.*

In this chapter, I begin with the sketch of a joint activity that denotes a typical *fureai* experience at Kotoen. Then I pursue the various themes that emerge from the empirical description. These include the "take and give" rationale in an institutional context, where engagement as a "grandparent" can be explained as one form of reciprocity in a social welfare institution, and the beneficial effects of *fureai* to the elders and children. The latter is based in part on comments solicited from parents of children who currently attend the nursery and of graduates. The chapter concludes with a comparison between natural grandparents and Kotoen grandparents as one way to examine the advantages and limitations of reengaging the alternate generations in an extrafamilial context.

A Drawing Activity

It was a cool winter morning. After morning exercises outside, the second-floor residents returned to their rooms upstairs. Few residents were seen along the corridor. At about 10:15 A.M., the caregivers on duty on the second floor started to lay newspapers on the floor outside the caregivers' station. I helped them to fasten the papers onto the floor with tape. This area would serve as the boundary of activity when the children came up for a joint activity later.

Mrs. Tanaka was sitting on the couch beside me. She took a piece of the leftover newspaper and was using a marker to draw something on it. Suddenly she asked me, "Hey, what do the eyes of Anpanman look like?" Anpanman, the Japanese equivalent of Mickey Mouse, is a popular cartoon character that has captured the hearts of millions of Japanese children.

"Aren't they round?" I said. I had hardly taken a close look at Anpanman, had seen the cartoon on TV only once. Mrs. Tanaka drew two round eyes on the round face and then asked again, "What about the hair?" "It probably has no hair, does it? Since it is an *anpan* [round bread with mashed red bean filling]," I said. But when I looked at her picture later, I found that she had added some strands of frizzy hair on the head of Anpanman. She said she must practice drawing Anpanman because children nowadays ask her to draw characters like Anpanman and Power Rangers.

Mrs. Tanaka was preparing for the children to come. This was the third time in a week that the children would visit. A different age group of children came each time, and activities differed depending on the age of the children. Most of the activities are creative and interactive in nature, encouraging mutual help and contact between the two generations.

Next to Mrs. Tanaka, several residents began to gather and watch a documentary on monkeys. On one long sofa directly opposite the caregivers' station, there were three people; on the next sofa opposite the elevator were Mr. Ishii and Mr. Furuya, watching the same TV.

At 10:40 A.M. the children appeared with the shoes "they wear to go to Grandpa and Grandma's place." Today, it was the Lily group's first visit in five months. Seventeen of them lined up in twos and followed their teacher into the caregivers' station to make announcements. The teacher guided them on what to say as each child took a turn to say a sentence, such as "Let's play together" or "Please come out to play." When the messages were done, the remaining children simply announced their names over the PA system and said, "Let's play together!"

By this time, residents who were interested in the activity were already sitting round the area. Before the children got on to the newspapers, the teacher announced a few rules.

Teacher: The eldest sisters and brothers class of five-year-olds has come to play. We have brought drawing paper and crayons here. As each of you children has brought your own crayons, please lend the grandpas and grandmas your crayons.

Children: Yes.

Teacher: Place the drawing paper on the newspaper, and please draw on top of the newspaper, and not on the floor. There are grandpas and grandmas who have to sit on the chairs because their legs are weak and they cannot sit on the floor like you do. For these grandpas and grandmas, please bring your paper and crayons to where they are and draw with them. In this case you don't have to draw on the newspapers. Please remember that you should not draw on the floor.

Teacher: Another rule is never to run because there are newspapers on the floor and it is slippery. If you knock into a grandpa or grandma you will hurt them, and this is dangerous.

Teacher: Because it has been some time since you all have come to play at Grandpa and Grandma's place, you may have forgotten the rule—never go into a grandpa or grandma's room without seeking permission to do so. Please don't forget this rule.

Teacher: You may start now; please go slowly.

At the end of the teacher's announcement, one boy ran to Mr. Furuya, who was still sitting at the far end opposite the elevator. Mr. Furuya looked troubled; he seemed to say he couldn't draw and asked Mr. Ishii to draw for the boy. Then he got up and walked away.

Activity centered on the newspaper area. Eight residents had joined the children. Mr. Yama, the case worker, also joined in for a while and drew a gorilla. I was behind Mrs. Tanaka, taking notes and tape-recording the event when Mrs. Matsui came by. In her usual soft voice, she showed me her chapped palms and said she couldn't draw because of her hands.

"It's all right not to draw," I told her. "If you like, you may sit with the children and watch them draw instead." So she sat down beside Mi-*chan*.[1] The girl drew a rectangle and divided it by a few lines. She asked Mrs. Matsui to color them, "Any colors that you choose." They sat down to work together, and Mi-*chan* continued drawing lines on top of the rectangle and Mrs. Matsui coloring.

Mrs. Hara's room was just outside the activity area. She came out and watched the boys who were drawing besides Mi-*chan*. When she saw Mrs. Matsui's coloring, which was relatively simple, she joined her. Finally, they completed the picture—a big square filled with small colored squares.

Besides the group of Mi-*chan*, Mrs. Hara, and Mrs. Matsui, I observed four other elder-children groupings, which had emerged spontaneously.

Mrs. Tanaka and Mayi-*chan* formed another group. Mrs. Tanaka had remained seated on the same couch on which she was sitting before the activity began. Mrs. Tanaka walks with a cane because of her weak legs. She receives disability benefits because of this, and said she had first applied to a nursing home. However, she was asked to enter an old-age home instead, since she is really quite independent apart from her problems with walking. While she cannot go for morning walks with the children, she nevertheless engages actively with them; her enthusiasm is evident in her desire to learn how to draw Anpanman.

Mayi-*chan* stood by Mrs. Tanaka and put the paper on her lap, then they each drew on their own side of the paper. Mayi-*chan* drew a sun and flowers, while Mrs. Tanaka drew a house, a person, Anpanman and then a hut, later adding a little Anpanman inside. The drawing looked complete, and then Mayi-*chan* said, "Let's have a fountain," so they both added strokes together to create a fountain.

They decided the artwork was completed. "Good job!" I exclaimed. "How about your names?" At first, Mrs. Tanaka said "Tanaka"; then she changed her mind and said, "Kimi-*chan*, write Kimi-*chan*, kimi, kimi, ki—mi—." She pronounced as Mayi-*chan* wrote her first name down in hiragana, followed by "Mayi" in hiragana, and then she put a big "-*chan*" below. "This is our joint work!" Mrs. Tanaka said as she held it up. Both

---

[1]Names with the suffix -*chan* here refer to the names for children. It is common in Japan to add a -*chan* to a child's first name. This is usually done to girls and younger boys. Older boys usually add -*kun* to their first name.

of them looked pleased. After the names were written, Mayi-*chan* decided to add something more to the drawing, and she drew a bird on top of the hut. It was a big crow, and Mrs. Tanaka said, "This is such a big bird that the roof is going to collapse!"

Mr. Terada and Hirō-*kun* formed the third group. Mr. Terada is the most well-dressed among all the male residents. He wore expensive sweaters and shirts and always looked fresh and clean. I once asked Miss Matsu if Mr. Terada were particularly rich. She said no, but she commented that as he had quite a big pension, he probably become richer after entering the home. Mr. Terada is considered on the borderline between the second floor and third floor because his responses have deteriorated in the recent years, including walking and talking. He hardly talks at all, which makes it difficult to know what he wants or likes. He seems alone among the residents, always sitting by himself watching TV. However, he is always present for activities with the children. He was sitting on the couch next to Mrs. Tanaka and was drawing a rabbit for Hirō-*kun*. Because there was no communication, the boy seemed bored after awhile and soon took over the paper and started drawing by himself. He drew rockets instead. At this point Mr. Terada seemed to have withdrawn and to have become an observer watching the activity.

Unlike Mr. Terada, Mr. Ishii enjoys talking to the children. He had moved forward to join the children, though at first he had been sitting with Mr. Furuya at a couch further away. He moved forward to talk with Masa-*kun*, who was drawing. "How many siblings do you have?" he asked Masa-*kun*. Masa-*kun* answered, "Four." (Masa is the youngest in his family, with two elder brothers and one elder sister.) Mr. Ishii expressed astonishment, as most Japanese families today have only one or two children. Mrs. Shibuya, who was sitting beside Masa-*kun*, also joined in their conversation.

Masa-*kun* drew a rainbow and wrote the Japanese hiragana of *niji* on top of it. "You are good!" Mr. Ishii praised him. The teacher saw it and praised him as well. After that he started to use white crayons to draw clouds. Both Mr. Ishii and Mrs. Shibuya praised him again. He drew two of them and started to color them in white. "Isn't it all right to leave them just like that?" commented Mrs. Shibuya, but Masa-*kun* decided to continue coloring them. Mrs. Shibuya had turned her attention to Masa-*kun* after she had finished a joint project with Jun-*kun*.

Thirty minutes passed; most were done by then. The teacher announced a presentation time (*happyōkai*). All the children brought their work to the teacher; then they were asked to sit down on the newspapers.

The teacher showed Mi-*chan*'s picture first. When she asked her what the colored squares were, she said they were the shops at Disneyland.

Jun-*kun* filled the big orange drawing paper with many colorful flowers. When the teacher asked him what it was, he said it was a bouquet of orchids. On the back of the paper were the names of the "artists." He and Mrs. Shibuya had both written their names in hiragana. When the teacher asked Jun-*kun* who drew with him, he said, "Shibuya" and was about to say more when the teacher cut him off: "You shouldn't call her Shibuya, but should add grandma after the name."

Throughout the presentation time, seven boys crowded around Mrs. Tanaka, sitting on the arms of her couch and in front of her since her position faced the teacher directly. Mrs. Tanaka suddenly realized this and asked, "Why am I so popular among the boys today?" She grinned. I offered to take a picture for her with the boys.

Several children drew Anpanman during the activity. The teacher thus took this opportunity to explain about the character: Anpanman's head is made of *anpan*, and he will tear a part of his head out to give to people who are hungry. The teacher's explanation helped the residents to understand more about the world that fascinates today's children. Such knowledge helps the elders to interact with the children more effectively.

The activity lasted forty-five minutes. After the presentation, the children lined up and said in unison to the residents, "Thank you very much," while the residents replied, "Please come again." After a series of handshakes and hand waving, the children disappeared as they turned down the stairway.

"Take and Give"—Reciprocity in a Welfare Institution

Several interesting themes emerge in a reading of the just-described activity. The first is a depiction of the residents' perceptions of reciprocity in an institutional social exchange system.

Elders in a welfare institution are often perceived as engaging in a one-sided dependency, in which there is "no longer reciprocity but a fixed receipt with no return" (Hazan 1980, 37). One's ability to reciprocate in the social exchange system is an important factor that differentiates one's attitude toward care given by a welfare institution versus that given by one's family.

The issue of reciprocity in family care in Japan has been explored in various studies. Takie Sugiyama Lebra (1974) points to compensative transference through generational succession as a mechanism to validate reciprocity, in which parents have the right to demand care from their children as compensation for their caring for their own parents. Akiyama Hashimoto (1996) contends that a Japanese family's elders could retain a sense of self-worth while depending on their family, not merely because of the normative structure of filial obligation based on tradition but also because of the attitude that they have accumulated credit (by bringing up the children and enduring hardship for the family) and therefore deserve to be helped. Hiroko Akiyama, Toni Autonucci, and Ruth Campbell (1990), on the other hand, distinguish between symmetric and asymmetric rules of reciprocity in their study of relations between older mothers and their middle-aged daughters and daughters-in-law in Japan and America. They conclude that Japanese elders maintain reciprocity in exchange through many forms, not necessarily in kind. This includes "repaying to the grandchildren for the kindness of their daughters-in-law" (Akiyama, Antonucci, and Campbell 1990, 133).

I suggest that residents in old-age institutions adopt these mechanisms to legitimize the aid they receive. The residents, particularly elders in Japanese social welfare institutions, are caught in a dilemma of reciprocity. The negative stereotype attached to the institutions, intensified by the Confucian idea of filial obligations that children should render to their parents, has made residents who have children feel bitter about being neglected by them—in a way, not getting a return after paying their dues. On the contrary, their dependency on the institution (an outside entity when compared to the family) creates in them a sense of indebtedness and the feeling of "being taken care of," which cause them to feel constrained and obliged. It seems unrealistic to talk about "accumulated credits" in the larger social sense (such as through working for the society and fighting for the country); the issue of compensative transference is not appropriate here either. From the discussion of "event grandparenthood" and the grandparent obligation in Chapter 4, I thus suggest that reciprocity in a welfare institution is a process of "take and give"— first receiving from the welfare system, and later giving back indirectly in other forms when opportunity arises. Kotoen residents seem to have ample opportunities to "give"—thanks to their role as "grandparents" in the *daikazoku*.

Hence, according to this notion, when Mr. Okada and Miss Tsuji played the "loving grandparent" role during the graduation ceremony and Tanabata festival discussed in Chapter 4, they were obliged to do so because they feel "indebted" to the staff, who are manifestations of the

[123]

larger welfare system that supports them. Moreover, by fulfilling their obligations, they were also balancing the exchange system by "giving" back what they had "received" or "taken." This is analogous to Akiyama et al.'s example of repaying to the grandchildren what was "owed" to the daughter-in-law.

Similarly, when Mrs. Tanaka, Mrs. Shibuya, Mrs. Hara, Mrs. Matsui, Mr. Kurima, and the rest interacted with the children, it was a form of giving (*asonde ageru*—"play for you"), giving in return for what they had received from the institution. Such interactions may not necessarily be material, such as actually working together as in Mrs. Tanaka's and Mrs. Hara's cases; they could also take the form of praising the children for their good work.

Sometimes elders withdraw from an activity when they feel that they cannot "give." This may explain in part why some activities attract more residents than others. Drawing and clay modeling, for example, usually have lower attendance than paper drama (*kami shibai*) or panel theater. This can be inferred from such expressions as "I don't know how to relate to the children." This uneasiness usually arises when elders seem to feel that they are unable to give something to the children (such as playing with them, making them happy, or telling them stories) when they interact. During the drawing activity, Mr. Furuya and Mr. Terada withdrew, apparently because of this concern.

The social exchange model postulated by James Dowd (1975) could be used to explain the tendency to withdraw or disengage from activities in which one considers oneself inadequate. In the social exchange theory, a key factor in defining the elders' status is the balance between their contributions to society, which are determined by their control of power resources, and the costs of supporting them. The status of elders declines if they possess fewer power resources than younger people. Applying this to the level of individual behaviors, Dowd explains that elders disengage because they have little to exchange that is of value, forcing them to accept the retirement role in exchange for limited social services. Mr. Furuya and Mr. Terada both withdrew from the drawing activity because they felt they had inadequate resources to give, but Mr. Furuya discovers giving in other ways of interacting with the children. He spends a tremendous amount of time in such activities as caring for the one-year-olds during *Narashi* Childcare and playing with the children physically. Mr. Terada, with failing physical and mental health, finally adjourned to the third floor, where withdrawal becomes more acceptable.

The social exchange theory is useful in explaining withdrawal on two levels for institutionalized elders: On the first level, it explains the withdrawal of elders from the society as they enter the institutions; they are forced to disengage because they have few powerful resources with which to maintain reciprocity in the society. On the second level, it explains the continual salience of exchange mechanisms within an institution. The "take and give" system in the institution resembles a microsociety: Although elders consider themselves to be the disadvantaged group in the society—being "abandoned" by their families or with no family to turn to—they nevertheless view themselves as debtors in care within the institution. By recognizing their emotional and intellectual resources via the children, the elders, although they have limited material resources, are able to "return" indirectly by means of *fureai* with the children. When viewed in a *daikazoku* context, this resembles reciprocity in a family.

Giving also occurs in more direct forms, such as gifts. Although it is a rule that the residents should not give any gifts to the staff, residents nevertheless violate the rules time and again, reflecting their eagerness to strike a balance in the exchange relationship. Every morning, for instance, Mrs. Matsuda offers coffee to the staff who worked the night shift; residents often stuffed candies and other goodies into my pockets and a bag for my son ("Don't tell the other staff," they would say); when I was leaving at the end of my fieldwork, one resident even tried to give me money, a traditional gesture to someone who is leaving. They probably felt uneasy to have someone working for them unpaid, even though they were aware that I was no ordinary volunteer: In my own way, I was exchanging my services for research data.

That gift-giving is prevalent even in a welfare institution reflects the dominance of the custom in Japanese culture. The complexity of the act and art of gift-giving in Japan has motivated Harumi Befu (1974) to define gift-giving as an institution, in which people are motivated by social obligation to engage and maintain the institution. However, on a less-established scale, elder-children interaction at Kotoen also hinges on the same principle. Gift exchanges occur in a played-down scale. Staff supervise elders in making presents for the children's birthdays, Children's Day, and the graduation ceremony. Summer greetings are prepared by the staff for elders to write to the children. In return, children also prepare gifts for the elders, and with the help of their teachers, they also make presents for the elders' birthdays and send hand-drawn New Year's cards to them. Reciprocity with the neighboring elementary schools that send their students to work as volunteers at Kotoen is also emphasized.

[125]

Volunteerism, although an established practice in the West, has been vigorously promoted only in recent years in Japan. Volunteerism emphasizes altruism in which satisfaction is derived from the simple act of giving. However, the prevalence of reciprocity in gift-giving and indebtedness in the Japanese context has motivated Kotoen to repay the volunteers in some way. In return for their volunteer work, the assistant director, a staff member, and four to five second-floor residents visit each elementary school together annually to present to the representatives of the volunteers, in the presence of the school principal, their gesture of appreciation. These are usually dust cloths (*zōkin*) that were sewn during craft club on Saturdays. It is interesting that during one of the presentations, the assistant director said to the students, "Please use these dust cloths for more volunteer work," symbolizing the desire for continuity in exchange.

By perceiving reciprocity as an underlying principle at work in elders' contact with children, I am not claiming that the residents weigh their interaction with the children on a balance sheet. Rather, I argue that the emphasis to give helps foster positive attitudes toward engagements with the young. In this exchange, elders—many as "event grandparents" who limit their *fureai* with the children within the boundary of an activity—do benefit in various significant ways.

Anpanman and McDonald's Happy Meal

Interaction with the children can be a learning experience to the elders, helping to expand their understanding of today's young culture. Mrs. Tanaka's desire to draw Anpanman keeps her up to date with what interests today's children. On another occasion, Mr. Ishii learned about the popularity of McDonald's restaurant from the children.

On this occasion, the Dandelion group (three-year-olds) brought clay to the second floor to play with the residents. Like the drawing activity, they settled to play on the area covered with newspapers outside the caregivers' station. Eleven residents joined in with nine children in clay modeling. Mrs. Hara, as usual, came out of her room and started to make something beside a boy. She made a doughnut and gave it to the boy, "This is a doughnut, eat it; it's delicious!" she said. At eighty-five, Mrs. Hara is amazingly receptive to youth culture. She keeps herself up to date by being conscious of the likes of the children, even visiting bookstores to read books that interest the children. It therefore comes as no surprise that she would mold a doughnut (a Western product) for the boy instead of a *dango* (a traditional Japanese dumpling made from flour).

Mrs. Tanaka is good with clay. She was receiving orders from the children, making cute little animals such as rabbits and turtles. Some other residents who were not working with clay just looked on or chatted with the children as they worked. Mr. Ishii seemed fascinated by something a boy was making and asked him what it was. "McDonald's Happy Meal!" the boy shouted and caught all of our attention. "What is that?" Mr. Ishii was puzzled. "Grandpa knows nothing more than the food served at the cafeteria here!" Everyone roared with laughter, but at the same time, the elders must have admitted that they had again learned something new from the children.

The panel theater (*panaru shiataru*) activity the elders experienced when the Lily group visited them also proved a learning experience. Twenty residents came and filled the chatting corner for this activity. The teacher came with a white board and a big brown envelope. The children who followed her came and sat among the residents. "Today, we are going to make curry rice together," the teacher said. It was imaginary cooking time. Along with hamburgers, curry rice (*karei raisu*) is one of the favorite foods among children in Japan now. Although it originated in India, curry rice, like Chinese noodles (*ramen*), has become a part of Japanese food culture. In recent years, "curry rice shops" have sprung up alongside the "ramen shops," and an increasing variety of brands of curry paste and instant curry packets line the shelves of supermarkets.

The whole session resembled a school lesson. The teacher started by inquiring what kind of curry they should cook. She then gave a quiz about the types of curry available. "What are the names of *karei* [curry] with *butaniku* [pork], *gyūniku* [beef], and *chikin* [a Japanized word for "chicken"]?" Some residents were not sure, thinking that it should be *butaniku karei* for pork curry and *gyūniku karei* for beef curry. "No, *butaniku* with *karei* is called *pōku karei*, *gyūniku* with *karei* is called *bīfu karei*, and *chikin* with *karei* is called *chikin karei*," the teacher explained. Some elders gave a nod of understanding and seemed satisfied to have learned something.

Rapid changes in contemporary Japanese society today often challenge the elders' knowledge. The mass importation of English into the Japanese language (Stanlaw 1992), such as *pōku*, *bīfu*, *raisu*, and *panaru shiataru*, is one such change that contributed to the elders' isolation from contemporary culture, distancing them from their own language. This has made the elders as much learners from the children and the staff as they are teachers to the children.

After the cooking session, the teacher proceeded to tell a children's story using the panel and some stickers—a story about why the carrot is red, the radish is white, and the *gobō* (burdock root) is brown. She said this is because when they went to the bath, the carrot stayed too long and turned red; the radish kept brushing herself and became clean and white; but the *gobō,* refusing to clean herself, remained brown and dirty. The moral of the story, she said, is that we should take a bath and clean ourselves like the radish. At this point, she took the opportunity to educate the elders, talking to them as though she were talking to the children: "Grandpa and Grandma, please also go to the bath. Among you there are carrots, radishes, and *gobō,* but please don't say it's too troublesome and refuse to go to the bath." Then she invited the elders to go swimming with the children as the pool was already opened for summer. (No elder, however, has ever gone swimming in the pool at Kotoen.) The activity time ended after a short time for *fureai,* during which the children were encouraged to talk to the elders about their recent activities. Because it was near the summer festival, many of them had been spending time practicing *taiko* (drum beating) for the festival.

The panel theater received a good response from both the children and the elders. The elders seemed to have enjoyed learning and interacting with the children. However, compared with work activities such as clay modeling and drawing, in panel theater, *fureai* is restricted, as the elders join the children to become learners and listeners.

"Teach Me How to Make a GI Hat!"

During the panel theater time, Mr. Ishii and Mr. Terada were sitting beside each other, farthest from the teacher. Like two juveniles in a classroom, they sometimes turned to make funny comments to one another and giggled at their jokes while the teacher was talking.

Residents who gather for activities with children find it a good opportunity for *fureai* among themselves, too. While Mr. Ishii remained an audience member in the panel theater session, he somehow turned into the group's teacher during a session of "playing with newspaper" (fourteen residents joined the Rose group). He didn't mean to become the center of attention. At the beginning of the activity, he sat beside Shun-*kun* and said, "Tell me what you are doing." Shun-*kun* murmured, "Airplane." Mr. Ishii wasn't sure how to fold one, so he took a piece of the newspaper and folded a hat for him instead, "a GI hat." He said he had learned it during the Occupation time when he was a young adult.

The residents beside him saw the hat on Shun-*kun*'s head and were interested in learning how to make one, too. "Teach me how to make a GI hat!" Mrs. Shibuya at the side said. With Mrs. Shibuya, Mr. Furuya, and Mrs. Kanda watching, Mr. Ishii gave a demonstration. Soon, the three of them were folding hats for the children.

Soon the teacher joined in and asked Mr. Ishii to teach her, too. A few children now had the GI hats on, made by Mr. Ishii or one of his "students." Other children saw them and began to crowd around Mr. Ishii's area, requesting a hat for themselves. Mrs. Shibuya folded one wrong, and brought it to Mr. Ishii to have it corrected. When he handed the hat back to Mrs. Shibuya, she jokingly said in a childish tone, "Thank you; I am from the Rose group." At the end of the activity, with a GI hat on each of them, the children and the teacher bowed to say "Thank you."

As the elders were folding the hats, they talked to one another, to the staff, and to the children casually. Mrs. Kita chatted with other residents about how they learned to fold things; she said they had to create their own toys and other things from waste paper when she was young because they were poor.

Joint activity time provides opportunities and subject matter for communication among the residents. During a drawing activity, Mr. Ishii and Mrs. Shibuya engaged in a conversation about the number of children in Japan in the past and today, after they heard that Masa-*kun* has three siblings. During clay modeling time, a girl made a clay figurine of a mother holding a child in her arms, and the elders sitting beside her were so impressed with her creativity that they talked among themselves about it. One of the elders present was Mrs. Noyama's roommate. Mrs. Noyama had to visit the clinic that day. When she returned, her roommate told her about the figurine. I was at the door, about to say, "*Ojamashimasu*" ("I am disturbing you"), when I heard her roommate saying, "The kids here are so cute and so creative. When I encounter smart kids, I am so happy."

Intergenerational programs and activities focus on communications between generations to help provide meaning to the elders. Observations at Kotoen show that by bringing the generations together, they also create moments that enhance relations among the elders. Many have enjoyed such moments while keeping in touch with the children.

[129]

The Pickled Plum Group

Residents at Kotoen are accustomed to the presence of children. Many think it would be horrible without children to break the monotony of the environment. The presence of children also makes life a fun to many.

After lunch during one Open Childcare, elders were sitting on the floor of the nursery area for the Lily and Rose groups, waiting for the children to pass them by and say "Thank you" before heading to their futons in the hall for naps. The children had brushed their teeth and were dressed in pajamas. "Starting with the Lily group," the teacher said, "please stand and say 'Thank you' to the grandpas and grandmas." The children turned toward the residents, bowed, and said, "Grandpa, Grandma, thank you very much." Then the teacher counted, "One, two, one, two . . ." as the children marched out.

After the Lily and Rose groups had marched past, Mrs. Mitani said to the resident besides her, "Then the teacher would say, 'Grandpa, Grandma, stand up, one, two, one, two!'" The few of us who heard it giggled at her funny idea. The teacher overheard it and joined in, "Well, Grandpa and Grandma, what group name should you have?" Someone called out, "Let's call ourselves the pickled plum group!" The rest chuckled. It seems a perfect choice, as elders love to eat pickled plums. Mrs. Mitani said, "In that case, we are rolling out!" The group name was decided, and the teacher repeated the same pattern he used earlier, "Pickled plum group, stand up, one, two, one, two . . ." They marched happily like the children out to the hall.

"Get the Children Out Quickly; I Want to See Them!"

Because of their physical and mental constraints, Riverside Green residents have significantly less contact with the children than do their second-floor counterparts. Sometimes the teacher will bring the children for a stroll to the third floor, but such visits cannot be considered frequent.

Most children have contact with Riverside Green residents only during morning exercises. Most of these residents like children, but many show little confidence in interacting with them. They feel incapable in comparison to the second-floor elders. The children, however, seem to be at ease with elders in wheelchairs. It is a common scene after the morning exercise to see children making their rounds among the frail elders. Some elders who look as if they are sleeping lift their heads and smile at the children as they approach. One elderly woman in a wheelchair, who hardly responds to anything, will not fail to beam at the children and even struggles to move her fingers to play *jan-ken-pon* with them.

Mrs. Sugi, when interviewed by the media, claimed that interaction with the children has a significant positive impact on the frail elders. She cited instances of frail elders who tried hard at rehabilitation in the hope of holding the children one day. Some elders were able to improve well beyond the expectations of the staff. No drastic changes were apparent during my stay, although I have observed Mrs. Kondo (mentioned in Chapter 4) changing her attitude and smiling more as her *fureai* with the children improved.

Elders who attend rehabilitation at the center can observe the children playing from the rehabilitation area. Because there are no walls separating them, the teachers sometimes stay for a short while to chat with the elders. Once the head teacher joined the elders and the caregiver while the children were having afternoon snacks after their nap. One of the elders said, "Get the children out quickly; I want to see them!," knowing that they would have free play in the big hall after their snacks.

During *Narashi* Childcare, Riverside Green residents, too, share the excitement of meeting the cute toddlers. During such less structured times, elders in wheelchairs who have requested to meet the children can be seen, accompanied by the caregivers, popping in at the one-year-old area to hold them.

"Working Grandparent" Role

Every year, the nursery solicits the residents' help for *Narashi* Childcare. Residents do not need to sign up to help, but after the first few days, core caregiver elders were recognized.

Eighty-eight-year-old Mrs. Hoya was one of them. She has participated in almost all of the *Narashi* Childcare sessions since she came here five years ago. Being able to take care of the children appears significant to her sense of self-worth. When I asked her during the graduation ceremony if she felt sad that the children had graduated, her reply was the same as Mrs. Tanaka's: "Not at all. New children will soon come." To Mrs. Tanaka, this means that there will always be children around, and she will not have to worry about being left all alone like a grandparent at home as the children grow up. Mrs. Hoya, though, senses her responsibility with the new one-year-olds; as she said, "They will come, and they will be crying and crying all the time; we become very busy."

She did become very busy in April. The first week, only four out of ten children began childcare. The sessions started at two hours and extended a bit every day, depending on the children's adaptability to the institution. After two weeks, all the ten children had graduated into full-time childcare (eight hours). Mrs. Hoya had already "gained" herself a "grandson" by the end of the first week, as Yu-*chan* became particularly attached to her. Our conversations pretty much circled around Yu-*chan* during that week. When we chatted on Friday, she kept repeating, "On Monday, all ten will come; it's going to be tough!" Patting her on the shoulder, I said, "Do take a good rest over the weekend; please *gambatte* [persist] from Monday on!" She laughed and said, "Yes, yes!"

Besides *Narashi* Childcare, Mrs. Hoya was also kept busy in April by the biannual bazaar held on the last Sunday of the month. She had been a seamstress in the past, and she only participates in the handicraft club at Kotoen. But being good at handicrafts, she had commissioned herself to make as many candy boxes as possible. These are beautiful octagon-shaped boxes made from milk cartons and covered with rice paper. She has a shelf full of the boxes in different sizes, and she sometimes gives them as gifts to visitors.

Mrs. Hoya is a "workaholic" among the elders. After the "childcare duty" in the mid-morning, she went back to her room and spent all day making the candy boxes. When she fell sick two weeks later, Mrs. Tanaka, her roommate, claimed she had overextended herself unreasonably.

In the social exchange analysis, Mrs. Hoya's diligence is interpreted as an act of "clearing her debt" with the welfare institution, possibly reversing the balance sheet to accumulate some credit if she can. However, her overwhelming sense of responsibility to both the *Narashi* Childcare and the bazaar could afford a second interpretation: Through caregiving in *Narashi* Childcare, she has gone beyond the symbolic (and ceremonial) grandparenting role to the actual "working grandparent" role, and it is the work role accompanying these tasks that has given her a sense of fulfillment and satisfaction.

Role perspective has dominated social theories of aging (Hooyman and Kiyak 1996). Role theory posits that roles are the basis of an individual's self-concept, and role loss can lead to an erosion of social identity and self-esteem (Rosow 1985). Old age, accompanied by retirement and widowhood, presents the dilemma of role loss. How people cope with role changes in old age thus leads to two widely debated theories of successful aging: activity theory and disengagement theory (Hooyman and Kiyak 1996, 67). These theories and the challenges they present are undertaken again in the next chapter. Here I discuss activity theory as it applies in this context.

Mrs. Hoya's maintenance of the work role supports the activity theory, which suggests that elders will be more satisfied if they can maintain as many middle-aged activities as possible, substituting new roles for those that are lost. Although Mrs. Hoya "complained" that she was too busy and burdened with "work," she was at the same time feeling useful and satisfied with her self-imposed work obligations and responsibilities.

This sense of usefulness is also felt among residents when they can contribute through teaching and consulting roles. Both formal and informal interactions between the elders and the children provide ample opportunities for the fulfillment of this role. Mr. Ishii, for instance, taught the children about worms at a chance meeting before the morning exercise.

One summer morning, Mr. Ishii arrived at the courtyard early. Two children (one from the Lily and the other from the Rose group), who were also out early, discovered a caterpillar near the flowers planted by Mrs. Hoya. They asked Mr. Ishii to come and see it. Mr. Ishii stood down to watch it with them and said, "This worm does not curl up; if it does it is called *tama-mushi.*" It became a lesson on nature for the children as he talked a bit about the worms he knew while the children listened and watched the caterpillar.

Imparting knowledge to the children may occur in any situation. Children bring big handkerchiefs to spread before them as place mats during meals. It is common for these handkerchiefs to have English words printed on them—most children's goods, in fact, have English letters printed on them to play up the merchandise's trendy image. While the children and the elders were waiting for their lunch during Open Childcare, Mr. Yamazaki noticed the English letters on the handkerchief of one girl, and he began to read the words and explain the meanings to her.

Sometimes the nursery teachers create an opportunity for the elders to be the teacher. In another Open Childcare session, halfway through singing a traditional children's song at the assembly of children and elders in the big hall, the chief teacher asked the "grandparents behind" about the correct lyrics. Such public recognition of the elders' knowledge helps the children to perceive the elders as capable. Just as the elders benefit from their role, enhancing their sense of usefulness, the children also benefit from learning through the elders.

Benefits of *Fureai* with Elders on Children

Every morning, the children shouted to the residents at the morning exercise assembly, "Grandpa, Grandma, good morning!" Like most urbanites in Japan, most of the nursery children live in nuclear families (justifying their application to the nursery). Many of their grandparents live out in the country, which means they get to meet only once or twice a year during festive seasons. If their parents had not chosen to send them to the nursery at Kotoen, these children would have had very little opportunity to greet a "grandpa" and "grandma" in the morning.

Parents commented that the elders' presence in the nursery supplemented the nuclear family. Through their interactions, the elders could gain from the children's vitality, while the children could learn to adjust to the pace of the elders and be more patient with them.

Fureai with elders has provided "precious experience in a nuclear family," as one parent asserted. Parents claimed that the experience at Kotoen had given their children a positive perception of the aged. Children are reported to have become helpful and kind to the weak and the handicapped. Daily kinship with the elders has helped foster intimacy between the children and their own distanced grandparents. They feel more attached to their own grandparents because of their Kotoen experience. Lily group children whom I interviewed claimed that they enjoyed the elders' presence. All said they would love to live with their grandparents: "How nice if Grandpa and Grandma could live with us!" one girl said.

The one-year-olds who were experiencing institutional care for the first time, too, found the transition relatively easy because of the individualized attention provided by the elders. Besides this, the accessibility of nursing staff in case of emergency is also reassuring to the parents.

In some instances, mothers developed relations with the elders whom their children befriended, resulting in three-generational *fureai*. A few mothers still bring their children to visit the elders who have been transferred to Riverside Green, especially during festive seasons such as the New Year. Ninety-one-year-old Mrs. Chiba, who entered the home seventeen years ago, recalled being close to a girl and her mother some fifteen years ago when the nursery was still located separately from the old-age home. She recalled times when she was invited for a cup of tea as she passed by their house. "It's a pity," she sighed, "to have lost contact not long after the child graduated."

Children (and mothers) who lack contact with elders seem more likely to display negative attitudes toward the aged, particularly if they are frail and institutionalized. When we brought some Riverside Green elders in wheelchairs to a neighborhood playground one spring afternoon, the children playing there responded with puzzled and unfriendly looks, no mothers or children greeted the elders, and one child questioned aloud, "What are they doing here?" even though the playground is a public space.[2]

It is common for children at Kotoen to resist interacting with the elders when they first enter the nursery. During morning exercise time, children who had just entered Kotoen and those who were "veterans" were distinguishable through their attitudes toward the elders. "Veteran" children swung from one elder to another, shaking hands, playing finger games, and chatting with them, sometimes even leading the newcomers to greet the elders. Newcomers, however, were reserved, and some even cried when they were led by their teachers to greet the frail elders. Nonetheless, after a month in the nursery environment, they were also running to greet the elders and taking the initiative to hold elders' hands. Their resistance had diminished with frequent contact (figure 6.1).

Do children who have attended Kotoen grow up with more positive perceptions about elders as compared with children who do not? Kotoen has little follow-up data on the graduates. Therefore we cooperated in drafting a questionnaire to survey a sample of graduates.

Children's Perceptions of Elders

We mailed fifty-five questionnaires to a selected groups of graduates— those who had graduated three, five, and seven years ago. Although a stamped return envelope was enclosed with each survey, after two months, only eleven copies had been returned. A 20 percent response rate to a mail survey is considered reasonable, but to the administrators and me, it was unbearably low as we were counting on at least 80 percent to respond to their alma mater's inquiries. Kotoen tried to contact the

---

[2] The neighborhood playground in Japan is an informal gathering place for young mothers and their children living nearby. Over time, an informal young mothers' group may be formed at the playground. They are usually housewives, living in nuclear households in small apartments. The social and emotional supports derived from such informal gatherings are important to these mothers. These groups may sometimes ostracize outsiders not belonging to the group.

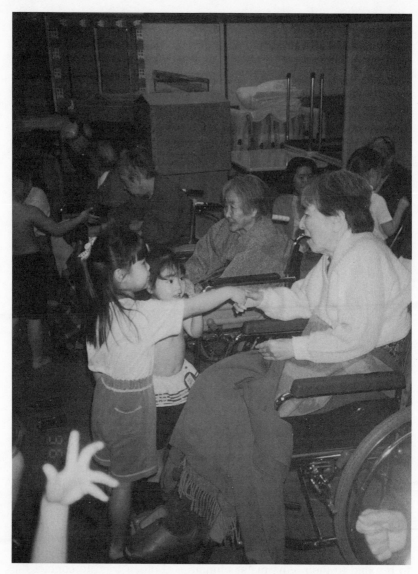

Figure 6.1. Children shake hands with elders in wheelchairs.

nonrespondents, but apparently many had moved away from their last known address. The data are thus limited in their representation of the graduates; I also interpret this response group as a self-selected subset who cared enough to respond.

The administrators characterized the respondents as children whose mothers are more responsible (*shikkari shiteiru*). Eight of the eleven mothers had written additional responses in space provided on the last page of the survey. These responses further imply that respondents are a subset of parents who feel more connected with Kotoen, particularly by a sense of indebtedness. One mother, for example, started her comment about Kotoen's influence on her children with "My three children have received your good care."

All eight mothers commented that engagements with elders at Kotoen has helped develop good characteristics within their children. They noted that their children have developed empathy toward elders or the frail. One mother wrote, "When we returned to the country and were in my granduncle's shop, my daughter readily offered to help an older woman to bring her packages home. When I looked at both of them walking off, I knew she had developed such empathy because of her experience at the nursery, and I was grateful."

The mothers' perceptions of their children are supported by a comparison of the Kotoen graduates with children in neighborhood schools. The latter group consists of students in an elementary school and a junior high school that are both about a fifteen-minute walk from Kotoen. A similar survey was conducted among a class of the third-, fifth-, and seventh-graders. The smallest classes in each group contained twenty-eight, thirty-four, and forty students, respectively, amounting to a total of ninety-two responses. The small size of the Kotoen data limits comparisons and restricts the possibility of making broad generalizations; nevertheless, they provide some interesting insights into children's perceptions of elders in contemporary Japan.

Some Observations

Living Arrangements

The two groups in the survey support the theory that Japan is moving toward a nuclear family structure: 71 percent (73) do not live with their grandparents. Of the 29 percent (30) who do, about 67 percent (20) rank their frequency of contact with their grandparents as frequent on the scale of "frequent," "moderate," and "few." In contrast, only 20 percent (16) perceive their interactions with grandparents who live separately from them as "frequent."

Perceptions of Age-Integrated Facilities

Although children in the neighborhood school group attend schools near Kotoen, 23 percent said they were not aware of the existence of age-integrated facilities. Of those who were, all mentioned Kotoen. A few third-graders who did not know the name of Kotoen and referred to it as being in front of a classmate's house, while that classmate wrote, "in front of my house." It is interesting to note that this student was one of two who replied "bad" to the question, "What do you think of age-integrated facilities?" He commented, "It is better for adults to be with adults and children to be with children." As a neighbor of Kotoen, his extremely negative image of the place would be upsetting to Kotoen, which hopes to extend its network and *fureai* with the neighborhood. However, could his negative image be a result of his distance with the elders? Perhaps his perception would be different if he had attended Kotoen nursery.

In general, most children in both groups replied "very good" or "quite good" (on a scale of 1 to 5 [bad to very good]) to the question "What do you think of age-integrated facilities?" More Kotoen graduates perceived age-integrated facilities as "very good." In both groups, more girls than boys answered "very good." More third-grade girls from the neighborhood school group also gave comments in response to the question. Such comments included "It's nice because it looks fun," "Grandparents can look after the toddlers," and "I hope all [generations] can stay on good terms." Younger children seem more idealistic and positive regarding *fureai* with the old.

Interest in Volunteer Activities

Volunteer activities in school are often regarded as part of intergenerational programming, as student volunteers usually help in old-age institutions. In the neighborhood school group, 27 percent (25) indicated that they had participated or were participating as volunteers. These children had visited Kotoen as members of the schools' volunteer clubs. There were four times more girls than boys in this group. As the school volunteer clubs enroll only students in the fourth grade and older, there were no third-graders among them.

When those who were not currently volunteering were asked if they were interested in volunteer activities, 57 percent (16 out of 28) of the third-graders, 55 percent (12 out of 22) of the fifth-graders, and 23 percent (7 out of 30) of the seventh-graders answered yes. Girls composed 69 percent (24 out of 35) of this group.

Among the Kotoen graduates, four out of eleven had done volunteer work. When asked if they were interested in returning to Kotoen as volunteers, six out of eleven said yes.

The response implies a declining interest in volunteering as children become older. As examination pressure intensifies among the junior high students, we can assume that affirmative answers to this question would decline further among older students. Past experience at Kotoen did not seem to affect the children's desire to volunteer much. There seems to be a gender difference in the interest in volunteering, indicating that girls are more inclined toward caring for others.

Perceptions of Old Age

When the children were asked to indicate how old are people considered elders, 51 percent (47 children) in the neighborhood school group and 73 percent (8 children) in the Kotoen group indicated 70 years and above. Among these children, a higher percentage from the Kotoen group answered "80 years and above." The Kotoen group seems more realistic in their age estimates than the others, which is no doubt due to their greater experience with the elderly.

To assess children's perceptions of elders, the survey adopted the Semantic Differential Study used in CATE, Children's Attitudes toward the Elderly Instrument, developed by R. K. Jantz et al. (1976). The reliability of this technique for children has been cited in many related studies (Phenice 1981; Nakano 1991). We selected ten items from Ikuko Nakano et al.'s (1994) modified version on the Semantic Differential of bipolar adjectives. They were evaluated on a scale of one to five.

The response shows that the Kotoen group tended to regard elders as warmer, happier, friendlier, cleaner, and better than did the neighborhood school group. But the Kotoen also tended to perceive elders as less healthy, weaker, and less sharp. In the neighborhood school group, the seventh-graders tended to have a less positive image than the others. In both groups, girls tended to perceive the elders as weaker and more in need of help than did the boys. This correlates with their interest in volunteer work. When asked what kinds of volunteer activities they wished to engage in, most answered with activities relating to helping elders.

The survey shows that Kotoen graduates have contradictory perceptions of elders—they are friendlier yet weaker, happier yet less sharp. It is easy to classify the contradictions as an indication that the Kotoen children are not as positive in their perception of old age after all. However, these children have grown up in an environment where they meet frail elders every day. They could merely be perceiving reality as they have experienced it, in which "weaker" or "less sharp" do not carry the stigma of stereotypical old age.

Combining the children's contradictory images of old age with their high age estimates, I thus suggest that past experience in *fureai* with the elders reduced their stereotypical thinking and positively influenced their perceptions of old age. This agrees with the contact hypothesis theorists, who proposed that children form more positive attitudes about elders with increased contact because it facilitates their ability to differentiate among age groups and to form more accurate perceptions of them (Caspi 1984, 74).

Kotoen Grandparenthood versus Natural Grandparenthood

How do Kotoen grandparents compare with natural grandparents? Children in Kotoen seemed to have learned to differentiate between the two. When I asked the five-year-olds how they felt about having elders in the nursery, they said they liked the idea because the elders could play with them. Children could readily mention some activities they did with the elders here. Kotoen graduates in the survey, too, remembered going for walks with "grandpas" and "grandmas," playing together and learning origami from them. When asked about their own grandparents, some children mentioned that their grandparents play with them, too. But one said that his grandparents were too busy working, and they had no time to play with him.

One difference between natural grandparents and Kotoen grandparents is that the latter seem to have more free time to accommodate the children. Vern Bengston's (1985) analysis of the variability in grandparenting warns that natural grandparents may have their own jobs and leisure and family activities. Takie Sugiyama Lebra's study (1979) on Japanese women has also shown some grandmothers too preoccupied with *ikigai* ("purpose in life") activities to have time for grandchildren. As one child's claim of her grandparents as being too busy shows, most grandparents of nursery-age grandchildren are still in their late fifties and sixties, a considerably young and energetic age in the context of Japan's long life expectancy, and many may still be in the workforce.

Some children also mentioned that they like their grandparents because they receive pocket money from them whenever they meet. Receiving pocket money, especially from grandparents who live separately, has become one of the established exchanges between grandparents and their grandchildren in Japan. In surveys on Japanese grandparent-grandchildren relations, "receiving pocket money" is listed as one of the most common things children like about their grandparents (Tsukamoto 1978; Chōfu-shi 1989).

Monetary and material gifts from grandparents are a common way for most grandparents to express their love to their grandchildren, especially when the forms of communication are limited by distance. This sometimes becomes a burden to the elders. One elderly woman who lives in the community has two great-granddaughters. When I asked her if she meets them often, she shook her head and said, "No, I don't meet my great-grandchildren much. It costs a great deal to give pocket money! One of my granddaughters who was in Chiba has three children, and if all three come, it will cost a lot in train fare and other things. I have to give each one 5,000 yen and three of them would cost 15,000 yen."

On the contrary, "collective grandparenting" practiced at Kotoen discourages Kotoen elders from showing affection to a particular child through monetary and material means. Besides, most Kotoen elders have limited financial resources, which would make it difficult to engage in such a practice.

The types of interactions experienced by Kotoen "grandparents" and natural grandparents are also different. Kotoen staff plan activities and events where the elders interact as a group. Within the boundary of the programs, *fureai* can be meaningful, as we have seen earlier in the chapter. The natural grandparents in my data (elders in the community), however, when mentioning *fureai* with their grandchildren, focus on taking care of them, sharing meals, and watching TV together.

Moreover, natural grandparents experience a decline in contact with their grandchildren as they grow up. Most natural grandparents in the same data set claimed that they did not see their grandchildren much, now that they had grown up. One respondent commented that although she used to take care of her two grandchildren, as they are teenagers now, they look in her direction only when they receive pocket money from her. Kotoen grandparents have no worries about missing little children, because as the bigger children graduate, small toddlers are added to their "grandchildren group."

However, even when grandchildren grow up and grow away, natural grandparents are still connected to their grandchildren by serving as a link between the younger generations and their family history (Hagestad 1985). The lack of family connection and temporal continuity is the fundamental difference between natural grandparents and Kotoen "grandparents." In the idealized village of the past, many elders probably had long-term ties with the neighborhood children and could say they had watched them grow up. Kotoen, located in the *shitamachi*, apparently hopes to revive such ties, as many children live in the neighborhood. In reality, however, graduates grow up and grow away like most grandchildren; they seldom return, and relations with a child usually end with his or her graduation from the nursery. As shown in Chapter 4, even when some return, they come with a new identity as school volunteers and may not show much interest in meeting the elders.

Eighty-four-year-old Miss Umeda, a Riverside Green resident, is an exception. She still maintains ties with a boy and his mother even after they moved away from the neighborhood. Miss Umeda moved to the third floor after staying on the second floor for nine years. The caregivers remember her as an active "grandma" in the past. As she had been a seamstress before "retiring" to Kotoen, she had used her expertise to make costumes for the children in drama performances and other events. One year, she even sewed kimonos for the children during the *shichigo-san* (a traditional event in Japan for children at three, five, and seven years).

Miss Umeda's close relationship with Tabi, a boy who graduated three years ago, continues through occasional correspondence. Tabi and his mother used to visit Miss Umeda until they moved to Chiba Prefecture two years ago. As we talked, she showed me the three New Year's cards, two letters, and a photograph she had received from him since he graduated. The New Year's cards and one letter sent in the first two years were written by Tabi's mother. Tabi wrote the latest New Year's card and letter, as he is now ten years old. The letter was written in Tabi's big handwriting, but the phrases were well constructed and polite, obviously taught by his mother. The letter thanked "Grandma" for the New Year's card and the *otoshidama* (money children receive from adults in the New Year), implying reciprocity in the relationship. Miss Umeda's relations with Tabi resemble that of natural grandparents who are distanced from their grandchildren physically. In this case, Tabi's mother is instrumental in maintaining the ties. Miss Umeda is the only case of continual interaction at Kotoen now. With "collective grandparenting," ties beyond the institution will continue to be rare. Instead of an ideal situation in which graduates maintain ties with the elders, many Kotoen residents instead derive a sense of symbolic continuity with the graduates through photographs and fond memories. Mrs. Mitani, for example, keeps on the display cabinet in her room a photograph she had taken with a child who had graduated years ago. "That's my grandson—oh, not the real one," she likes to say.

Intimacy and *Fureai*

In their model of Japanese interpersonal relationships, Kinoshita and Kiefer (1992) describe three levels of intimacy. Level 1 is the most intimate, referring to relations that allow one to be in *amae* (indulgence); these include family, close friends, and "consociates"—people to whom one relates across time and with intimacy (Plath 1980). Level 2 is less intimate and is comprised of relations that are governed by *enryō* (restraint or holding back), *giri* (obligation), and social *amae*. In Level 3, casual contacts and anonymous social relations dominate (Kinoshita and Kiefer 1992, 28–29).

With this definition, most *fureai* between the elders and the children falls into the second or even third level. Even with Mrs. Mitani and Mrs. Chiba, who have contacts with the children and their mothers, the relations still lack the quality of "consociates." No elders have ever been invited by a mother or child to their house for meals or to an outing together, other than those organized by Kotoen.

Kinoshita and Kiefer suggest that the model is not static. *Fureai* between the old and the young, too, is not static. The old and young at Kotoen have much potential to move into intimacy at Level 1, as they stay in close proximity and sustain frequent contact across time (from one to six years old). In this chapter, we further see how the *fureai* programmed by Kotoen has encouraged spontaneous contact and benefited the generations. Through play and the limited caregiving made possible through *Narashi* Childcare, children probably have more consistent and frequent *fureai* with the Kotoen elders than with their natural grandparents.

[143]

Elders and children have constructed meaningful interactions among themselves within the boundary set by planned activities. At the same time, however, drawbacks remain. Besides limitations placed by the emphasis on group contact, other factors such as declining health, personal backgrounds, and attitudes also affect alternate-generation contacts. These factors are discussed in the following chapter.

[7]

Fureai: Realities

In the media portrayal of Kotoen and during the Golden Fair, the elders and the children in the *daikazoku* appear to live happily together ever after, and *fureai* seems consistent over time. In reality, however, changes in *fureai* are apparent over the past decade. This chapter examines changes in the frequency and types of programs to promote *fureai,* changes in the participation levels of the residents, and the issue of increasing involvement of male residents (the "grandpas").

Changes in the programs to promote *fureai* through the years reflect staff efforts to plan appropriate programs for both groups. When examining changes in the residents' participation levels, I highlight the reality of declining health among the residents and suggest that the common notion of passive *fureai* used among the administrators is a strategy to keep the elders engaged even when they are frail. When analyzing changes in participation levels of elders over time, I challenge the activity and disengagement perspectives in social gerontology and propose a continuum from active to passive interaction to better understand engagements in old age. I further adopt the person-environment fit theory in social gerontology to frame the dynamics of generational contact, where physical competence, attitudes, and the nature of the activity interplay to determine the most comfortable level of *fureai.*

Finally, I analyze the increasing involvement of "grandpas." With the longer life expectancy of men (along with women) and lesser social constraints in contemporary society to restrict men's "impulse" to nurture, such an encouraging sign of change is challenging the typical images of the grandmother as the focus of *fureai* with children.

Experimenting with Various Innovative Activities

One of the aims of the Committee to Promote *Fureai* is to plan activities and programs to encourage alternate-generation contact. As a pioneer in the nation with no model to follow, Kotoen has relied on its staff's creativity to design innovative programs. Many programs have been tried and modified over the past decade; as a result, some longtime residents are nostalgic for certain programs in which they participated in the past.

"One of the most memorable episodes of *fureai* with the children to me," said the ten-year resident Miss Kusumoto, "was attending nursery with the Dandelion group [three-year-olds]."

She was referring to a program Kotoen implemented when the two groups first began living together. According to the current nursery principal, Mr. Hitachi (who was then a caregiver), the program aimed to encourage the initially quite reserved residents to interact with the nursery children. This program was omitted after the first year, as elders and children gained the momentum of *fureai*. Miss Kusumoto attended the three-year-old class with Mrs. Shibuya. Like Miss Kusumoto, Mrs. Shibuya still cherishes the memories of her "nursery days":

> Miss Kusumoto and I played with the Dandelion children every morning. We did many things together. We even had an attendance booklet like the children's. It was like attending a nursery ourselves; when the teacher marked attendance, she said, "Grandma Shibuya," and I lifted up my hands like the rest of the class. . . . I went for more than six months but had to stop in October when I caught the flu.

During the same period, the "visit to elders' quarters" program was also initiated. As the program name implies, the children did visit the elders' bedrooms at the beginning; five or six children crowded at the bedside to play with an elder. The children used to visit both the second- and third-floor residents every day and engaged in activities such as origami, drawing the elders' faces, or simply chatting. Such room visits were later changed to the present form of joint activity at the chatting corner (or in front of the caregivers' station) where more residents could participate. The frequency of visits was also reduced to three or four times a week for the home residents and even less frequently for Riverside Green residents. The frequency of helping the children with changing clothes has also been reduced in recent years. At the beginning, the elders also helped the children to change into pajamas before their naps, but after a few years, the request for help before the nap was dropped. Several other activities, such as the elders and the children cooking together or lunching together in the cafeteria, were also experimented with, but have not been planned in recent years.

Open Childcare, started in 1989, is about the only activity that has increased in frequency through the years. In its first four years, this program was implemented three to four times a year; in 1992, it increased to eight times, and it reached the present level (twelve times a year) in 1994.

On the one hand, the changes in frequency and forms of intergenerational programs throughout the years reflect the programs' experimental nature. On the other hand, they reveal the dilemma of the residents' weakening health. Through the years, many residents have experienced a withdrawal of *fureai* from an active to passive nature as their health deteriorated. This is a common phenomenon faced by age-integrated facilities. An age-integrated institution in Tokyo, which combines a nursing home with a nursery, also sees a decline in activities between the children and the elders as it entered its eighth year of *fureai* activities. The administrator interviewed claimed that the institution has had to reduce the frequency of *fureai* in recent years to accommodate the residents, who have become weaker and require more attention to daily health and hygiene care.

"You Will Understand [My Position] by the Time You Turn Eighty"

Mrs. Shibuya is an example of someone whose weakening health has caused her to withdraw from *fureai* with the children. She had attended the nursery with the Dandelion group and adores children:

> I have looked after my grandchildren before. The children here remind me of my grandchildren; they were that small once, too. . . . When I feel down, I go down to watch the children play, and that makes me feel good. After a while, I return to the second floor feeling refreshed and happier. . . . The children somehow feel attached to me; they like me.

The children indeed became attached to her readily. One winter morning, after the regular morning exercises in the courtyard, the children and the elders went for a walk around the block. Two girls from the Rose group (four-year-olds) held Mrs. Shibuya's hands as they walked. They

[147]

chattered on the way; one girl told Mrs. Shibuya that they had received a box of grapes from her grandmother in the country the night before, and that they were delicious. When they came to a stony path, she said, "Grandma, be careful, please watch your step." She went on to say that she had hurt herself here once when she was a Dandelion child. It was refreshing to start the day with a stroll with the children, and I assumed that Mrs. Shibuya must have enjoyed the walk as well.

A couple of weeks later, there was another morning walk. When the caregiver asked Mrs. Shibuya to go, she refused. I was surprised and was unable to comprehend why she would turn down the invitation, being an attached "grandma" to the children. When I asked her, she said, "I don't hate it at all." She repeated this several times to emphasize that, in fact, she was reluctant to say no. "But I can't keep up with the kids; they walk too fast, and I am pulled along. My legs are weak. I really wish to go, but I need to take care of my legs, too."

Before I could find the words to console her, she looked right into my eyes and sighed, "You will understand [my position] by the time you turn eighty." Then she pointed to Mr. Furuya and said, "That grandpa is going." Mr. Furuya is one of the regular attendees of the morning exercises. In winter, there are usually fifteen to twenty residents at the morning exercises. Sometimes half of them are elder men. The exercises are usually held in the open courtyard, despite the low temperatures. The cold sometimes discourages residents' attendance; some who do attend return indoors immediately after the exercises, without even interacting with the children.

Mrs. Shibuya, however, did not head right to the door after the exercises. As she waved to the last child who had left for the walk, she got up, walked to the gate, and chatted with some other residents who were already there waiting for the children to return. When the children were in sight, she joined the rest to clap and shout "Keep it up!" Mrs. Shibuya still remains an active participant in joint activities and Open Childcare, and she is always excited about the children's presence on the second floor. However, she has recently resigned herself to the cheering role instead of walking or running with them. Now eighty-one, Mrs. Shibuya entered Kotoen eleven years ago and claimed to be very active in the past:

> I have done many things in the past, like calligraphy, flower arrangement, folk dance; I did it all before. In the past we had thirteen people in the dance group, but now [there are] only two. We represented Kotoen by performing in various cultural events in the community. We practiced a lot in

the past, in the morning and in the afternoon; did I dance too much? Perhaps my legs became weak because of dancing. . . . After my legs started to hurt, I began to lose interest in everything.

Mrs. Shibuya 's withdrawal from active *fureai* with the children is typical of the residents. Many nursing home residents who formerly stayed on the second floor have experienced the same withdrawal process.

Ninety-five-year-old Mrs. Tochida, the oldest resident in Kotoen, represents an extreme in withdrawal. Mrs. Tochida entered the old-age home eighteen years ago and was transferred to the nursing home fourteen years later. In recent years, her health has deteriorated considerably: She suffers from hearing and vision loss and stays in bed almost all day. Mrs. Matsuki, the nursing home's case worker, recalled Mrs. Tochida as a very active woman who loved dancing. Mrs. Matsuki's two children, who are now college students, were very attached to Mrs. Tochida when they were attending nursery here. Mrs. Tochida's smile had appeared in various magazines featuring *fureai* at Kotoen. In failing health, she now retreats from interacting with others (including the children). "Have I done anything wrong to live such a long life?" she said in one of our conversations. "Every day I pray to be received by the other world soon."

Most residents agree that declining health negatively affects active *fureai* with children. Mrs. Noyama, who acted as the Kotoen Grandma during the Golden Fair, was forced to stay in bed often because of her liver problem; many others complain of back and limb aches that force them to reduce all forms of physical activity. With further health deterioration, they will be promoted to the third floor in time, and their *fureai* with the children will be reduced to a more passive nature.

Passive *fureai*—characterized by nonverbal expressions such as watching, touching, smiling, or giving an encouraging pat on the head—are equally encouraged by the staff. It is a strategy recognized by both the staff and the elders to remain engaged. A report by Kotoen staff about *fureai* during the morning exercises stated that "although an increasing number of residents are not able to join the children in active exercises and marathons, they could still achieve ample communication with the children while sitting down."

The acceptance of passive communication resembles observations of passive interaction by Japanese mothers in the caretaking of their children. A study on maternal care and infant behavior in Japan and America by Caudill and Weinstein (1969) shows that although mothers in both cultures spend about the same amount of time during the daytime hours in caretaking, American mothers interact more vocally with their infants and stimulate them to greater physical activity and exploration. On the contrary, Japanese mothers interact with their infants in a more passive manner, engaging in greater bodily contact and instilling a physical quiescence and passivity with regard to environment.

Passive Communication

Age-integrated facilities in Japan generally recognize such passive communication as a form of *fureai* and even therapy for elders. Most programs to promote *fureai* in other age-integrated facilities I have surveyed are event-based; that is, children and elders get together to celebrate certain festivals. During these events, the elders are usually the audience watching the children sing, dance, or compete. Besides these events (which should also be considered passive), many administrators mentioned daily interaction in the form of passive communication. An administrator of a combined institution in western Tokyo that offers similar services in the same vicinity as Kotoen said,

> Elders in the nursing home have limited formal interactions with the children. They get together only for annual events such as sports day, tea ceremony, Respect the Elders Day, and Tanabata. But they have informal *fureai* every day because the children play on the rooftop of the nursing home building every morning. When they go there, they will pass by the elders, at which time they sometimes hold hands and interact. . . . Besides the annual events, they have a joint singing session every month. . . . Some old-age home elders stand at the gate waiting for the children to arrive and go home every day; they wave and talk to them. . . . The children sometimes go to the old-age home to play at the small pond there. . . . The residents also stand at the side to see the children playing on the open ground next to the home. . . . Elders have become happier and gentler with the presence of the children. Even to watch the children helps.

The close proximity of the old-age institutions to children's institutions allows elders to communicate passively with the children through watching. Some such passive *fureai* occurs in the gardens of the nursing homes, as nursery children often play in the nursing home's gardens if they are bigger than the nurseries' playgrounds. During such times, elders sit at the side watching the children become immersed in their laughter and songs. Perhaps they experience the same therapeutic effect as Mrs. Shibuya, who "goes down to watch the children play when she feels down." The conceptualization of old age in traditional Japanese culture helps to explain the recognition of passive interaction between the elders and the children. Unlike the youth-oriented culture in the United States, for example, which expects elders to conform to the activity level of the middle age, Japanese culture tends to encourage withdrawal from active engagements in old age. In traditional Japan, elders are dressed with bright red garments on their sixty-first birthday to symbolize their relinquishment of responsibilities; when they turn sixty, they also become known as *go-inkyo-sama*, an honorific indicating their retired state (Smith 1961, 96). It is expected that elders will depend on the family and be indulged by them (Benedict 1947).

The Japanese acceptance of such passive modes of communication as a form of *fureai* often puzzled the intergenerational program administrators in the United States. Matt Kaplan claims that "in the United States, intergenerational interaction is understood to always mean direct, overt communication" (1996, 18). Communication by watching thus could be patronizing to the elders, as it implies that "as a result of physical disability, their preferred mode for engaging with the world's activities has been reduced to one of passive observation" (Kaplan 1996, 19).

A Volunteer Just by Being Present

In Japan, "passive observation," is regarded as a form of activity. I suggest it as a strategy for elders to remain engaged in the face of frailty. In the video *A Volunteer Just by Being Present*, which was made by the National Old Age Club Federation (1995), passive observation is introduced as a form of volunteer activity for the elders. The video, a production to promote senior volunteerism among Japanese, begins with a Christmas concert at Kotoen, focusing on a song performance by the elders before exploring the various volunteer opportunities available to elders. One form of volunteering, as the title suggests, requires the elders merely to be present with the children. The video shows elders sitting on park benches, watching the children play. Takahisa Kihara, the producer, then comes on to explain the rationale of becoming "a volunteer just by being present":

As one ages, one gets less obsessed with the importance of blood-connectedness. It does not matter whose child it is; with affectionate eyes, they attend to the children who are there. The children, too, notice these

[151]

elders and feel reassured. This is a trivial task, but the elders are also performing a role this way. It is good to have more active social participation, but to participate simply by watching, anybody can do it; isn't that so?

The video emphasizes the roles that elders could play with children. "Children are the lovers of elders," it asserts, claiming that elders and children are natural companions for each other. The video's last segment shows high school students working as volunteers in a nursing home. As they help the bedridden elders, the video claims that the elders are also working as "volunteers of the heart" (*kokoro no bora*) for the students because "they bring out the sense of empathetic feeling in the youth."

In the exchange perspective, recognizing elders as volunteers in their interactions with children attempts to restore the reciprocity between the two, implying that declining health does not impair elders' values in the exchange: They still possess valuable resources even when bedridden.

Kihara's effort to integrate volunteerism in elders' passivity is a unique concept; it also reflects the dominance of the activity theory that has resulted in the desire of the welfare personnel to justify passive behavior by linking it with a concept that has an activity connotation. The activity theory (developed by Havighurst 1963) assumes that a person's self-concept is validated through participation in roles characteristic of middle age; therefore, elders who are active, who maintain as many middle-age activities as possible, and who substitute new roles for those that are lost through widowhood or retirement will be more satisfied and better adjusted than less active elders (cf. Hooyman and Kiyak 1996, 67). Volunteering is said to substitute one role for another and to help achieve higher life satisfaction and self-esteem among elders (Swartz 1978).

In a way, implying that elders do not necessarily disengage with increasing frailty but may maintain a useful role serves to critique the disengagement theory. First formulated by Elaine Cumming and W. E. Henry in 1961, disengagement theory is another of the most widely known and controversial theories in social gerontology. It views disengagement as an adaptive behavior; thus the process whereby elders decrease their activity levels, seek more passive roles, and become increasingly preoccupied with their inner lives is seen as normal, inevitable, and personally satisfying (cf. Hooyman and Kiyak 1996). Both the activity and disengagement theories have been widely criticized for their limitations in explaining social aging. I offer another argument to these perspectives: Rather than categorizing the behavior of passive interaction under the umbrella of either theoretical perspective, with one's physical well-being a variable factor, I propose that the elders' interactions with the children be viewed as a continuum from active interaction to passive interaction. Elders move from one step to another, depending on their physical condition. This is not necessarily a one-way process; for example, Mrs. Noyama disengages when ill and reengages when her health improves.

If we evaluate the nature of the Kotoen elders' *fureai* with the children on this continuum, Mr. Furuya and several other male elders are on the active side of the continuum; Mrs. Shibuya is in the middle, with a tendency toward passive interaction; and Mrs. Tochida would be at the extreme end of the continuum, withdrawn and disengaged as she has claimed but probably still a spontaneous passive "volunteer" in Kihara's conceptualization.

Personal Backgrounds and Attitudes

Although physical weakness may be a major factor limiting elders' interaction with children, other factors, such as personal background and attitudes, also influence interactions. The elders often relate to past experience with children in justifying their present level of interaction with them. Mrs. Shibuya thinks that the children attach to her easily because she used to take care of her grandchildren, claiming that residents who have no such experience are not as fond of children. The handful of residents who have "confessed" to having little interest in children indeed fit into this category; however, many who like children and make conscious efforts to interact with them also belong to this category. The short and jovial Miss Sakada, although never married, engages actively with children. To her, even physical condition is not a barrier to interaction; she feels that it is a matter of one's attitude: "As long as you want to do it, you can." This is echoed by the childless Mrs. Hara, who agrees that "if there is a barrier, it would be more mental than physical." On the contrary, eighty-six-year-old Mrs. Minai, who has grandchildren and greatgrandchildren, for instance, feels that it is hard to develop close attachments to the children because "they are other people's children" (*tanin no ko*). Therefore, the elders' personality and attitude—whether one is outgoing, optimistic, reserved, or resentful of change—also appear to be valid factors affecting interaction.

One's attitudes to children may sometimes change with increasing exposure to them. Miss Tsuji, who repeatedly claimed that she did not fancy children when she first entered Kotoen, gradually changed her attitude in the later months as she became attached to Judy. She consequently asserted that she could not handle toddlers because they were too small and found interacting with older children more comfortable.

It is evident that various factors intertwine to influence elders' interaction with the children. I would like to introduce the person-environment fit theory—a recent and popular theory in social gerontology—to help frame the dynamics in *fureai*. The theory suggests that "the environment is not a static backdrop but changes continually as the older person takes from it what he or she needs, controls what can be manipulated, and adjusts to conditions that cannot be changed" (cf. Hooyman and Kiyak 1996, 5). Hence, attaining an optimal level of interaction with the children is a process of adjusting to the environment (the presence of children) according to individual competence. To attain the most comfortable level of *fureai*—be it active or passive or somewhere along the continuum of interaction—one's physical competence and attitudes, as well as the nature of the activity (whether it demands physical strength, such as a marathon, or is a quiet one that demands skill, such as drawing), converge to determine the most comfortable fit.

Fureai and Different Age Groups among Children

The age of Kotoen's children ranges from one to six. Likewise, the age range within the elders varies widely, from the sixties to the nineties. Faced with such age differences within the two groups, are there differences in the characteristics of *fureai* between different age groups?

Age relates to *fureai* because elders in the younger old-age cohort tend to be healthier. This partly explains the prominence of "grandpas" at Kotoen. But this study also suggests that health, rather than age, may be a more salient factor affecting *fureai*, combined with one's perception of one's aging. One's physical condition is a more apt indicator that one is aging (or has become old) than is the number of years one has lived. Mr. Yokohira will continue to feel young until his declining health one day takes him by surprise. Mrs. Shibuya, too, had been active until her legs started hurting when she turned eighty. The average age of third-floor residents, for example, is 82.3 years, only about two years more than the average age of the second-floor residents. When other factors such as attitude and motivation are taken into consideration, age seems to become a less salient factor in elders' interaction with the children.

Instead of correlating the age of children with the age of the elders, it seems more appropriate to correlate the health level of the elders with the age of the children. In this study, however, I contend that regardless of physical condition, elders relate most spontaneously to the younger children, particularly the one-year-olds. The one-year-olds seem to attach most easily to the elders, and elders also find themselves better able to keep pace with these toddlers who still walk unsteadily. They also derive a greater sense of usefulness from this group through caring for them. Compared with the children in other age groups, the one-year-olds seems to evoke a stronger sense of "impulse to care" among the elders. On interacting with the children, one elder commented, "We can mix only with the one- and two-year-old kids. The four- and five-year-olds, when they become that old, they grow away from us. They have developed strong preferences of likes and dislikes by then, but little kids have not."

The tendency for spontaneous interaction with younger children is obvious during the monthly Open Childcare. During the free playtime in Open Childcare, elders are usually seen talking and playing with the one- and two-year-olds. With older children, they mostly engage in parallel activity with the older girls; that is, they may be doing coloring or origami side by side, with little *fureai*. Older boys, however, are mostly running around, playing "sword fighting" or jumping from a tower of blocks. *Fureai* with the older boys, thus, is more at the spectator level—the passive *fureai* of watching. Even the healthier elder men do not engage in physical activities with the older boys, because doing so could be dangerous.

The significance of planned programs is felt more in interactions with the older age groups. Although *fureai* with older children tends to be passive during free play, elders and older children may still become engaged with one another during programmed activities.

In the earlier chapters, I raised the issue of programming as limiting the depth of *fureai* among the elders and the children. On the contrary, programming is significant in promoting *fureai*, as shown in Chapter 6. With a wide range of programs, Kotoen is more committed to *fureai* than are many other age-integrated institutions. These programs are useful not only in providing opportunities for elders and children in different age groups to reengage (with general and age-specific programs such as Open Childcare and joint activities, respectively), but also in providing a more negotiable environment to help elders find a comfortable level of *fureai* with the children most compatible with their abilities.

"The Children Prefer Grandpas to Grandmas"

In recent years, "grandpas" have gradually replaced "grandmas" to become the representative image of "grandparents" at Kotoen. Even the elder women are well aware of this emerging phenomenon and make remarks such as "The children prefer grandpas to grandmas." Although most elder men appear to enjoy *fureai* with the children, I recognized three residents as forming the core of the "grandpa" group during the year. In the following profiles of them, I focus on their attitudes toward *fureai* with children to show their zest in engagement. They imply changing attitudes among elderly men toward the nurturing role primarily delegated to women and suggest the need to provide opportunities for men to become more involved with generational reengagement.

Of the three, Mr. Furuya is the most committed. All three are relatively young, below the average age of 75.53 years for male residents, and they are in general good health. They are all divorced, and each has fathered at least two children.

Mr. Yokohira

In his sixth year at Kotoen, seventy-four-year-old Mr. Yokohira is considered a longtime resident in comparison to the other two "grandpas." He somehow strikes me as still a boy at heart. His hobby is keeping *suzumushi* (a kind of cricket), which he keeps in a bucket. He often spends hours observing them on the balcony. When his pets begin "singing" in early summer, he carries the bucket of *suzumushi* up to show to his friends on the third floor. Mr. Yokohira is helpful to other residents. He thinks young and shows it by wearing colorful shorts and shirts more appropriate to his own perceived age than his actual age. I said to him on Coming-of-Age Day (January 15), "Mr. Yokohira, you, too, celebrated such a day once, didn't you?"[1] He sounded serious while joking: "Oh no, I am still three years away from adulthood."

During a later interview, he said, "I can't imagine myself as an old man already. . . . I used to think that one's life stops in one's twenties. When I

[1]All Japanese who turned twenty in the previous year celebrate Coming-of-Age Day (*seijin no hi*) on January 15. This is a national holiday. Young Japanese men and women in formal dress attend the Coming-of-Age Ceremony held by their respective cities or wards on that day. Young women usually wear beautiful kimonos with long flowing sleeves, and men wear Western coats, although some also wear the traditional Japanese formalwear, called *hakama*.

[156]

entered here, I realized my life leaped—no, not in the order of spring to summer to autumn to winter, but it leaped over them all at once. . . . It's already fifty years after the war now; the nursery kids who were just crying yesterday have turned into university students overnight."

Thinking of himself as young did not particularly disturb his identification as a "grandpa" here. He said, "I love to play with the children. In the past, I was the only grandpa, and before me, only grandmas interacted frequently with the children. But this year it suddenly increased—like Ishii and Furuya. This is a good sign. We go running together, we spend more time with the children, and in this way, the children become attached to us naturally. . . . It is important to have frequent contact with the children, as the longer you are separated from them, the more distant they are to you."

While most of the residents, particularly the women, feel that a frequency of two to three times a week was adequate for joint activities with the children in their living quarters, Mr. Yokohira thinks otherwise:

> For joint activities such as clay modeling and drawing, if possible, the children should come every day. In this way, it is easier to develop intimacy with each other. . . . The more contact the better; we should feel that we are living with each other. This is a plus for the elders, too. It is hopeless to cling to the shell like a bagworm [he made an action of putting his palms together], and we have to try our best to get out of the shell to interact with others. But if we cling only to the adults, it is bad, too. It is ideal to have children around. . . . Rather than playing gateball or [the board game] *Othello*, it is better to have *fureai* with the children. It is good to develop some hobbies, but we shouldn't stick just to one . . . and anyway, we can only do things that the children do; with age, we return to become children.

Mr. Ishii

Seventy-four-year-old Mr. Ishii is another good-humored man among the residents. When I asked him about his *fureai* with the children, he said, "The most difficult thing is to have to endure not seeing them when I catch a cold. Usually, when I hear the announcement from the children saying, 'Grandpas and grandmas, please come down and help us change,' I can't wait to fly to them!" When the children come for joint activities, Mr. Ishii is always present; he even follows the children to the stairway to wave goodbye to them as they return to the nursery downstairs after the activities.

Mr. Ishii had lived in Kotoen for only nine months when I interviewed him in May. Prior to the interview, I had noticed his increasingly active contact with the children as he became one of the regulars during joint activities on the second floor and at other events. He said it took him a while to become acquainted with the children. He wanted to become involved from the start but was afraid that it is not what a man should do. He was brought up to think that childcare is a woman's responsibility, and like most Japanese men of his age, he was not really involved in caring for his two daughters when they were young.

"Do you find the children here noisy?" I asked.

"No, well, if they cry, I simply hand them back to the teacher. I am glad I can do that, though," he said with a chuckle, referring to the one-year-olds that he had helped care for briefly during the *Narashi* Childcare.

He enjoys talking to the children, something that most male residents are quite poor at. Compared with the women, the men tend to be *mukuchi*—silent, not talkative and sociable, although they display affection for the children.

Mr. Furuya

Compared with Mr. Yokohira and Mr. Ishii, sixty-nine-year-old Mr. Furuya is *mukuchi*. His quiet disposition is partly due to his impaired speech. When I first started my fieldwork in November, he appeared to be stern, isolated, and nonresponsive. He spends almost all of his time in solitude, writing calligraphy in his room without even interacting with fellow residents. This has gained him the nickname of "master of calligraphy" among the residents.

However, by the time I was preparing to leave the field ten months later, he had transformed himself into becoming a popular "Kotoen grandpa." He had become a more lively, responsive, happy, and communicative person in that short time span. When the television station came to film Kotoen, Mr. Furuya was highly recommended by the staff for close-up interviews. But as he spoke little during the interviews, he was introduced solely through narratives in the documentary.

The development of Mr. Furuya's *fureai* with the children was gradual. I noticed it beginning in early January, when the nursery teacher began to engage his help in drawing white lines on the courtyard before morning exercises by pushing the marker cart. After the exercises, when the children and the elders engaged in the routinized *fureai* of shaking hands, playing *jan-ken-pon,* and engaging in small talk, he somehow started to create his own form of *fureai* with them by lifting up one child at a time and swinging him or her. The children were thrilled with this, and soon a line formed in front of him every morning—mostly one- and two-year-olds, but occasionally older children. This has motivated other healthy elder men to do the same thing.

The morning routine of *fureai* between Mr. Furuya and the children is envied by the "grandmas." Mrs. Hara, who complains of weakening knees, said, "Mr. Furuya is very popular among the little ones; he can lift them and swing them, but I can't do it." One spring morning, when Mr. Furuya was absent because of a medical appointment, Mrs. Tanaka, who has to sit on a bench to exercise, tried to imitate Mr. Furuya. Obviously it was almost impossible to lift and swing a two-year-old while sitting down!

Mr. Furuya is always one of the last elders to part with the children after the morning exercises. After this, he returns to his room to write calligraphy. As mentioned in Chapter 6, he participates in joint activities with the children, depending on the activity. Nevertheless, he will at least come out of his room to meet with the children for a while.

Even when he decides to participate in a joint activity, he remains quiet and communicates only through working. Once the Rose group came with a bunch of empty bottles, tape rings, empty tissue boxes, and other used materials for an activity called "playing with waste"—creating and building something out of waste materials. He participated by spontaneously pairing up with a boy. They stayed in one corner, trying to run a string through a few plastic cups. He helped the boy to punch holes through the cups; the whole time, there was no verbal communication. Although they worked in silence, both seemed committed to the project.

Mr. Furuya is one of the few elders who consistently helps the children change clothes every afternoon. Instead of waiting for the announcement like Mr. Ishii and the others, Mr. Furuya arrives at the nursery around half-past two, ten minutes before the announcement, and starts to help change the one-year-olds who wake up earlier. By the time the announcement is made, Mr. Furuya is almost done with the one-year-olds, and he and other elders move to the two-year-old area to help them. Mr. Ishii and Mr. Yokohira usually chat a little with the children, but Mr. Furuya simply does his routine without much verbal interaction. The children feel at ease with him anyway. A couple of boys drag their pajama bags to him and wait for their turns to be dressed by him; one or two may lie on his lap and refuse to leave after being changed.

Studies of intergenerational programs in the United States have reported older men's anxiety that behaviors such as holding or hugging a girl might be misinterpreted (Hutchinson and Bondy 1990). Sexual issues, however, do not seem to be a concern in intergenerational programs in Japan. The men undress and dress the girls, too.

In Japan, more so than in the West, gender differences seem to fade into the background and are often overlooked as one gains the status of "elder." The misconception that older people are asexual seems to be sustained in Japanese old-age institutions. At Kotoen, there have even been instances of unrelated female and male residents pairing up as roommates in the hope that this would reduce the roommate conflicts that occur primarily among the women. Mr. Yamaki maintained that there are no such mixed-sex roommates now simply because no one has requested such an arrangement recently.

Once the children are changed, they say "Thank you" to indicate the end of the elders' task. Mr. Furuya is always among the first to leave the nursery at this time. But he is not gone for long; fifteen minutes later, he comes back to play with the children during their free playtime in the big hall. He usually waits at the edge of the hall for the children. Once I joined him to wait for the children, who were later than usual, and heard him murmuring to himself while gazing into the empty hall, "Are they coming out to play here today?" He beamed when the children finally appeared and quickly joined them.

The nursery's usual childcare hours end at 4:30 P.M. Only a handful of children stay for extended hours until 6:00 P.M. Children begin to play freely in the hall starting at 3:30 P.M., as parents or guardians come in to pick them up. The nursery welcomes the elders to come and play with the children during this time, but Mr. Furuya seems to be the only one who does so.

On one winter day, he played blocks with them, held them in his arms, or carried them on his back. When one boy came to him with a running nose, he took a tissue from his pocket to wipe his nose. Then a Dandelion girl brought a mini director's chair to him. She sat on it and let him lift the chair up to walk around the hall. After one round, a boy came by; the girl got up to let the boy sit, and Mr. Furuya went through the same routine again. After this had been repeated with several children, he noticed a group of bigger children sitting on an exercise mattress. He went over and pulled the mattress, to the children's delight. Some rolled off along the way while others tried to get on "the boat." By the time most of the children had left (a little after 4 P.M.), he was apparently tired.

Mr. Furuya's *fureai* with the children can be observed from the rehabilitation area. Residents and elders from the community who attend physiotherapy always watch their *fureai* affectionately and seem to enjoy the noise and laughter of the children. They are also benefiting from passive *fureai* at the same time.

After living at Kotoen for more than a year, Mr. Furuya had added children to his daily routine, which had initially been limited to calligraphy. However, it was his devotion to the *Narashi* Childcare in April that made him known as the ultimate "Kotoen grandpa." Although Mr. Yokohira claims to have initiated the commitment of elder men into grandparenting at Kotoen, it is Mr. Furuya who has consequently promoted it to become a widely recognized norm.

Narashi Childcare and "Grandpas"

The Kotoen elders regard April as a busy month. Like teachers who gear up to receive their new students in schools nationwide, the elders gear up to receive new children at Kotoen. The one-year-old group is always the center of attention among the elders. Elders seem to relate the best with them: They can better keep pace with the toddlers who still walk unsteadily, and they derive a greater sense of usefulness from those who need the most care. Compared with the children in the other age groups, the toddlers elicit a strong caring impulse among the elders.

During the Home Residences meeting with the staff in early April, the chief nursery teacher appeared to "recruit" elders to volunteer in *Narashi* Childcare. Many residents expressed interest but felt reserved about committing to it because of health concerns (Figures 7.1 and 7.2).

In the first week of *Narashi* Childcare in April, three men (Mr. Furuya, Mr. Ishii, and Mr. Yokohira) and three women (Mrs. Hoya, Miss Murakami, and Miss Sakada) appeared to form a babysitter group. Other than diaper changing, which was handled by the teachers, the elders helped in all other aspects of childcare, such as feeding the children, playing with them, and putting them to sleep. They relieved the tasks of the two teachers greatly, and their presence smoothed the toddlers' adjustment into the nursery environment. Sometimes when there were enough elders to look after all of the toddlers, the teachers joked about having nothing to do, as all the children were being taken care of.

There are ten toddlers—eight boys and two girls—in the Cherry group. In April, there were an average of seven toddlers every day as some began childcare a few days later than the others; fever and cold also caused some to be absent on some days. The elders' attendance also fluc-

[161]

Figure 7.1 *Narashi* Childcare

tuated. Nevertheless, by the end of the first week, I was able to identify five elder-child dyads that had emerged spontaneously over a few days of *fureai:* Mrs. Hoya "adopted" a boy, Miss Murakami's "grandchild" was a girl who looked like her; Mr. Yokohira, Mr. Ishii, and Mr. Furuya each formed bonds with boys, too; at the same time, Mr. Furuya was sought after by the eldest toddler of the group (two years old).

Mr. Yokohira and Gaku, the youngest among the boys (thirteen months old), formed one prominent dyad. Mr. Yokohira is patient and communicative, and when he carried Gaku, who cried most of the time on the first few days, he soothed him by talking to him in a soft and gentle voice. Once or twice when Gaku cried, Mr. Yokohira looked up at the other quiet toddlers playing with their grandparents and turned to ask Gaku caringly, "They are all not crying; why are you crying?" After two days with Mr. Yokohira, Gaku began to calm down more in his arms. By the end of the week, everyone was already identifying Gaku as Mr. Yokohira's "grandson"—the little crying one who often fell asleep in Mr. Yokohira's arms, still sucking his thumb.

Gaku had gained a reputation among the residents as the "crybaby," as he cried the most among the toddlers. One morning, several elders stopped by to visit the toddlers after morning exercises. Mr. Yokohira was

Figure 7.2. *Narashi* Childcare

holding Gaku, and Mrs. Tanaka looked at the little boy and asked, "Is he the youngest; he must be the crybaby!" Mr. Yokohira got quite protective and sounded unhappy: "Who said he is a crybaby?"

Mr. Furuya's "grandchild" was easier to please than Gaku was. Tomi smiled happily when Mr. Furuya put him in the yellow toy box, lifted him up, and carried him around. He also enjoyed sitting on Mr. Furuya's lap to play with blocks or a ball. Tomi appeared satisfied when held by his favorite "grandpa," although Mr. Furuya could not tell stories like others. Sometimes Tomi fell asleep on Mr. Furuya's lap. Mr. Furuya would then place him on the futon and begin to attend to other toddlers.

By the second week of *Narashi* Childcare, Tomi had already "declared"

Grandpa Furuya to belong only to him, and was attached to him as soon as he arrived at the nursery at 8:30 A.M.

Kazu, the eldest boy in the Cherry group, was also fond of Grandpa Furuya. Kazu was a fairly independent boy who did not seem attached to any elder. One morning, the elders were attending to their "own grandchildren"; Tomi was sitting in front of Mr. Furuya and playing with little plastic blocks with him, while Kazu played by himself in a corner. But when Kazu accidentally bumped himself, he quickly ran to Mr. Furuya and buried himself in his lap. Tomi immediately felt jealous and pushed Kazu away, saying "No, no" at the same time, and climbed to sit on Mr. Furuya's lap instead. Kazu got up and moved away for a while; then he brought some blocks and came back again to play beside Mr. Furuya. Tomi had now moved down to his former position in front of Mr. Furuya, but he looked cautiously at Kazu over his shoulder, aware of his presence and apparently prepared to ward off Kazu if he tried to intrude on his territory again.

These dyads, however, did not remain constant throughout the *Narashi* Childcare. During the second week, Mr. Ishii stopped coming because he caught the flu, and Mrs. Hoya was also absent soon thereafter because of an illness; a few other elders filtered in and out. The "grandmas" seemed more relaxed now, and by this time the toddlers had become more familiar with the environment and began to venture out on their own. The elders simply sat around to chat while keeping a watch on them. Mr. Yokohira and Mr. Furuya were the only two with more "demanding" toddlers. Mr. Yokohira, however, also stopped babysitting by the end of the third week. By this time, Tomi and Kazu had already left the arms of Mr. Furuya, but instead of announcing his duty completed, Mr. Furuya took over Mr. Yokohira's duty and "adopted" Gaku instead. Mr. Furuya had extended his hours of babysitting beyond the requested duties of grandparents, staying with the toddlers until they took their afternoon naps. The teachers discussed this among themselves, and decided to let him do so as long as he did not upset the nursery's tempo, such as by putting Gaku to sleep before naptime. It is common for *Narashi* Childcare to end in a month, once the toddlers have become accustomed to nursery life. Mr. Furuya's almost indispensable service to the toddlers, however, seemed to extend it into infinity. Mrs. Sugi jokingly commented on several occasions that she would be obliged to pay him if this continued.

Mr. Furuya's bonding with Gaku turned out to be more enduring and soon widely known. A week after the "adoption," nobody mentioned Gaku as Mr. Yokohira's "grandchild" anymore. At the beginning, Mr. Furuya once even "kidnapped" Gaku to the second floor before morning exercises. Miss Matsu was alarmed when she saw them and had to inform the nursery immediately. In a casual conversation I had with Miss Matsu about Mr. Furuya, she burst out, "To him, everything circles around Gaku!"

Gaku apparently felt the same about Mr. Furuya. Once when Mr. Furuya was absent in the morning, the nursery teacher brought Gaku to Mrs. Tanaka, but he seemed uneasy; the teacher remarked, "Gaku is a 'grandpa' person; he wants only Grandpa Furuya!"

Mr. Furuya stopped his babysitting duty after the *Narashi* Childcare was announced to be officially over at the end of May. Gaku, however, was still attached to Mr. Furuya. During morning exercises and other gatherings, Mr. Furuya continued to stay near the one-year-olds. During a safety talk by two traffic policemen from the community in the big hall one morning, the residents sat on the steps near the Cherry group. Gaku eagerly looked around, and when he spotted Mr. Furuya among them, he left the group and walked unsteadily toward him. Mr. Furuya gave him a hug and carried him back to his group. Elders and children always sit separately during assemblies. During free activity in Open Childcare and before pick-up time in the afternoon, Gaku can be found clinging to his "grandpa," along with other toddlers who also like to throw themselves on Mr. Furuya. These are the times when Mr. Furuya's smile lingers the longest on his otherwise stern face.

Did Mr. Furuya have a special aura that made the children attach to him so readily? His unfailing patience and persistent commitment to the children appear to be the major reasons for his popularity. Throughout his *fureai* with the children, he maintained his quiet disposition. He is popular with all of the children, but he is particularly committed to the younger ones. This, he told a member of the nursing staff, was because his health does not allow him to play physically with the stronger and more active older children. His speech impairment, too, makes him more comfortable playing with the younger toddlers, with whom he can use more nonverbal communication. Mr. Furuya is able to maximize his physical capabilities and downplay his verbal deficiencies to reach a comfortable level in interacting with the children. His positive attitude also influences him. On a rare occasion in which we talked about *Narashi* Childcare, he commented that although other men think that it is only for the women, he did not think so, and he wanted to try it and see. His efforts benefited not only him but the children and the staff as well.

[165]

The staff themselves are pleased with the transformation of Mr. Furuya and see the children as a form of therapy for him. Mr. Furuya had virtually lost contact with his family members after his divorce twenty-five years earlier. Mr. Yama is trying hard to reconnect him with his two daughters. His elder daughter, however, refused to meet her father; his second daughter, who lives in the neighboring prefecture, said she had no memory of her father, but she expressed a willingness to meet him if the time was right. Mr. Yama feels that Mr. Furuya's active engagement with the children was probably prompted by missing his daughters and grandchildren. After these few months of observation, Mr. Yama feels that Mr. Furuya is now quite prepared to meet his family and is planning to arrange a reunion for him soon.

Why "Grandpas"?

Why did "grandpas" at Kotoen become more actively engaged with the children? Eighty-year-old Mr. Tane said, "Because the grandpas have nothing to do compared to the grandmas, who can find interests in knitting, flower arrangements, and other feminine hobbies. That's why we devote more time to the children." Mr. Tane is not as active as the three core "grandpas," but he is characterized as the elder who is fond of embracing as many children (normally four to five older children) as he can in his arms during the *fureai* routine in the morning. When he once tried to do the same during a joint activity on the second floor, some elders beside him said, "You need to share the children; you can have only one." He then unwillingly let the other children go, leaving only one child to sit with him.

Mr. Tane's reasoning is supported by the core "grandpas." None of the three had joined any hobby clubs. Men, on the whole, participate less in hobby clubs than do women. However, in addition to spending time and energy on club activities, women also visit clinics (as patients) more regularly than the men, which sometimes causes them to miss the interaction activities.

From a psychological perspective, the caring and nurturing roles displayed by the men in their engagement with the children seem to support personality theories that claim that with aging, men tend to reveal a more feminine side of their personality, while women show more masculine traits (Gutmann 1974; Gutmann et al. 1980). However, I argue that such personality change depends on opportunities available for change in a particular social context.

In Japan, traditional sex roles, which clearly separate men's and women's responsibilities, are all the more dominant among the older generations, who are more traditional. The initial concerns of the core "grandpas" about men's involvement with children reflect their awareness that childcare traditionally and culturally belongs to the women's sphere. Being of the younger cohort (below age seventy-five) as well as having the opportunity for involvement has probably influenced their decision to follow their "impulse" rather than conforming to the rigid traditional role.

Research on grandparenthood and popular discourse on grandparenthood in Japan reflect parallel changes. Recent serial dramas about Japanese families increasingly show the desire of grandfathers (instead of grandmothers) to babysit the grandchildren (for example, a drama series called *Wataru Ningen Oni Bakari* shown on the Fuji Television Network in 1996). A report on the relationships between grandparents and grandchildren in Hyōgo Prefecture (1994) also revealed that grandfathers were more willing than grandmothers to accept the role of caretaking.

Psychosocially, this may be an unconscious attempt by older men to redress their lack of past opportunity to care for their own growing children. When the staff viewed children as a form of therapy for Mr. Furuya, they may have been reasoning along the same lines. Mr. Furuya had left his children when they were young to work in the city, and thus he may see active *fureai* with the children as making up for his loss of the joy of watching his own children and grandchildren grow up.

On the other hand, can we propose that the lesser commitment among the elderly women who participate in *Narashi* Childcare is a result of the opposite reason—that is, that they have already had their share of work in taking care of their own children or grandchildren? In a supportive finding, Lilian Troll (1985) argued that grandparents prefer to do new things rather than to repeat earlier behaviors, "no matter how enjoyable they were the first time around" (149). Furthermore, unlike grandmothers in a family, who may sometimes be forced into childcare so as to "bind the daughter-in-law into looking after them in old age" (Lebra 1979), the elders here have no such worries, as they know that they already had their old age well taken care of the moment they entered Kotoen.

The Kotoen data cannot conclusively justify this assumption, as a complexity of reasons (including health, attitudes, and backgrounds) influences one's commitment to childcare. The control data from other old-age homes also show little support for the proposal. One resident, though, replied that she does not need to have children around now, as she has taken care of them before.

Aside from these reasons, the prominence of "grandpas" at Kotoen can be explained in terms of attributes such as younger age (the "grandpas" are five years younger than the "grandmas" on average), better health, and therefore more energy to interact with the children. It is interesting that women usually refer to their relations with the children in terms of how they can help. Men, besides helping, are equally at ease with their role of "playing" with the children. The dominance of elder men at Kotoen offers encouraging empirical evidence to support theories that elder men in Japan are increasingly taking on nurturing roles. When the Kotoen's logo was conceived a decade ago, the dancing "grandma" was the stereotype of elders' *fureai* with children. A decade later, with longer life expectancy for both men and women, the image of a dancing "grandpa" is now integral for a more realistic portrayal of generational reengagements.

[8]

Window to Society

Kotoen represents one attempt to address the dilemma of generational disengagement in contemporary Japanese society. This is an age-integrated facility that has received widespread media publicity and has been claimed as a successful model of the welfare society. To recapitulate, the aim of this study is to examine Kotoen not as a model but as a case study to understand the extent to which contact between the young and the old can be made meaningful in an extrafamilial context. The first section of this concluding chapter summarizes the inquiry and the hope that lessons from this study can illuminate the significance of generational reengagement. Then I broaden the discussion by stepping back to the larger Japanese society. I hope that knowledge on the larger societal context will elucidate the urgency of generational reengagement and provide a rationale for the significance of deliberate attempts to link the generations.

Lessons from Kotoen: Ironies in Generational Reengagement

Throughout this study, I have focused on the ironies found in an attempt to connect the generations. These ironies are framed within the concepts of *daikazoku* and *fureai*.

I argue that there are two levels of ironies. On the macro level, the *daikazoku* ideology suggests a romanticized image of the traditional Japanese family system, where three generations live together harmoniously. The acceptance of the Kotoen ideal by the media and television viewers, as shown in Chapter 5, suggests that the ideology does not simply address a private dream; it is also a dream yearned for by the wider public. However, this contradicts the present social reality, for age segregation is becoming a norm, and all indications are that it will become a more established trend in the future.

On the micro level, the controversy between the ideal and practice of *fureai* in a *daikazoku* exists. I had expected intimate, dyadic ties to develop between the elders and children. Most of the children in the nursery stay in nuclear families; hence, to many, their contact with Kotoen elders is closer and more frequent than that with their natural grandparents. In practice, however, *fureai* at Kotoen is characterized by the notions of "event grandparenthood" and "collective grandparenting." In the former, the grandparenting role is perceived by the elders as contained within the boundary of an event or an activity; when outside the frame, life goes on as a typical old-age institution. The latter defines grandparenthood as a collective identity, where elders and children classify one another in different age grades. These notions have limited the potential for more *fureai*. With these notions in mind, the emphasis on alternate-generational ties beyond the institutional setting becomes ironic.

One of the aims of the Committee to Promote *Fureai* is to encourage the graduates of Kotoen to return to visit the elders, and if possible, to serve as volunteers at the center. A project called Time Capsule initiated during my fieldwork serves as an example. This project began with combined efforts to make a "big egg" out of cardboard and colored paper during joint activity time. Then all three generations at Kotoen wrote letters expressing what or who they wanted to be three years later and placed them inside the "big egg." The egg was scheduled to be opened during the Golden Fair in 1999. However, it is uncertain to what extent the project will be successful; most children do not return to visit even when they live in the neighborhood. Besides the new friends and examination pressure that have more salience in their lives, the absence of close relations fostered with a particular grandparent as a result of collective socialization also deters the desire to return.

Two important factors help to explain the controversy between the ideal and practice in linking the generations. First, the group orientation or group consciousness prevalent in Japanese society deemphasizes individual identities and constrains dyadic interactions between the children and the elders. Such a cultural characteristic forms the background for promoting group interaction in alternate-generation *fureai* by the staff.

[170]

Miss Umeda's gift incident and the practice of leaving the addressee as anonymous in summer greetings to the children illustrated in Chapter 5 are examples of the stress on collectivity. This is reinforced by the *daika-zoku* framework, wherein children and elders become essential not as individual selves but for their roles as grandchildren and grandparents who will in turn be succeeded by the next generation of elders and children. As the elders cheerfully send off the graduates and wait eagerly for the next batch of children, the children also view their graduation as the point where they relinquish their Kotoen "grandchildren" role.

Second, when perceived within the reciprocal structure of "take and give" in a welfare institution, "event grandparenthood" also suggests obligation in *fureai,* where elders respond to the grandparent role as a way to repay what they have received as a welfare recipient (that is, as an old-age home resident).

Under these notions, many residents do not seem to care to foster intimate relations with the children. Most, in fact, do not know the children's names and could not recall being close to any one child before. Nonetheless, I argue that within the disjuncture of ideology and practice, meaningful relations have flourished, and the "spontaneous" has been encouraged through programming.

The "we as a family" feeling has developed spontaneously among the Kotoen residents as a result of constant reinforcement of the concept by the administration and the media. Such feelings are especially felt at competitions with other institutions, such as the Joint Quoits Meet or the Joint Nurseries' Sumo Competition. Aspects of grandparenting are evident among the residents, too, as elders discuss their common feelings about children. The passionate involvement of some elders such as Mrs. Hoya and Mr. Furuya reveal the possibility for greater involvement beyond "event grandparenthood" and "collective grandparenting."

These exchanges and encounters are significant in various aspects. The institution's open architectural structure and the presence of children have a rejuvenating effect that has enriched the lives of those whose worlds have physically shrunk to a few rooms and hallways. Keeping in touch with the children counteracts loneliness and isolation among the elders; it inspires them to learn more about the contemporary youth culture and enhances their *ikigai* ("purpose in life").

The children have displayed positive attitudes toward old age as a result of frequent *fureai* with the elders. Such positive perception discourages stereotypes about elders and prevent the development of ageist attitudes. Age-integrated institutions like Kotoen also destigmatize the negative image of old-age homes; the publicity of Kotoen as a *daikazoku* and the lively image of an old-age home with children have changed many people's negative perceptions of old-age homes in Japan.

I began this study with a brief sketch of Mrs. Noyama and her activities with the children. As the story developed, we learned that the ideal of alternate-generational interactions—the romanticized image of *fureai* in a *daikazoku*—remains ideal in practice. The ironies faced by Kotoen remind us that we cannot examine an institution outside of its particular cultural temporal context, and sometimes this means coming to terms with the contradictions and recognizing that positive meanings do develop within these parameters.

Significance of Programming

Studying *fureai* in Kotoen has shown that different generations coexisting in close proximity fulfills only one of the conditions necessary for *fureai*. There is also a need for explicit and conscious efforts to encourage the fostering of meaningful relations between the two groups. The Kotoen experience has highlighted the significance of appropriate planning and programming to enhance *fureai*.

At Kotoen, the range of activities planned by the Committee to Promote *Fureai* provides ample opportunities for elders to engage in *fureai*. It also allows them to shift between active and passive forms of *fureai*, depending on their health conditions, thus providing a more negotiable environment to accommodate elders with various levels of abilities in *fureai*.

In considering the issue of programming to promote generational contacts, the following points are useful. First, among the residents in old-age institutions, the Showa-*mono* generation—the younger, more energetic, and more highly educated—are gradually emerging to replace the older, more reserved, and traditional generation of elders. This group, both male and female, should be tapped as resources and encouraged to contribute innovative ideas to link with the young. Second, the emphasis of *fureai* only through play activities at Kotoen limits the breadth of contact that is possible in an age-integrated facility. Children, for instance, could volunteer in serving meals or accompanying the elders in wheelchairs for a stroll in the neighborhood. Third, there should be training programs to help enhance the staff's professional knowledge and expectations in dealing with *fureai* activities. Staff members at Kotoen often feel overburdened with the present volume of caregiving tasks and extracurricular events related to *fureai* activities. Appropriate training programs will reduce staff burnout and also encourage more meaningful exchanges between the staff and the elders.

Despite the prevailing ambiguities, Kotoen is successful in linking the old and the young. It is a significant attempt to address the dilemma of generational disengagement and provides us with a point of departure for thinking about ways to keep the generations in touch. It may be argued that Kotoen is successful because of its *shitamachi* surroundings. However, integrating old-age homes and nurseries as exemplified by Kotoen is only one way of bringing the generations together; age-integrated facilities should be encouraged in as many different settings as possible to cater to a diverse population of different socioeconomic backgrounds. For example, nurseries or after-school care centers can be integrated with day service centers for elders or private retirement homes in the suburbs. Age integration can take many forms—the key is keeping in touch.

Aging Society: An Era of Change

The discussion up to this point has concentrated on Kotoen as a case study in reengaging the generations. My point, however, is not to linger on Kotoen per se but to place generational reengagement within a larger sociocultural context and to view Kotoen as a window on Japanese society as well as other societies that are currently facing the same dilemma of generational disengagement.

In Japan, the aging society is only beginning to pick up its momentum: In 1995, people 65 and older made up 14.92 percent of the population, but 30 years later, this percentage is expected to increase to 25.79 percent, and the old-age dependency ratio will reach 43.2 percent. In other words, there will be only slightly more than two persons of working age available to support one elderly person (Table 8.1).

Demographic research has shown that the sharp decline in the fertility rate is the major factor contributing to Japan's rapidly aging population (Kuroda and Hauser 1981; Ogawa 1996). After the 1947–49 postwar baby boom, fertility declined sharply. In 1960, the total fertility rate (TFR) had already fallen by more than half, to two children per woman.

Table 8.1
Trends in Population Structure: 1920–2075

Year	Population Composition by Major Groups			Age Dependency Ratio		
	0–14	15–64	65+	Total	Children	Elders
1920	36.48	58.26	5.26	71.6	62.6	9.0
1925	36.70	58.24	5.06	71.7	63.0	8.7
1930	36.59	58.66	4.75	70.5	62.4	8.1
1935	36.89	58.46	4.66	71.1	63.1	8.0
1940	36.08	59.19	4.73	69.0	61.0	8.0
1947	35.30	59.90	4.79	66.9	58.9	8.0
1950	35.41	59.64	4.94	67.7	59.4	8.3
1955	33.44	61.24	5.29	63.3	54.6	8.7
1960	30.15	64.12	5.72	55.9	47.0	8.9
1965	25.73	67.98	6.29	47.1	37.9	9.2
1970	24.03	68.90	7.06	45.1	34.9	10.3
1975	24.32	67.72	7.92	47.6	35.9	11.7
1980	23.50	67.35	9.10	48.4	34.9	13.5
1985	21.51	68.16	10.30	46.7	31.6	15.1
1990	18.24	69.69	12.08	43.5	26.2	17.3
1995	15.90	69.28	14.82	44.4	23.0	21.4
2000	15.18	67.79	17.03	47.5	22.4	25.1
2005	15.64	65.24	19.12	53.3	24.0	29.3
2010	16.37	62.35	21.28	60.4	26.3	34.1
2015	16.34	59.53	24.14	68.0	27.4	40.5
2020	15.45	59.04	25.51	69.4	26.2	43.2
2025	14.50	59.71	25.79	67.5	24.3	43.2
2030	14.17	59.81	26.02	67.2	23.7	43.5
2035	14.59	58.82	26.58	70.0	24.8	45.2
2040	15.34	56.68	27.98	76.4	27.1	49.4
2045	15.79	55.82	28.37	79.2	28.3	50.9
2050	15.74	56.09	28.17	78.3	28.1	50.2
2075	17.09	57.32	25.58	74.5	29.8	44.6

Sources: (Up to 1995) Institute of Population Problems, Ministry of Health and Welfare, Latest Demographic Statistics, 1995, Tokyo; Statistics Bureau, Management and Coordination Agency, Quick Report on One-percent Sample Tabulations of the 1995 Population Census, Tokyo, 1996. (From 2000) Institute of Population Problems, Ministry of Health and Welfare, Population Projections for Japan: 1991–2090, Tokyo, 1992 (cited in Kono 1996, 10–11).

Between 1971 and 1974, there was another baby boom on a much smaller scale (2.14 children per woman in 1973), but after that it fell continuously, reaching a record low of 1.43 in 1995 (Ogawa 1996, 54).

Relating the phenomenon to women's increased participation in the labor force and the increasing age at which most women have their first child, some critics interpreted the fertility rate decline as women's revenge against patriarchal society and male-dominated and institutions. Shigemi Kono (1996, 32) further cited competitive entrance examinations—an ordeal that may begin as early as preschool age—to be conducive to low fertility in Japan, as it causes children to "become financially and psychologically expensive."

The fertility rate decline further contributed to the rapid change of the ratio[1] of elders to children: In 1986, the ratio was about 50 elders to 100 children; in 1997, it will level off at 100 to 100; and by 2025, elders will outnumber the children by a ratio of 177 to 100 (Kono 1996, 15).

Rapid demographic changes that occur too quickly, before people and the society are ready for them, may have grievous consequences. The rapid increase in the elderly population has been identified as a "social problem" that is expected to strain both public and private resources, causing widespread concern (bordering on panic). Some even equate population aging with the doom of Japan's future. Kono (1996, 27) calculated that if the present fertility rate and life expectancy hold constant, "the population of Japan will become extinct." Following this pessimistic projection, he commended that "if such an extraordinary population aging ever comes to the seashore of Japan, it has been argued that Japan would collapse under the heavy dependency burden of the elderly."

Japanese concern and anxiety over the future of an aging society (and one's own old age) stem from the lack of an updated map to redefine and resituate oneself in this new age of mass longevity. Postwar changes in family structure and the erosion of traditional ideals have made the traditional model of old age based on filial piety, valid only a generation before, increasingly obsolete. Until a new model is established to provide a guide, the anxiety will remain.

Changing Family Structure

Recent studies on aging in Japan have focused on the postwar decline in the proportion of multigenerational households and related concerns of decline in family care for elders. Many see this as an alarming indication of the deterioration of filial piety among Japanese. Critics use the data to justify the urgent need for a welfare system to provide alternate housing and to replace the traditional reliance on daughters and daughters-in-law

---

[1] The elderly population (age sixty-five and above) divided by the population of children (age fifteen and below) multiplied by one hundred.

as caregivers. They cite the figures as reflecting the reality of the un-desirability of three-generational living. Kazunori Yamanoi (1995), an advocate of the Swedish welfare state model, has cited cases of family abuse in elders, called "silver harassment," and the high suicide rate among elders living with their families to advance his argument.

On the other hand, some argue that three-generational living contin-ues to be an attractive lifestyle to most Japanese, citing as evidence for this the increasing number of three-generational living arrangements (Yuzawa 1991).

In using the data to support the claim that the alternate generations in Japan are increasingly isolated from one another, I would argue that even when there is a statistical increase in actual numbers of three-generational families, the trend of the distancing of alternate generations continues for the following reasons.

First, the cohabitation rate is higher among the old-old (75 years and above) than the young-old (65 to 74 years). In 1995, the percentage of three-generational cohabitation was 25.3 percent for those 65 to 69 and 32.6 percent for those 70 to 74. The figure increases with an increase in age groups; the 80 and above age group shows the highest cohabitation rate at 53.1 percent (Kono 1996, 44). By the time most grandparents who live with their grandchildren are 75 and over, their grandchildren are most probably of school-going age. These children would be spending more time outside the family, attending schools and "cram–schools," which prepare them for tedious entrance examinations. Actual inter-action between the generations would thus be minimal.

Second, we need to redefine the term *three-generational family* in relation to statistical data. An increasing number of three-generational families today are housed in "two-household housing" (*nisetai jūtaku*)— a term commonly seen in housing advertisements in Japan. Such housing is comparable to the concept of "mother-in-law apartments" in the West, but in a much more scaled-down size. Typically, the grandparents re-side on a different floor or different side of the house with their own kitchen, bathroom, and sometimes entrance. Kikuko Kato (1988, cited in Morioka 1996, 518) proposes to call such an emerging variation of stem family "modified stem family" because although it appears to be a three-generational cohabitation on the outside (sharing the same address), in essence it operates as two nuclear families in successive generations. Thus the rising number of modified stem families in Japan today should be interpreted as an increase in the conjugal family system rather than a persistence of the stem family system (Morioka 1996, 518). Along with providing more privacy for the two households, such living arrangements reduce the frequency of intergenerational interaction that was more likely in the traditional stem family, when the activity space was shared.

Third, alternate-generational relations cannot be assumed to be the same as in the past, even when the three generations are living in a traditional stem family structure—that is, sharing the same activity space. Nobuko Fujimoto (1976) noted an increasing tendency for the children's (nuclear) family to become the center of the three-generational household, with grandparents being pushed to the boundary or periphery. In this way, the relationship between grandparents and their grandchildren is hindered by the middle generation.

In addition, as suggested by the surveys, the proportion of three-generational households is expected to decrease further. In a question regarding the support of one's parents in an international comparative survey, Japanese youth between the ages of 18 to 24 who answered "I will support them by all means" decreased from 47.5 percent in 1976 to 22.6 percent in 1993, ranking Japan the lowest in the ten countries surveyed (Sōmuchō 1993).[2] A comparison of this survey with a 1994 opinion survey of women between the ages of 20 and 49 on family planning shows that similar attitudes prevailed among the future elders. To the question "Do you expect to rely on your children in your old age?," 50.3 percent of the respondents said no, 14.2 percent said yes, and 34.2 percent expressed indifference. This was particularly so among those 20 to 24 years old (58.2 percent) (Okazaki 1996).

These surveys also point to a projected increase of elderly-only households in the future. In the Tokyo metropolitan area, single elder households are expected to increase from 11.1 percent (1.87 million) in 1990 to 24.8 percent (4.76 million) in 2010. Many of them, inevitably, would be among the emergent affluent elders who want to remain self-reliant. Kiyomi Morioka and Itsuki Nakabayashi (1994) refer to this group of emerging urban elders, mostly retired salarymen, as changing the elder culture of Japanese society. They refuse to stay with their children, have less connection with the community, are not the types who will join old-age clubs or play gateball; they are basically not the elders stereo-

[2] Responses from youth in some other countries included in the survey are as follows: United States, 62.7 percent; United Kingdom, 45.9 percent; Sweden, 36.8 percent; Korea, 66.7 percent; Thailand, 59.3 percent.

typed by the government. An increasing number of this group of elders are exploring the option of private retirement housing. The "silver business" of retirement housing has become a booming industry in Japan since the 1980s.[3] It addresses the demand of a growing middle class of elders who either cannot or prefer not to stay with their children, but who still desire appropriate housing conditions that can also accommodate their health needs (Kinoshita and Kiefer 1992).

Along with an increase in affluent elders, there is also an increasing number of the less fortunate ones who are forced to live alone and who fear dying alone. The number of "lonely deaths" (*kodokushi*) among elders, seen as people who are "falling through the cracks between absentee relatives and the few local agencies that aid the elderly" (*Newsweek*, October 28, 1996), has nearly tripled since 1983, reaching 1,049 cases in Tokyo in 1994. These extremely disadvantaged elders not only lack alternate-generational contact but are also alienated from the more fundamental human contact that is ironically absent in a densely populated urban city.

Compared with elders living in three-generational households, those in elder-only households are more isolated from children. Outside the family, elder-children contacts are limited, as most educational, recreational, and social opportunities are set up on an age-specific basis. Interactions with neighboring children, both in the rural and urban areas, are also less likely nowadays.[4] Moreover, Japanese are also found to have less contact with their children (and grandchildren) than other nationalities when they do not live together. Only 14.3 percent of Japanese 60 years and above reported that they see their children every day, and 17.2 percent said they meet them more than once a week. This is significantly lower than the American sample, which recorded 21.2 percent and 40.8 percent, respectively (Sōmuchō 1990).

In an aging society, more Japanese are growing old in relatively good physical and mental health. In fact, more than 70 percent of elders become bedridden only in their last week of life (Kōseisho 1996), and most do not become senile with age, as senility occurs in fewer than one in

---

[3] The types and conditions of retirement housing vary greatly in Japan. Entrance fees for this housing are expensive. In the Tokyo area, for example, the average entrance fee is about 25 million yen (Hino, cited in Urban Life Research Institute 1991, 9).

[4] The International Comparative Survey on the Lives and Consciousness of Older People shows consistently from five surveys between 1981 and 1995 that more elders in Japan than in other countries answered "Almost not at all" to the question "How many times a week do you talk to people staying near you?" (Sōmuchō 1996).

twenty (Koyano 1993). The growing number of healthy elders, however, fear declining life satisfaction and face isolation and loneliness. This is aggravated by the emergence of an age-segregated society.

The Dilemma of Reducing Old-Young Contacts

Most literature on the interactions between young and old begins with an indictment of age segregation as "violating the continuity of the wholeness of the life cycle" (Kuhn 1989, xi) and as being "one of the most unnatural occurrences in our society" (Rosenberg 1993–94, 4). An increasing amount of research has found negative effects of age segregation on both the young and the old. Matt Kaplan (1993, 71–72) summarizes the negative consequences: a reduction in the extent and quality of both the children's and the elders' social support networks; an increase in feelings of loneliness and increased vulnerability to depression experienced by the elderly; an increase in the younger generation's negative perceptions of, and informational inaccuracies about, the aging process; and a decrease in people's familiarity with aging as a natural process in the continuum of life.

Most studies in Japan on perceptions of elders focus on high school and university students as subjects. These studies have all concluded that the attitudes of Japanese youth toward elders are characterized by negative stereotypes (Koyano 1989). An international comparison of college students' perceptions of elders in Japan, the United States, Great Britain, and Sweden has further shown that more young Japanese perceive elders as grouchy and stubborn, and fewer see them as kind and honest than do peers in the other three countries (Koyano 1993). These findings imply that more young Japanese have "ageist" attitudes toward the old. This is an alarming contrast to the idealized images of respect and care for elders that dominate social scientists' writings about Japan (for example, Benedict 1947; Palmore 1975; Palmore and Maeda 1985).

Wataru Koyano attributes this discrepancy between ideal and actual images to the *tatemae* and *honne*[5] mentality of the Japanese. *Tatemae*, as Erdman Palmore has observed, is manifested in the "silver seats" that exist on every train, the Respect the Elders Day held every Septem-

---

[5] Koyano (1989) states that *tatemae* is an ideal, culturally defined, normative meaning, whereas *honne* indicates actual meaning or feeling. He notes that the proper use of *tatemae* and *honne* may signify the generally realistic, rather than idealistic, nature of Japanese thinking, as it implicitly permits the presence of something far from ideal.

ber 15, and the Law for the Welfare of the Elderly (enacted in 1963), which declared in Article 2 that "the elderly shall be loved and respected as those who have contributed toward the development of society for many years, and shall be warranted a healthful and peaceful life" (Koyano 1989, 342). *Honne,* on the contrary, is characterized by negative images of elders as silly, senile, weak, and stubborn.

Negative perceptions of elders, however, are not supported by a study of the perceptions of children between the ages of nine and twelve (Nakano 1991). However, in a similar later survey of junior high students (Nakano et al. 1994), the research team found that positive images of elders declined with the rising age of the children. Both studies concluded that "favorable experiences with elders" were consistently the most important factor affecting Japanese children's formation of positive attitudes toward elders. The 1994 study also suggests that, rather than assuming that cohabitation with grandparents would definitely result in positive images of the elders, the nature and content of the interactions are also influencing factors not to be overlooked. Their findings support my survey mentioned in Chapter 6.

Relating the research results to what I argued about three-generational living and alternate-generational contact earlier in the chapter, the increasingly negative stereotypes of elders among junior high students may be influenced by the age of the grandparents they reside with; most have probably already entered the category of old-old by the time their grandchildren are in junior high school. In addition, they may also be influenced by the negative stereotypical images of elders that dominate the media (Koyano 1993). Hence, although past favorable experiences with elders will certainly help to foster positive images of aging, these positive perceptions and experiences can only remain constant if they are continually strengthened as the children grow up.

Japanese society today is increasingly afflicted with deviant behavior and violence among children; such behavior includes bullying, suicide, and delinquency. This has caused great concern among educators, parents, and social commentators, who wonder if they can rely on these children to be responsible citizens in supporting them in the future. The increase in the proportion of nuclear families, resulting in a lack of grandparents to serve as moral guide posts (transmitting desirable social values to the young and imparting proper child-rearing attitudes on the middle generation), is seen as a significant cause of the emerging problems (Yoshizawa 1989).

The middle generation participants in K.S. Elliot and Ruth Campbell's

(1993, 131) study on reciprocity in three-generational families provide some evidence of long-term benefits of cohabitation with elders. One participant said, "If you are nice to old people, the children will see this, and when you grow old, they will be nice to you. This is teaching through your own action."

Age segregation and the consequent negative perception of aging and old age, therefore, foretell concerns on different levels, from personal concerns about children's attitudes toward their own aging parents in the future to the wider social implications of the aging society's future survival.

"Service of the Heart"

One of the indications of the yearning for reengagement in Japan is the "Service of the Heart," a "rent-a-family" service (Kaplan and Thang 1997). One such company that was established in 1990 reported that they are doing so well they have to place many elderly couples or individuals on the waiting list for visits from their purchased "family members." A typical rent-a-family session simulates a three-generational family setting. The "daughter" or "daughter-in-law"—a trained entertainer— would prepare meals where all would eat together, and there would be other "family" events such as "family" walks in the park, gift giving, singing, chatting, and playing with "grandchildren." The "grandchildren" usually climb into the "grandparents'" laps for intimate games with them. The advent of such business ventures in Japan signals a need for initiatives beyond the family to reconnect the generations. If elders who desire intergenerational contact do not have access to their own grandchildren, they should at least have access to somebody else's grandchildren.

In the midst of this tide of change in the larger society, the linking of generations becomes a more pertinent task. Kotoen has shown the merits of reengaging the generations. It represents an effort in the emerging "field" of intergenerational programming that reveals the urgent need to bring the generations together.

Intergenerational Programming in Japan

In Japan, intergenerational programs are termed "intergenerational interaction activities" (*setaikan kōryū katsudō*). Defined as people from various ages getting together to do something in an extrafamilial setting, they have a connotation of three-generational interaction, including the middle generation (Saito 1994, 161). However, the programs typically involve cooperation, interaction, or exchange between people over sixty and people under twenty, with little, if any, involvement by the middle generation.

Programs for alternate-generational contacts were in existence before the awareness of the "dilemma" of changing family structure in an aging society. Most, if not all, old-age welfare institutions are visited by children from nearby schools on an infrequent basis. In the early 1970s, with the first wave of public awareness of aging problems,[6] the Youth Red Cross members in Fukushima Prefecture, for example, initiated a "one-voice campaign" (*issei undō*), in which they greeted the single elders in their neighborhood before and after school (Miyazato and Tsushida 1994, 146). More intergenerational programs, however, began to appear throughout the country in the 1980s.

Support for intergenerational programs first appeared in aging policy under the "measures for learning and social participation" in the 1986 Policy Guidelines for a Long-lived Society. Often seen in the framework of the "lifelong learning" movement, a wide spectrum of learning experiences for people throughout the life span (Thompson 1996), it is included as one of the six pillars of the Ministry of Education's "comprehensive projects to promote *ikigai* of elders."[7] As such, it is often sponsored by local projects through specific national programs such as the Model Municipality Project (Saito 1994).

The new Fundamental Law on Policies for Aging Society adopted by Prime Minister Hashimoto's Cabinet in July 1996 continues to show an interest in intergenerational programming. This law, which replaces the 1986 Policy Guidelines, states: "In order to build energetic local communities as well as to help the elderly play an active role in them with something to live for, the elder's environment in social activities will be facilitated. To achieve this goal, opportunities will be provided for the elders and young generations to promote mutual exchange, and voluntary activities of the elders will be supported" (Maeda 1996, 131).

[6]In 1970, when Japan first met the statistical criteria of an aging society, the instances of increasing suicides and lone deaths among elders brought to public awareness the existence of old-age problems in Japan. To counter these problems, the National Social Welfare Organization initiated several campaigns such as the National Campaign for Aged Welfare (1971) and Zero Lone Death Elders Campaign (1973) (Miyazato and Tsushida 1994, 146).

[7]The categories are (1) projects for conferences to promote education for elders, (2) elders' classrooms, (3) volunteer training seminars, (4) effective use of elder resources, (5) counseling, and (6) intergenerational interactions (Saito 1994, 167).

Connecting with the "active social participation" of elders—an arena much promoted recently—thus causes intergenerational programming to take on a special sense of relevance and urgency.

Intergenerational programs occur in a variety of educational, recreational, and social welfare settings. Some of these are connected with national programs that are overseen by separate ministries; many more are local initiatives, planned and implemented by local government agencies, nongovernmental neighborhood governing associations (*chōnaikai*), and other community organizations, such as youth and elders' organizations and clubs (Kaplan 1996). With few guidelines other than "getting the generations together," the programs usually leave their style and content to the imagination of the planners.

Intergenerational programs are receiving increasing media attention. As these programs are a relatively recent phenomena, literature on them is limited.[8] Through a review of available interdisciplinary scholarly materials, newspaper articles, popular arts and literature, television documentaries, and interviews and site visits, I offer an overview of the "field" to date.

I place the intergenerational programs into four identifying categories, based on the groups that initiate them: initiatives from the young, the elders, or the community, and initiatives in age-integrated facilities like Kotoen.

Initiatives from the Young

This category refers to intergenerational programs initiated by youth-related institutions—mainly schools, kindergartens, and nurseries.

The volunteer school program for both private and public schools, started in 1977 by the Ministry of Education, provides a major impetus to schoolchildren's involvement with the elders. Serving as a form of welfare education, the program aims to promote the understanding and awareness of social welfare among schoolchildren.

A school is selected as a "volunteer school" for three years and receives a funding of 100,000 yen annually for the period. Most participating schools are elementary schools. In 1993, 60 percent of the 4,600 partici-

[8] There are only three known English sources (Yamazaki 1994; Kaplan 1996; and Kaplan et al. 1998). Various significant reports have been added to the Japanese literature since 1992 (Chōju Shakai Kaihatsu Sentā 1992; Aoi 1994; Eijingu Sōgō Kenkyū Sentā 1994; Yasuda Kasai Chōju Raifu Sapōto Kabushiki Kaisha 1995). Based on its study in 1994, the Eijingu Sōgō Kenkyū Sentā published a guidebook on how to plan an intergenerational program.

pating schools across the nation were elementary schools; junior and senior high schools constitute 30 percent and 10 percent, respectively. The program has received positive feedback, and this volunteer experience is said to have influenced some student to embark on a career in welfare services.

Most schoolchildren in such programs visit old-age institutions or elders living alone in the community. Interaction with the elders include written correspondence, playing traditional games together, learning about traditional crafts and history from the elders, and helping with cleaning. Elders are invited to attend Sports Day, musical concerts, Respect the Elders Day, and culture festivals at the schools. Sometimes the students have joint sports activities with the elders such as gateball and golf. Most of the school volunteers who visit Kotoen are involved through this type of program.

Some schools develop a "foster grandchild system" in which children pair up with elders in a particular nursing home for frequent and intimate interactions. One elementary school in Higashiyama City (Tokyo metropolitan area) allows the children to bring the elders out shopping in their wheelchairs as the children reach sixth grade. Such consistent contact has encouraged the development of long-lasting relationships.

Students in a senior high school in Edogawa Ward interact with elders by volunteering at a special nursing home near the school monthly; they also stay in the home for summer camp.

During the three-year volunteer school period, one high school in Ibaraki Prefecture introduced new courses in the home economics curriculum: besides lessons such as sewing, cooking, and childcare, there were lessons that included practical activities in understanding social welfare for the students. Students in the cooking class also started a monthly meal service that they called the Heart of Grandchildren. The box lunches were wrapped with lunch mats made by the sewing class, while students from the childcare class delivered the box lunches to the elders and ate with them (Eijingu Sōgō Kenkyū Sentā 1994).

One drawback of the scheme is a lack of continual funding for the projects that have been started during the volunteer schools period. Some schools are forced to cut back on costly projects, but an increasing number reported that new funding from local administrative bodies has enabled most activities to continue uninterrupted (Saito 1994, 177).

Nurseries and kindergartens, too, initiate intergenerational programs to promote alternate-generational interaction. In 1994, 146, or about 10 percent, of the (licensed) nurseries in Tokyo reported having some

[184]

form of intergenerational program with the elders. Most were event-based, such as concert performances at old-age homes and invitations to schools' sports days. A few schools also invited community elders to play with the children on a regular basis. A nursery in Tama City, Tokyo, for example, has held a designated Grandma's Day monthly for twenty-five years—essentially an open house day for community elders to come in and play traditional games with the children (Higashi Fukushi Kyōkai Hoikubu Tsūshin 1995).

For the past eight years, a nursery in Arakawa Ward, Tokyo, has let its three- to six-year-old children interact monthly with elders in a special nursing home nearby. After a year of group interaction, the children pair up with the "grandparent" of mutual choice and continue with more intimate dyad relations.

In 1987, another nursery in Itabashi Ward, Tokyo, initiated an experimental meal service to elder-only households in the community. The meals for the twice-weekly service are prepared in the nursery's kitchen and distributed by the nursery teachers and the children. The following year, a Life Support Service Center began in the nursery to provide services ranging from counseling new mothers to providing home help for community elders (Tatsunoko 1988).

Initiatives by Elders

Elders also play an active role in initiating contact with the young. Most old-age clubs interact with elementary school students (Saito 1994, 166). Many old-age clubs initiate interaction through traditional games, crafts, food, and cooking. Some programs, such as teaching children to plant and harvest rice, seek to restore past living experiences (Kobe-shi Rōjin Kurabu Rengōkai 1991).

Similar to the United States' Foster Grandparent program (begun in 1965), "foster grandma" schemes have also been established in several parts of Japan. Nada-Ward in Kobe City, for instance, began the scheme in 1992 to provide telephone consultation and home visits by elders to new mothers in nuclear families in the community. This program was started under the *ikigai* policy for elders (*Kobe Yomiuri Shinbun*, April 19, 1993).

Many individual elders serve the children in productive ways: as volunteers in after-school centers (Suginami Ward, Tokyo), as mentors for elementary school students (Saitama Prefecture), as consultants and teachers of carpentry and traditional crafts in the Children's Society

(Higashiyama city, Tokyo), as employed assistants in children's welfare institutions (Shiga Prefecture), and as teachers to urban children in farm experience schools (Shinagawa Prefecture) (Tokyo Volunteer Center 1993a, 25).

Perhaps the most popular example of productive elder-young interaction is the experimental town of Kasakake's after-school children's center in Gumma Prefecture. Since its establishment in 1977, the center has employed elders as part-time caregivers. The twenty elder caregivers registered at the center rotate to work weekly. Every day, there are three elder part-time caregivers present at the center; they are supervised by two full-time staff, to serve fifty children ranging in age from five to ten years old (Eijingu Sōgō Kenkyū Sentā 1994). Employing seniors as child caregivers is still relatively rare in Japan as compared with doing so in the United States, where guidelines on working as senior caregivers along with appropriate training workshops for them have been designed to encourage participation.

Intergenerational programs initiated by elders are a comparatively recent phenomenon, reflecting the changing cohort of Japanese elders who are beginning to see beyond the family in serving and interacting with younger generations. In recent years, more emphasis has been placed on encouraging volunteerism among the elders. In Tokyo, a senior volunteer program has been initiated. The word *senior* in senior volunteer has been in use since 1992. According to the Tokyo Volunteer Center—an organization founded to promote volunteerism in Tokyo in 1981—the word *senior* has replaced *silver* to change the negative image of the latter: "The word 'silver,' such as silver hair or white hair, equals aging. As in 'silver seat,' it implies a passive existence, as the object of needing a helping hand" (Tokyo Volunteer Center 1993b, 4).

It is thus hoped that the the word *senior* will bring a new image to elder volunteerism and encourage participation among those who have hesitated to do so because of the stigma attached to *silver.* In other words, while *silver* means "frail," "passive," and "unproductive," *senior*—a relatively new English-Japanese word adopted into the Japanese vocabulary—depicts an emerging group of "newly old" in today's aging society. *Seniors* are healthy, active, and productive; they are separated from the frail elders whom they volunteer to help.

Besides redefining elderly volunteers as "senior volunteers," the Tokyo Volunteer Center (1993b, 9) has also redefined the benefits of volunteerism for seniors. It stresses volunteerism as bidimensional, that in giving, the volunteers also "receive *ikigai.*" It emphasizes that even bedridden persons can volunteer, for example, by communicating with children about the past and telling folktales. It promotes the concept of "volunteer therapy" which claims that volunteer activities have the effect of improving the mental and physical health of the persons who do them. Emphasizing volunteerism as beneficial to both the volunteer and those helped, and as beneficial not only in psychological but also physical aspects, aims to match the objectives of senior volunteerism with the elders' *ikigai*. Close to 100 percent of Japan's elders see "keeping healthy" as their *ikigai* (Chōju Shakai Kaihatsu Sentā 1992, 28).

Initiatives in the Community

I define community-based organizations and groups broadly here, including social organizations such as neighborhood associations, local volunteer groups, self-governing bodies, charity organizations, and private business groups that initiate intergenerational activities and programs.

An overwhelming number of activities in this category are event-based and annual, or "one-shot deals." They include festivals and events that promote cultural and religious themes, seasonal events, activities tied to environmental appreciation, and preservation themes (Kaplan 1996).

One characteristic of community-based programs is their emphasis on three-generational interactions. Examples of these initiatives are "Apple Picking," "Annual Festival of *Fureai* and the Future," "Neighborhood Barbecue Party," "*Soba* [wheat noodle] Making," and "Japanese Songs: 100 Years' Concert" (Yasuda Kasai Chōju Raifu Sapōto Kabushiki Kaisha 1995). Some organize more regular programs. The town of Kamou in Kagoshima Prefecture designates the third Saturday of the month as the Intergenerational Interaction Day, in which all civic halls (*kōminkan*) organize activities such as "listening to the experience of the elders," "learning about local history," sports, volunteering, and crafts to enhance interactions across the generations (Eijingu Sōgō Kenkyū Sentā 1994). Ehime Prefecture started a program for "open space for little children and elders' interactions" to encourage interactions among the community elders, nursery and kindergarten children, and the children's mothers (Miyazato and Tsushida 1994, 154).

This category also relates to lifelong learning activities, such as hobby clubs, that integrate members of different generations. In recent years, more and more communities have also been creating space for the old and young to interact; these initiatives include building "elders' space" in children's playgrounds (Hyōgo Prefecture), establishing a children's library in an old-age home (Saitama Prefecture), and placing swings and slides in the open ground of old-age home.

Initiatives in Age-Integrated Facilities

Kotoen belongs to the final category in the classification of intergenerational programming. Age-integrated facilities are an emerging trend in Japan. These facilities often cite practical reasons such as effective use of limited land and resources and the "emotional" reason of providing *fureai* to both the old and the young as the main reasons for the combination.

Age-integrated facilities, however, are not recognized by the government as "functionally complementary"; rather, they are simply seen as "built together" because of "limited land." The enhancement of the linkage between the old and young is seen as a secondary effect of the combination (*Rōjin Hoken Fukushi Janaru* 1993, 8). There is no government department to coordinate integrated facilities across generations. Many integrated facilities for elders and children have faced initial difficulties in trying to convince the different departments involved of the merits of such a complex combination.

Despite these difficulties, the number of age-integrated facilities in Japan is increasing. Facilities can become age-integrated either by moving into an existing service or by constructing new projects with the goal of integrating services for different generations.

In the recent years, many day service centers or other elderly services have been set up in the empty classrooms of schools and nurseries. The declining birth rate in Japan has caused many schools to become underenrolled. In 1994, there were more than 50,000 empty classrooms in elementary and junior high schools nationwide (*Yomiuri Shinbun,* June 23, 1994). On the other hand, the shortage of land has forced many old-age services to move to the suburbs or the country, further removing the elders from the community. Establishing service centers for elders in schools thus allows easy access to community elders as well as to opportunities to promote their interactions with children.

The frequency of interaction between children and elders in the same building greatly depends on administrative planning. The students in a school in Saitama Prefecture, for example, have frequent get-togethers for lunch with the day center's elders (*Yomiuri Shinbun,* June 23, 1994). Students in a school in Hiroshima Prefecture sometimes take classes with the elders from Senior University (Tokyo Volunteer Center 1993a). In Akita Prefecture, although little active interaction occurs between the nursery children and day service elders who use their empty classrooms, passive *fureai* is reported: Elders seem satisfied to hear the laughter and singing of the children and watch them playing in the open through the windows (*Asahi Shibun,* November 6, 1995).

In the spring of 1996, the Ministry of Education announced for the first time that it was acceptable for elders to use empty classrooms for day activities (*Asahi Shinbun,* November 16, 1996). Setting up services for elders using empty classrooms in schools is a major breakthrough in bureaucracy. Schools come under the legislation of the Ministry of Education, whereas elderly welfare is overseen by the Ministry of Health and Welfare. Until the pressing need for increased elderly welfare was felt, transferring the "property" of one ministry to another was almost impossible. With the anticipated increase in elderly service centers in the New Gold Plan (see Appendix B), more schools will see elders in their compound in the near future.

Another form of combining the old and young is age-integrated facilities that are constructed to accommodate both generations. No studies or surveys have been conducted on such facilities nationwide, but diversity among them can be seen through scattered reports and media attention they have received. They differ from each other much as modified three-generational arrangements among Japanese families differ today.

Most age-integrated facilities are found in urban areas that are faced with the pressure of limited land space. There is no official count available of the number of these facilities, as there is no governmental department to oversee them. Using various sources (such as government agencies, news reports, and newsletters from welfare service organizations), I identified thirty-nine age-integrated facilities in Tokyo. Among them, I visited five (in addition to my field site) and surveyed twelve other facilities by telephone. They are a good cross-section of various combinations.[9]

A study of these age-integrated facilities shows that living close by does not necessarily facilitate frequent interaction. Some attribute their combination purely to land pressure. While Kotoen mentions the savings in

[9] I surveyed these age-integrated facilities: three combinations similar to Kotoen; one nursing home with nursery and junior high school; four nursing homes with nurseries; one old-age home with nursery; two day service centers with nurseries; two day service centers with children's after-school centers; one day service center with elementary school; one elders' rest center with nursery; one elders' rest center with children's after-school center; one elders' rest center with both a children's after-school center and silver pia housing; and one elder care house with university students' dormitory.

overhead costs that results from the combination, other facilities that have different organizations in charge of different services find that combinations make calculating utility and maintenance costs confusing.

Administrators' attitudes and efforts to provide programs and activities, therefore, is the driving force in encouraging interactions. In an after-school children's center that was built above a day service for elders (operated by two different social welfare organizations), children do not see the elders, as they use the outside stairs. An administrator for the day service for elders said that the children's center and the day service have joint events only twice a year: a fire drill and *bon* dancing during the summer. Another similar combination facility, however, reported active interaction between the two age groups, especially during summer and winter school vacations. While Kotoen's administrators have explicitly presented it as a "big family" with *fureai,* the administrator of a similar age-integrated facility stressed that the facility was not integrated; the children and elders were simply coexisting. Many administrators claim that they have no particular plans for more interactions because planning such programs is time-consuming.

One central Tokyo nursing home that combines a nursery and a junior high school has received much publicity since its opening in 1991, being the only one in Japan featuring such an "ambitious" combination. Many reports favorably emphasized the benefits of children interacting with elders and junior high students serving as volunteers. Interviews with the nursing home's administrator, however, showed that interacting activities with the children occurred only about once a month; interaction with the junior high students is even more limited. Many students visit the home only once as part of their curriculum during their first year. Very few students serve as volunteers, and they are also not particularly encouraged by the school to do so, as students are expected to spend most of their time preparing for examinations.

Several administrators claim that they faced opposition from parents— the middle generation—when age-integrated facilities were first proposed. Parents objected on the grounds of hygiene and worried that elders would transmit diseases to children. The director of a day service center combined with an elementary school in central Tokyo attributed PTA members' initial objections to the media's negative portrayal of elders as senile and therefore potentially harmful to children. The PTA members' opposition had delayed the interaction between the elders and the children for two months. However, the parents' attitudes changed gradually as they realized the merits of linking the generations.

Many age-integrated facilities do not share utility spaces, and none except Kotoen shares kitchens and offices. Some share an entrance, but many have separate entrances. Kotoen seems to share the most common spaces and utilities among the facilities I surveyed. If most institutions are analogous to the diverse, modified three-generational households, then Kotoen resembles a traditional large, multigenerational family. Close proximity between the generations in a facility does not necessarily link the generations: Appropriate planning and programming are important to make *fureai* happen.

Characteristics of Intergenerational Programming

An overview of the intergenerational programs shows a diversity of activities and programs framed under "intergenerational interactions." Without an overarching theoretical framework or well-stated interagency and cross-disciplinary collaborative arrangements (Kaplan 1996), the intergenerational programming "field" seems somewhat haphazard in comparison to that in the United States. Nonetheless, the programs reveal a pattern consistent with their cultural and social context.

In general, the pattern of healthier elders teaching the young, and frail elders served by the young, prevails. Contact with elders in different health conditions helps the young to understand the process of aging and removes negative stereotypes about elders.

A dominant feature of intergenerational programming in Japan is its emphasis on the past. Many activities for the old and the young hinge on elders' knowledge of traditions, culture, and history. During these intergenerational meetings, children gain knowledge about the past from activities that range from learning about agriculture to more conventional Japanese pastimes such as origami, bamboo crafts, rope crafts, and childhood games to those with *furusato* ("old community," "hometown") flavor. Elders also visit schools or children's clubs to talk about the past, such as their war experience and the community during their childhood, which contributes to the youths' understanding of local history.

An emphasis on the past reflects how rapid postwar modernization has transformed Japan (and the world) in the course of a generation to make "revitalization of traditional cultures" necessary. Such emphasis on learning from the wisdom and experience of elders is also beneficial to elders, as it emphasizes their productive role as teachers.

Even contact between frail elders and the young reveals connections

[191]

with past ideas. One report on intergenerational activities claims that these activities "provide the opportunity for the young to learn how to take care of their own aging parents in the future" (Eijingu Sōgō Kenkyū Sentā 1994, 31).

Besides reconnecting the loosened ties between the generations, intergenerational programming also represents efforts to reunite the whole community and the multiple generations within it. Age-integrated facilities further have a nostalgic implication for the cultural ideal of three-generational living structures.

An emphasis on the past connects intergenerational programming to the larger ongoing project of *furusato-zukuri* ("old village"-making)—efforts on the national and local levels to integrate "present-day activities and interpretations with past events, and to set in motion the construction of an 'authentic' image [flavor] of the future" (Robertson 1991, 14).

Hence, apart from merging the generations so that they benefit from each other mutually, intergenerational programming is at the same time an attempt to recapture the human relations, community spirit, and family structure of the past. This implies the tendency in Japan to return to postfigurative culture—to use the term defined by Margaret Mead (see Chapter 1). Underlying this attempt is the sentimental belief that the past is ideal; maybe it offers some answers to the dilemma we are facing in an aging society today.

I agree that the past may offer some hints for us to tackle the present. But with the drastic sociodemographic changes occurring in Japan today, is a reversion to the postfigurative viable? What is the future direction of generational reengagements?

I suggest that we return to Mead for a clue. Mead's (1970, 83) proposal of a prefigurative culture in which it will be "the child—and not the parent or grandparent—that represents what is to come" offers a scenario quite different from what intergenerational programming in Japan tries to restore. I am doubtful of literally declaring the young as the leaders. However, turning our attention to the young provides new insights into the issues of linking the generations.[10]

In observing elders teaching children to play traditional games at Kotoen, a caregiver in her mid-twenties commented, "The elders now at least have knowledge in traditional crafts and games to teach the

[10]The "Hope for the Children" project in Rantoul, Illinois, a child-centered model of building a multigenerational and multiracial community, is one way of focusing on children in generational relations and programs.

children; I will have nothing to teach little children when I grow old." Mead's contribution is timely in helping us to think beyond the post-figurative culture in reengaging the generations. Moments at Kotoen when elders learn from children about Anpanman and McDonald's Happy Meals represent the potential of learning from the children as much as teaching them.

To say that the pattern of future generational relations is one in which only the children will lead the elders may be too simplistic. As pioneers in life, elders will continue to play significant roles in teaching the young to be pioneers in life as well. Nevertheless, we can visualize a better and more caring society if policy planners emphasize integrating, rather than segregating, the generations.

Appendix A

Residential Care Facilities
for the Elderly in Japan

There are four main types of residential care facilities for the elderly in Japan:

1. Special Home for the Elderly Care (Nursing Home) (*tokubetsu yōgō rōjin hōmu*). This is for those who are over sixty-five and who require nursing care because of physical or mental impairments.
2. Home for the Elderly Care (Old-Age Home) (*yōgō rōjin hōmu*). This is for those who are over sixty-five and who cannot maintain independent living because of physical, mental, environmental, and/or financial reasons.
3. Home with Moderate Fees (*keihi rōjin hōmu*). This is a form of boarding facility for those who are over sixty who have special housing or family problems. There are two subtypes in this category: Type A offers meal service; Type B requires the elder to cook for him- or herself.
4. Private Retirement Homes (*yūryō rōjin hōmu*). This is for elders with substantial financial means.

The first three types of homes are designated as welfare facilities under the 1963 Welfare Law for the Elderly. They receive national, prefectural, and/or local government funds. Many of these homes are managed privately through social welfare corporations (*shakai fukushi hōjin*), although many have been built with public funds.

Nursing homes are the fastest-growing segment among the four types of residential care for elders. Such facilities have grown from 80 beds when they were first built in 1963 to 206,600 beds in 1995. Most facilities were targeted to have 290,000 beds by 1999, according to Japan's New Gold Plan (see Appendix B). On the contrary, occupancy rates for old-age homes have been declining in the recent years: occupancy peaked at 71,352 beds in 1977; by 1994, however, it had declined slightly to 67,500. The new regulations by the Ministry of Health and Welfare require old-age homes built (or remodeled) since 1973 to have single- or double-occupancy rooms. This requirement, coupled with the fact that no new old-age homes were built after 1976, helps to explain the decline of old-age home residents.

In contrast, the homes with moderate fees have grown steadily through the years. In 1963, there were 1,082 residents in such homes; by 1994, the figure had increased to 23,700. Daisaku Maeda (1996) claims that homes with moderate fees have longer waiting lists than do the old-age homes, because of the differences in admission procedures (one applies directly to the former but applies through the city welfare office for admission to the latter) and the stigmatized image of the latter.

Since 1989, a new residential form called "Care House" was added to the category of homes with moderate fees. The Care House allows elders to engage help from outside caregivers when they become frail. This allows them to continue to stay in the same place instead of being transferred to a nursing home. There were 6,853 Care Houses in 1993; 100,000 were expected to be built by 1999 under the New Gold Plan (see Appendix B).

Private retirement homes are part of the booming "silver business" ongoing in Japan since the 1980s. Most of such facilities provide lifelong care support for frail elders. Their occupancy increased from 6,813 residents (in 90 homes) in 1982 to 18,700 residents (in 250 homes) in 1994. With the rising segment of elders who are financially affluent and prefer to live independently from their children, the demand for such homes is expected to increase in the future (Kinoshita 1992; Morioka 1994; Maeda 1996).

Appendix B

The New Gold Plan

**Target and Expansion in Services for Elders:
Comparison of the Gold Plan (1990) (Actual Data in FY 1993)
with the New Gold Plan (1994) for 1999**

	Gold Plan	Actual (1993)	New Gold Plan
1) In-home service			
Home helpers (persons)	100,000	69,298	170,000
Short-term stay service (beds)	50,000	22,054	60,000
Day service centers (places)	10,000	3,453	17,000
Home care support centers (places)	10,000	1,238	10,000
Visiting nurse stations (places)			5,000
2) Institutional service			
Nursing homes for the elderly (beds)	240,000	207,235	290,000
Health care facilities for the elderly (persons)	280,000	88,828	280,000
Care houses (a new type of home for the elderly with moderate fees) (persons)	100,000	6,853	100,000
Multipurpose senior centers in depopulated areas (places)	400	°101	00

Source: Ministry of Health and Welfare (cited in Maeda 1996, 98).
°denotes actual data in FY 1992

The 1994 New Gold Plan is a revised version of the 1990 Gold Plan ("Ten Year Gold Plan for the Development of Health and Welfare Services for the Elderly"), which was promulgated by the Japanese national government. Its goals were to be reached by 1999. One objective of the Gold Plan is to increase services and facilities to enable elders to stay at home as much as possible. A revision of the goals in 1994 reflects the inadequacy of the 1990 plan in meeting the predicted future needs of an expanding elder population. The New Gold Plan expands the level of services for elders greatly, although the goals still fall far below the levels of services in other developed countries. When the goal for home helpers was reached in 1999, the ratio between home helpers and the population aged 65 and older was 1:127.6. In Sweden, this ratio is about 1:50. Moreover, 2.6 percent of the elderly population was institutionalized by 1999, when the goal for long-term institutional care (nursing home and health care facilities for the elders) was reached, as compared with approximately 5 percent in countries in Western Europe and North America (Maeda 1996, 100).

In addition to expanding the just-described services, the New Gold Plan does the following (Maeda 1996, 101):

- It increases the number of qualified workers through strengthening various training programs. By the end of 1999, the number of qualified caregivers was to have increased by 200,000, the number of trained nurses by 100,000, and the number of trained physical therapists by 15,000.
- It institutes round-the-clock visiting personal care services by home helpers.
- It improves nursing home facilities so that they can offer more private rooms.
- It strengthens the family doctor system.
- It establishes a meals-on-the-wheels service.
- It improves personal care service in long-term-care hospitals for elderly patients.
- It modernizes nursing homes through the provision of grants for purchases of technology.
- It expands community-based rehabilitation services.
- It improves and develops services for demented elders, especially through the expansion of group-home services.
- It expands educational facilities and in-service training programs for caregivers and social workers working for the welfare of the elderly.
- It develops technical aid service systems, including the strengthening of the research and development system.
- It designates voluntary and private services for the diversification of service resources and for flexibility of the service delivery system.
- It expands specially designed public housing for elders.
- It improves the physical environments for the elderly and the disabled.

References

Akiyama, Hiroko; Toni Antonucci; and Ruth Campbell. 1990. "Exchange and Reciprocity among Two Generations of Japanese and American Women." In *The Cultural Context of Aging: Worldwide Perspectives*, edited by J. Sokolovsky, 127–42. New York: Bergin & Garvey.

Amoss, Pamela, and Steven Harrell, eds. 1981. *Other Ways of Growing Old*. Stanford, Calif.: Stanford University Press.

Angelis, Jane. 1992. "The Genesis of an Intergenerational Program." *Educational Gerontology* 18 (4): 317–27.

Aoi, Kazuo. 1992. *Chōju Shakairon*. Takegazakishi, Ibaraki-ken: Ryūtsū Keizai Daigaku Shuppankai.

———. 1994. *Koreika Shakai no Sedaikan Kōryū*. Tokyo: Chōju Shakai Kaihatsu Senta.

Aoi, Ken. 1987. "'Joshiki,' 'Seido' o norikoete Hoikuen to Rōjin Hōmu o 'Gattai.'" *Nikkei Architecture*, June 15, 132–36.

Apple, Dorrian. 1956. "The Social Structure of Grandparenthood." *American Anthropologist* 58: 656–63.

Asahi Shinbun. 1996. November 16.

Befu, Harumi. 1974. "Gift-Giving in a Modernizing Japan." In *Japanese Culture and Behavior: Selected Readings*, edited by Takie Lebra and William Lebra, 208–21. Honolulu: University of Hawaii Press.

Ben-Ari, Eyal. 1997. *Body Projects in Japanese Childcare: Culture, Organization, and Emotions in a Preschool*. Richmond, England: Curzon Press.

Benedict, Ruth. 1947. *The Chrysanthemum and the Sword: Patterns of Japanese Culture*. Boston: Houghton Mifflin.

Bengston, Vern L. 1985. "Diversity and Symbolism in Grandparental Roles." In *Grandparenthood*, edited by Vern Bengston and Joan Robertson. Beverly Hills, Calif.: Sage Publications.

Bestor, Theodore. 1989. *Neighborhood Tokyo*. Stanford, Calif.: Stanford University Press.

References

Bethel, Diana L. 1993. "From Abandonment to Community: Life in a Japanese Institution for the Elderly." Ph.D. dissertation, University of Hawaii.

Campbell, Ruth. 1984. "Nursing Homes and Long-term Care in Japan." *Pacific Affairs* 57 (1): 78–89.

Caspi, Avshalom. 1984. "Contact Hypothesis and Inter-Age Attitudes: A Field Study of Cross-age Contact." *Social Psychology Quarterly* 47 (1): 74–80.

Caudill, William, and Helen Weinstein. 1969. "Maternal Care and Infant Behavior in Japan and American." *Psychiatry* 32: 12–43.

Chōfu-shi. 1989. *Sofubo to Mago ni kansuru Chōsa.* Japan: Chōfu-shi.

Chōju Shakai Kaihatsu Sentā. 1992. *Koreisha no Ikigai ni kansuru Shisaku, Jirei oyobi Kanren Chōsa Shiryōshu.* Tokyo: Chōju Shakai Kaihatsu Sentā.

Clark, Scott. 1992. "The Japanese Bath: Extraordinary Ordinary." In *Re-made in Japan: Everyday Life and Consumer Taste in a Changing Society,* edited by Joseph Tobin, 89–105. New Haven, Conn.: Yale University Press.

Cohen, Lawrence. 1994. "Old Age: Cultural and Critical Perspectives." *Annual Review of Anthropology* 23: 137–58.

Cumming, Elaine, and W. E. Henry. 1961. *Growing Old: The Process of Disengagement.* New York: Basic Books.

Doi, Takeo. 1973. *The Anatomy of Dependence.* Tokyo: Kodansha.

Dowd, James J. 1975. "Aging as Exchange: A Preface to Theory." *Journal of Gerontology* 30 (5): 584–94.

Edwards, Walter. 1989. *Modern Japan through Its Weddings: Gender, Person, and Society in Ritual Portrayal.* Stanford, Calif.: Stanford University Press.

Eijingu Sōgō Kenkyū Sentā. 1994. *Sedaikan Kōryū ni kansuru Chōsa Kenkyū Hōkokusho.* Tokyo: Eijingu Sōgō Kenkyū Sentā.

Elliot, K. S., and Ruth Campbell. 1993. "Changing Ideas about Family Care for the Elderly in Japan." *Journal of Cross-Cultural Gerontology* 8: 119–35.

Erikson, Erik. 1964. *Insights and Responsibility.* New York: W. W. Norton.

Firth, Raymond William. 1936. *We, the Tikopia.* London: Allen & Unwin.

Foner, Nancy. 1994. *The Caregiving Dilemma: Working in an American Nursing Home.* Berkeley: University of California Press.

Fortes, Meyer. 1960. "Oedipus and Job in West African Religion." In *Anthropology of Folk Religion,* edited by Charles Leslie. New York: Vintage.

Fujimoto, Nobuko. 1976. "Sofubo to Mago." In *Sansedai Kazoku: Sedaikan Kankei no Jitsushō no Kenkyū,* edited by K. Masuda and T. Kamita. Tokyo: Kakiuchi Shuppan.

Geertz, Clifford. 1973. "Thick Description: Toward an Interpretive Theory of Culture." In *The Interpretation of Cultures.* New York: Basic Books.

Goffman, Irving. 1961. *Asylums: Essays on the Social Situation of Mental Patients and Other Inmates.* Garden City, N.Y.: Anchor Books.

Gutmann, David L. 1974. "Alternatives to Disengagement: Aging among the Highland Druze." In *Culture and Personality: Contemporary Readings,* edited by R. A. Levine. Chicago: Aldine.

——. 1985. "Deculturation and the American Grandparent." In *Grandparenthood,* edited by Vern Bengsten and Joan Robertson. Beverly Hills, Calif.: Sage Publications.

Gutmann, David L., J. Grunes, and B. Guffin. 1980. "The Clinical Psychology of Later Life: Developmental Paradigm." In *Life Span Developmental Psychology: Transitions of Aging*, edited by N. Datan and N. Lohman. New York: Academic Press.

Hagestad, Gunhild O. 1985. "Continuity and Connectedness." In *Grandparenthood*, edited by Vern Bengsten and Joan Robertson. Beverly Hills: Sage Publications.

Hamaguchi, Haruhiko, et al., eds. 1996. *New Encyclopedia of Aging*. Tokyo: Waseda Daigaku Shuppanbu.

Hashimoto, Akiyama. 1996. *The Gift of Generations: Japanese and American Perspectives on Aging and the Social Sciences*. Cambridge: Cambridge University Press.

Havighurst, R. J. 1963. "Successful Aging." In *Handbook of Aging*, Vol. 1, edited by R. William, C. Tibbits, and W. Donahue. New York: Atherton Press.

Hazan, Haim. 1980. *The Limbo People: A Study of the Constitution of Time Universe among the Aged*. London: Routledge & Kegan Paul.

———. 1992. *Managing Change in Old Age: The Control of Meaning in an Institutional Setting*. Albany: State University of New York Press.

Hendry, Joy. 1986. *Becoming Japanese: The World of the Pre-school Child*. Honolulu: University of Hawaii Press.

Higashi Shakai Fukushi Kyōkai Hoikubu Tsūshin. 1995. October 20.

Hooyman, Nancy, and Asuman H. Kiyak. 1996. *Social Gerontology*. 4th ed. Boston: Allyn & Bacon.

Hutchinson, Sally A., and Elizabeth Bondy. 1990. "The Pals Program: Intergenerational Remotivation." *Journal of Gerontological Nursing* 16 (2): 18–26.

Hyōgo-ken Katei Mondai Kenkyūsho. 1994. *Sofubo to Mago no kakawari ni kansuru Chōsa Kenkyū Hōkokusho*. Hyōgo, Japan: Katei Mondai Kenkyūsho.

Ivy, Marilyn. 1995. *Discourse of the Vanishing: Modernity, Phantasm, Japan*. Chicago: University of Chicago Press.

Jantz, R. K.; C. Seefeldt; A. Gaper; and K. Serock. 1976. *The CATE: Children's Attitudes toward the Elderly*. College Park: University of Maryland Press.

Jerrome, Dorothy. 1992. *Good Company: An Anthropological Study of Old People in Groups*. Edinburgh: Edinburgh University Press.

Kamata, Toji. 1993. "Gendai Ōdōron." In *Nijūiseki no Kōreisha Bunka. Chōju Shakai Sōgō Kōza, 21*, edited by G. Kabayama and Chizuko Ueno, 249–63. Tokyo: Daiichi Hōki.

Kaplan, Matt. 1993. "Recruiting Senior Adult Volunteers for Inter-generational Programs: Working to Create a 'Jump on the Bandwagon' Effect." *Journal of Applied Gerontology* 12 (1): 71–82.

———. 1996. "A Look at Intergenerational Program Initiatives in Japan: A Preliminary Comparison with the U.S." *Southwest Journal on Aging* 12 (1–2): 73–79.

Kaplan, Matt; Atsuko Asano; Ichiro Tsuji; and Shigeu Hisamichi. 1998. *Intergenerational Programs: Support for Children, Youth, and Elders in Japan*. New York: State University of New York Press.

Kaplan, Matt, and Leng Leng Thang. 1997. "Intergenerational Programs in Japan: Symbolic Extensions of Family Unity." *Journal of Aging and Identity* 2 (4): 295–315.

References

Kihara, Takahisa. 1995. *Iru Dake de Borantia.* Tokyo Shine Video: Zenkoku Rōjin Kurabu Rengōkai.

Kinoshita, Yasuhito, and Christie Kiefer. 1992. *Refuge of the Honored: Social Organization in a Japanese Retirement Community.* Berkeley: University of California Press.

Kobe-shi Rōjin Kurabu Rengōkai. 1991. Kobe-shi Rōjin Kurabu Moderu Katsudō Jigyō Jireishū.

Kobe Yomiuri Shinbun. 1993. April 19.

Kocarnik, Rosanne, and James Ponzetti. 1991. "The Advantages and Challenges of Intergenerational Programs in Long-Term Care Facilities." *Journal of Gerontological Social Work* 16 (1–2): 97–107.

Kōhō Edogawa. 1996 February 8.

Kono, Shigemi. 1996. "Demographic Aspects of Population." In *Aging in Japan,* edited by the Japan Aging Research Center, 5–52. Tokyo: Japan Aging Research Center.

Kōseisho. 1996. *Jinkōdōtai Shakai Keizaimen Chōsa no Gaiyō (Kōreisha shibō).* Tokyo: Tōkei Jōhōbu.

Koyano, Wataru. 1989. "Japanese Attitudes toward the Elderly: A Review of Research Findings." *Journal of Cross-Cultural Gerontology* 4: 3.

———. 1993. "Age-old Stereotypes." *Japan Views Quarterly.* Winter: 41–42.

Kuhn, Margaret E. 1989. Foreword to *Intergenerational Programs: Imperatives, Strategies, Impacts, Trends,* edited by Sally Newman and Steven Brummel, xi–xii. New York: Haworth Press.

Kuroda, Tashio, and Philip M. Hauser. 1981. "Aging of the Population of Japan and Its Policy Implications." *NUPRI Research Series No. 1.* Tokyo: Nihon University Population Research Institute.

Lebra, Takie Sugiyama. 1974. "Reciprocity and the Asymmetric Principle: An Analytical Appraisal of the Japanese Concept of *On.*" In *Japanese Culture and Behavior: Selected Readings,* edited by Takie Lebra and William Lebra, 192–207. Honolulu: University of Hawaii Press.

———. 1976. *Japanese Patterns of Behavior.* Honolulu: University of Hawaii Press.

———. 1979. "The Dilemma and Strategies of Aging among Contemporary Japanese Women." *Ethnology* 18 (4): 337–53.

Long, Susan Orpett. 1987. *Family Change and the Life Course in Japan.* Ithaca, N.Y.: China-Japan Program, Cornell University.

Maeda, Daisaku. 1996. "Social Security, Health Care, and Social Services for the Elderly in Japan." In *Aging in Japan,* edited by the Japan Aging Research Center, 85–112. Tokyo: Japanese Aging Research Center.

Mead, Margaret. 1970. *Culture and Commitment: The New Relationships between the Generations in the 1970s.* New York: Columbia University Press.

Miwa, Osawa. 1994. "Shakai Fukushi Shisetsu ni okeru Sedaikan Kōryū." In *Kōreika Shakai no Sedaikan Kōryū,* edited by Kazuo Aoi, 211–51. Tokyo: Chōju Shakai Kaihatsu Sentā.

Miyazato, I., and Yuko Tsushida. 1994. "Sedaikan Kōryū no Bolantia Katsudō." In *Kōreika Shakai no Sedaikan Kōryū,* edited by Kazuo Aoi, 142–59. Tokyo: Chōju Shakai Kaihatsu Sentā.

Morioka, Kiyomi. 1996. "Generational Relations and Their Changes as They Affect the Status of Older People in Japan." In *Aging and Generational Relations over the Life Course: A Historical and Cross-Cultural Perspective,* edited by Tamara K. Hareven, 512–23. New York: Walter de Gruyter.

Morioka, Kiyomi, and Itsuki Nakabayashi. 1994. *Henyōsuru Kōreishazō: Daitoshi Kōreisha no Raifusutaru.* Tokyo: Nippon Hyōronsha.

Myerhoff, Barbara. 1978. *Number Our Days.* New York: Touchstone Books.

Nadel, S. F. 1951. *The Social Foundations of Social Anthropology.* Glencoe, Ill.: Free Press.

Nakane, Chie. 1970. *Japanese Society.* Berkeley: University of California Press.

Nakano, Ikuko. 1991. "Jidō no Rōjin Imēji—SD Hō ni yoru Sokutei to Yōin Bunseki." *Shakai Rōjingaku* 34: 23–36.

Nakano, Ikuko; Yutaka Shimizu; Yomei Nakatani; and Jinko Baba. 1994. "Shōgakusei to Chūgakusei no Rōjin Imēji—SD Hō ni yoru Sokutei to Hikaku." *Shakai Rōjingaku* 39: 11–22.

New Collegiate Japanese-English Dictionary. 1983. 3d ed. Tokyo: Kenkyusha.

Newman, Sally, and Steven Brummel, eds. 1989. *Intergenerational Programs: Imperatives, Strategies, Impacts, Trends.* New York: Haworth Press.

Newsweek. 1996. "Lonely Deaths." October 28, 36–37.

NHK (Nippon Hōsō Kyokai). 1989. *Mago Hachijūnin no Daikazoku: Rōjin to Hoikuenji no Fureaiki.* April 27.

Ogawa, Naohiro. 1996. "Economic and Social Implications of Population Aging in Japan." In *Aging in Japan,* edited by the Japan Aging Research Center, 55–87. Tokyo: Japan Aging Research Center.

Ogawa, Naohiro, and Robert D. Retherford. 1993. "Care of the Elderly in Japan: Changing Norms and Expectations." *Journal of Marriage and the Family* 55 (3): 585–97.

Ōjima Shinbun. 1989. August 27.

Okazaki, Yoichi. 1996. "Characteristics of Family and Household Structure in Japan." Paper presented at the Nihon University International Symposium on Contemporary Family in Comparative Perspective, Tokyo, March 4–7.

Palmore, Erdman. 1975. *The Honorable Elders: A Cross-Cultural Analysis of Aging in Japan.* Durham, N.C.: Duke University Press.

Palmore, Erdman, and Daisaku Maeda. 1985. *The Honorable Elders Revisited.* Durham, N.C.: Duke University Press.

Peak, Lois. 1991. "Formal Pre-elementary Education in Japan." In *Japanese Educational Productivity,* edited by R. Leestma and H. Walberg, 35–68. Ann Arbor, Mich.: Center for Japanese Studies.

Phenice, L. A. 1981. *Children's Perceptions of Elderly Persons.* Saratoga, N.Y.: Century 21 Publishing.

Plath, David. 1980. *Long Engagements.* Stanford, Calif.: Stanford University Press.

———. 1988. "The Age of Silver: Aging in Modern Japan." *The World and I.* March: 505–13.

———. 1990. "Filed Notes and Conferring of Note." In *Fieldnotes: The Making of Anthropology,* edited by Roger Sanjek, 371–84. Ithaca, N.Y.: Cornell University Press.

References

Radcliffe-Brown, A. R. 1952. *Structure and Function in Primitive Society.* New York: Free Press.

Robertson, Jennifer. 1991. *Native and Newcomer: The Making and Remaking a Japanese City.* Berkeley: University of California Press.

Robertson, Joan. 1995. "Grandparenting in an Era of Rapid Change." In *Handbook of Aging and the Family,* edited by Rosemary Belleszner and Victoria Bedford, 243–60. Westport, Conn.: Greenwood Press.

Robertson, Joan; Carol H. Tice; and Leonard L. Loeb. 1985. "Grandparenthood: From Knowledge to Programs and Policy." In *Grandparenthood,* edited by Vern Bengston and Joan Robertson. Beverly Hills, Calif.: Sage Publications.

Rōjin Hoken Fukushi Janaru. 1993. "Hitotsu Yane no Shita' ni Atsumareba." October, 4–17.

Rosaldo, Renalto. 1989. *Culture and Truth: The Re-thinking of Social Analysis.* Boston: Beacon Press.

Rosaldo, Renato, Smadar Lavie, and Kirin Narayan. 1993. "Introduction: Creativity in Anthropology." In *Creativity/Anthropology,* edited by Smadar Lavie, Kirin Narayan, and Renato Rosaldo, 1–8. Ithaca: Cornell University Press.

Rosenberg, Marcia Kasper. 1993–94. "Making Friends at Friendship Corner." *Journal of Long Term Care Administration* 21 (4): 4–6.

Rosow, Irving. 1985. "Status and Role Change through the Life Cycle." In *Handbook of Aging and the Social Sciences.* 2d ed., edited by R. Binstock and E. Shanas, 62–93. New York: Van Nostrand.

Rubinstein, Robert L., ed. 1990. *Anthropology and Aging: Comprehensive Reviews.* Norwell, Mass.: Kluwer Academic Publishers.

Saito, Sadao. 1994. "Shakai Fukushi Bunya ni okeru Sedaikan Kōryū no Genjo—Fukushi Kyōiku o Tōshite." In *Kōreika Shakai no Sedaikan Kōryū,* edited by Kazuo Aoi, 160–205. Tokyo: Chōju Shakai Kaihatsu Sentā.

Shield, Renee Rose. 1988. *Uneasy Endings: Daily Life in an American Nursing Home.* Ithaca, N.Y.: Cornell University Press.

Shigaki, Irene S. 1983. "Child Care Practices in Japan and the U.S.: How Do They Reflect Cultural Values in Young Children?" *Young Children* 13: 13–24.

Smith, Robert. 1961. "Cultural Difference in the Life Cycle and the Concept of Time." In *Aging and Leisure,* edited by R. W. Kleemeier, 83–112. New York: Oxford University Press.

———. 1974. *Ancestor Worship in Contemporary Japan.* Stanford, Calif.: Stanford University Press.

Smith, Robert, and Ella Lury Wiswell. 1982. *The Women of Suye Mura.* Chicago: University of Chicago Press.

Sōmuchō. 1990. *Rōjin no Seikatsu to Ishiki ni kansuru Kokusai Hikaku Chōsa.* Tokyo: Sōmuchō Chōkan Kanbō Rōjin Taisaku Shitsu.

———. 1993. *Daigokai Sekai Seinen Ishiki Chōsa.* Tokyo: Seishōnen Taisaku Honbu.

———.1996. *Rōjin no Seikatsu to Ishiki ni kansuru Kokusai Hikaku Chōsa kekka no Gaiyō.* Tokyo: Sōmuchō Chōkan Kanbō Rōjin Taisaku Shitsu.

Stanlaw, James. 1992. "For Beautiful Human Life: The Use of English in Japan."

In *Re-made in Japan: Everyday Life and Consumer Taste in a Changing Society,* edited by Joseph Tobin, 58–76. New Haven, Conn.: Yale University Press.

Sugimoto, Yoshio. 1997. *An Introduction to Japanese Society.* Cambridge: Cambridge University Press.

Swartz, E. 1978. "The Older Adult: Creative Use of Leisure Time." *Journal of Geriatric Psychiatry* 11: 85–87.

Tatsunoko, Hōikuen, ed. 1988. *Hōikuen ga Fumedashita Zaitaku Fukushi Puran.* Tokyo: Daiichi Shorin.

Thompson, Chris. 1996. "Hitting the Yakuba Hall: The Politics of Lifelong Learning and Community Development in Towa-*chō.*" Paper presented at the Midwest Conference of Asian Studies, Champaign, Ill.. October 11–13.

Tobin, Joseph J.; David Wu; Y. H. Davidson; and Dana H. Davidson. 1989. *Preschool in Three Cultures.* New Haven, Conn.: Yale University Press.

Tokyo TV Network. 1996. *Fureai Rōjin Hōmu: Tōkyō no Naka no Chiiki ni Manabu.* September 12.

Tokyo Tokubetsuku Rengōkai. 1995. *Dai Jūgokai Tokubetsuku no Tōkei.*

Tokyo Volunteer Center. 1993a. *Senior Volunteers' Activity Manual.* Tokyo: Tokyo Volunteer Center.

———.1993b. *Senior Volunteers' Coordinators' Manual.* Tokyo: Tokyo Volunteer Center.

Troll, Lilian E. 1985. "The Contingencies of Grandparenting." In *Grandparenthood,* edited by Vern Bengston and Joan Robertson. Beverly Hills, Calif.: Sage Publications.

Tsuji, Yohko. 1997. "Continuities and Changes in Conception of Old Age in Japan." In *Aging: Asian Concepts and Experiences Past and Present,* edited by Susanne Formanek and Sepp Linhart, 197–210. Vienna: Der Osterreichischen Akademie Der Wissenschaften.

Tsukamoto, Tetsu. 1978. *Rōjin to Kodomo.* Kyoto: Minerubua Shobo.

Turner, Victor. 1974. *Dramas, Fields, and Metaphors: Symbolic Action in Human Society.* Ithaca: Cornell University Press.

Urban Life Research Institute. 1991. *Kōreika Shakai to Sumai.* Tokyo: Urban Life Research Institute.

Yamanoi, Kazunori. 1995. *Kazoku o Shiawase ni suru Oikata.* Tokyo: Kodansha.

Yamazaki, Takaya. 1994. "Intergenerational Interaction Outside the Family." In *Educational Gerontology* 20: 463–71.

Yomiuri Shinbun. 1994. June 23.

Yoshizawa, Eiko. 1989. "Chiiki ni okeru Torikumi no Kadai." *Gekkan Fukushi* 72 (6): 46–49.

Yasuda Kasai Chōju Raifu Sapōto Kabushiki Kaisha. 1995. *Chiiki ni okeru "Seidaikan Kōryū" no Genjō oyobi Suishin no tame no Hōsaku ni kansuru Chōsa Kenkyū Hōkokusho.* Tokyo.

Yuzawa, M. 1991. *Rōjin to Kodomo to no Kankei: Kazoku Mondai no Shakaigaku.* Vol. 4. Tokyo: Yasuda Seimei Shakai Jigyōdan.

Index

The Anthropology of Contemporary Issues

A SERIES EDITED BY

ROGER SANJEK